INDONESIA

A Study of the Educational System of the Republic of Indonesia
and a Guide to the Academic Placement of Students in
Educational Institutions in the United States

Karin Johnson
Education Writer and Editor
Jakarta

Wendy Gaylord
ELT Advisor
British Council ELT Projects Unit, Jakarta

Gerald Chamberland
Language Examiner, Educational Consultant
Indonesia-Australia Language Foundation, Jakarta

1993

World Education Series publication sponsored by the
American Association of Collegiate Registrars and Admissions Officers and
NAFSA: Association of International Educators

Washington, DC

Placement Recommendations Approved by the National Council on the
Evaluation of Foreign Educational Credentials

28257329

Library of Congress Cataloging-in-Publication Data

Johnson, Karin.
    Indonesia: a study of the educational system of the Republic of Indonesia and a guide to the academic placement of students in educational institutions in the United States / Karin Johnson, Wendy Gaylord, Gerald Chamberland.
        p.   cm. — (A PIER full country study)
Includes bibliographical references and index.
ISBN 0-929851-16-1
1. Education and state—Indonesia. 2. Education, Higher—Indonesia. 3. Universities and colleges—Indonesia—Directories. 4. School grade placement—United States. I. Gaylord, Wendy. II. Chamberland, Gerald. III. Title. IV. Series: World education series.
LA1271.J576   1993   93-14228
370'.9598-dc20   CIP

Publication of the World Education Series volume on Indonesia is funded by the United States Agency for International Development Jakarta and the Advising, Teaching and Specialized Programs Division of United States Information Agency.

Additional copies of this report may be obtained from AACRAO for $40 for AACRAO or NAFSA members ($60 nonmembers). For more information on available volumes in the World Education Series, contact the Publications Order Desk, c/o AACRAO.

Projects for International Education Research

Projects for International Education Research (PIER) is an interassociational committee of appointed representatives from the American Association of Collegiate Registrars and Admissions Officers (AACRAO), NAFSA: Association of International Educators, and The College Board. PIER is a 1990 merger of two committees of long-standing, the World Education Series Committee of AACRAO and the PIER Committee of AACRAO and NAFSA.

PIER is charged with assessing the need for information on education systems throughout the world that can be used by college and university admissions officers in the admission and placement of foreign students and scholars in institutions of higher education in the United States, publishing reports on these systems, and developing workshops and seminars on the admission and placement of foreign students.

Four types of publications make up the World Education Series: full country studies, workshop reports, special reports, and working papers. Among the topics covered are the different levels of education, admission and program requirements, grading systems, credentials awarded, study abroad programs, and institutions. Placement recommendations, when included, are approved by the National Council on the Evaluation of Foreign Educational Credentials. The PIER Committee oversees the selection of topics, authors, and reviewers.

Projects for International Education Research Committee
A joint committee of AACRAO and NAFSA

AACRAO Members
Chair: William H. Smart, Director of Sponsored Student Programs, International Education, Oregon State University, Corvallis, OR

Margery J. Ismail, Director Emerita of International Student Services, Purdue University, West Lafayette, IN

Sylvia K. Higashi, Assistant Dean, College of Continuing Education and Community Service, University of Hawaii at Manoa, Honolulu, HI

NAFSA Members
Kathleen Sellew, Research and Professional Development, Office of International Education, University of Minnesota, Minneapolis, MN

Patricia Parker, Assistant Director of Admissions, Iowa State University, Ames, IA

Cynthia Fish, Assistant Director of Admissions, CUNY-Baruch College, New York, NY

The College Board Member

Sanford C. Jameson, Director, International Education Office, The College Board, Washington, DC

Ex-Officio Members Without Vote

AACRAO—Wayne E. Becraft, Executive Director, AACRAO, Washington, DC

NAFSA—Naomi Collins, Executive Vice President & CEO; NAFSA: Association of International Educators, Washington, DC

Observers

Agency for International Development—Dale E. Gough, Director, AACRAO-AID/Office of International Education Services, Washington, DC

United States Information Agency—Mary Reeber, Chief, Advising and Student Services Branch, Office of Academic Programs, USIA, Washington, DC

Staff

AACRAO—Henrianne K. Wakefield, Assistant Executive Director of Communications and Membership Services, AACRAO, Washington, DC

NAFSA—Linda H. Callihan, Program Manager, Field Services; Jeanne-Marie Duval, Senior Director, Educational Programs; NAFSA: Association of International Educators, Washington, DC

The National Council on the Evaluation of Foreign Educational Credentials and the Placement Recommendations in this Full Country Study

The placement recommendations published in this PIER full country study have been approved by the National Council on the Evaluation of Foreign Educational Credentials (the Council) in consultation with its authors. The Council was established to provide guidance on foreign educational credentials for U.S. institutions of higher education. It is the only interassociational body in the United States specifically organized to perform this role.

Membership of the Council reflects the diversity of U.S. educational institutions for which recommendations are made. Member organizations are the American Association of Community Colleges (AACC), the American Association of Collegiate Registrars and Admissions Officers (AACRAO), the American Council on Education (ACE), The College Board, the Council of Graduate Schools (CGS), the Institute of International Education (IIE), and NAFSA: Association of International Educators. Observers from U.S. organizations interested in international education include the United States Information Agency (USIA), the Agency for International Development (AACRAO-AID), and the New York State Education Department.

Their representatives for 1992-93 are listed below. See pages 80-83 for a description of the Council's role, and a guide to the understanding of its placement recommendations for this volume.

Members of the National Council on the Evaluation of Foreign Educational Credentials

Chair: Caroline Aldrich-Langen, Associate Director of Admissions, California State University-Chico, Chico, CA (represents AACRAO)

Chair-Elect: Karen Lukas, Assistant Director of Admissions, University of Minnesota-Twin Cities, Minneapolis, MN (represents AACRAO)

Representatives of Member Organizations

AACC—M. Yukie Tokuyama, Director, International Services, AACC, Washington, DC

AACRAO—William H. Smart, Director of Sponsored Student Programs, International Education, Oregon State University, Corvallis, OR (Chair of PIER); Henrianne K. Wakefield, Assistant Executive Director of

Communications and Membership Services, AACRAO, Washington, DC
(observer only)

ACE—Barbara Turlington, Director, International Education, ACE, Washington, DC

The College Board—Marcelle Heerschap, Director, Office of Admissions, The American University, Washington, DC; Sanford C. Jameson, Director, Office of International Education, The College Board, Washington, DC (business meetings only)

CGS—James Siddens, Assistant Dean, Graduate School, Ohio State University, Columbus, OH

IIE—James O'Driscoll, Director, Placement and Special Services Division, IIE, New York, NY

NAFSA—Margarita Sianou, World Education Services, Inc., New York, NY; Richard B. Tudisco, Director, International Student Office, Columbia University, New York, NY; Robert Watkins, Assistant Director of Admissions, University of Texas at Austin, Austin, TX

Representatives from Observer Organizations

AACRAO-AID—Dale E. Gough, Director, AACRAO-AID/Office of International Education Services, Washington, DC

USIA—Mary Reeber, Chief, Advising and Student Services Branch, Office of Academic Programs, USIA, Washington, DC

NY State Education Department—Laura Lynch, Bureau of Comparative Education, State Education Department, University of the State of New York, Albany, NY

Contents

Tables

Sample Documents

Preface

Fourteen years have elapsed since the publication of the first World Education Series (WES) guide to the Indonesian educational system. In that time Indonesia, the fourth most populous country in the world, with a population of 185 million, has developed dramatically.

The educational system has experienced a period of great expansion as well. Enrollment at the primary and secondary levels expanded from 23 million in 1978-79 to 36 million in 1990-91. Expansion at the tertiary level has also been dramatic. Overall enrollment more than quadrupled from 386,000 in 1978-79 to 1,800,000 in 1990-91 while the number of tertiary institutions also grew apace. Four state tertiary institutions have been established since 1978 but the increase in the number of private tertiary institutions has been extraordinary; from 384 in 1979 to approximately 1,000 in 1993, almost all of which offer a three-year Diploma III (DIII) or higher qualification.

The introduction of a number of major educational innovations during the last 14 years has contributed significantly to qualitative changes in Indonesia's educational system. At the primary and secondary levels, the curriculum has undergone major revisions aimed at improving the quality of education. The definition of basic education itself will be expanded in 1994 to include nine years of schooling. At the tertiary level, many new undergraduate programs have been established, especially in science and technology. The reorganization of degree programs on a credit/hour basis has greatly improved the flexibility and efficiency of the system.

The expansion of the educational system is also reflected in the increasing number of Indonesians studying abroad. In 1991 Indonesia placed ninth, with 9,400 students, in the number of foreign students studying in the United States. Undergraduate enrollment made up 62% of this figure; graduate students 33%; and those enrolled in short courses, language training, or other nondegree programs 5%. These enrollments reflect an increase in both the number and quality of secondary school graduates as well as the capacity of Indonesia's expanding middle class to finance its children's undergraduate education abroad. Graduate enrollment, both in Indonesia and abroad, grew in response to the Indonesian economy's need for the specialized skills of graduate degree holders. In addition, since the early 1970s the Indonesian government, through a number of large multilaterally funded development projects, has sent thousands of civil servants abroad, including many to the United States, for graduate study. With Indonesia now preparing to enter the "take-off" stage of economic development, the number of Indonesians studying abroad, especially in the United States, is expected to grow.

This book presents an updated description of the structure and organization of the Indonesian educational system and a guide to the interpretation and evaluation of Indonesian educational credentials. It provides important information for admissions officials in U.S. educational institutions and will also help Indonesian educators and other training and development specialists obtain a more accurate picture of U.S. admissions criteria. Prospective students from Indonesia will thus be able to make more realistic educational plans and obtain more suitable placements in American tertiary institutions.

This book was researched and written in several stages over a period of 16 months, beginning in August 1991. Library research and data collection and analysis took place from August to October 1991 using published data sources, principally from the Ministry of Education and Culture, and data from other ministries (e.g., the Ministry of Religious Affairs) and other agencies (e.g., the World Bank and the United States Agency for International Development). The authors also interviewed educators and government officials in Jakarta. The book's extensive treatment of Indonesian tertiary education is based on a survey constructed by the authors and distributed to all tertiary institutions in Indonesia in October 1991. Information also comes from visits to state and private tertiary institutions throughout the country, including universities and institutes of teacher training, technology, and Islamic studies conducted by the authors in January, February, and March 1992.

Karin Johnson
Wendy Gaylord
Gerald Chamberland
Jakarta, February 1993

Acknowledgements

The history of this book began long before the authors put fingers to keyboard. In February 1991 it was merely a gleam in the eye of Ann Lewis, then Executive Director of the American Indonesian Educational Exchange Foundation (AMINEF) in Jakarta. Ann's determination to see a new World Education Series (WES) publication on Indonesia brought the authors together. Her encouragement kept us going through the endless process of proposal preparation and revision. Dr. Michael Orlansky, then assistant press attache at the U.S. Embassy, Jakarta, also provided valuable input at this stage. Our research was funded by USAID/Jakarta and jointly sponsored by USAID (United States Agency for International Development) and the Directorate of Private Higher Education, Directorate General of Higher Education of the Ministry of Education and Culture of the Republic of Indonesia. We are indebted to Dr. Norman Rifkin, then Director of Education and Human Resources at USAID/Jakarta for his support. At USAID our debt to our "caseworker," Gartini Isa, Education and Human Resources Project Officer, who provided us with much more than administrative assistance, cannot be forgotten. Also thanks to Isla Winarto, USAID Training Officer, who went out of her way to help us figure out the USAID bureaucracy.

We are also indebted to Prof. Dr. Sukadji Ranuwihardjo, Director-General of Higher Education, for authorizing this project, and to Prof. Dr. Yuhara Sukra, Director of Private Higher Education, who cosponsored the project. To Dr. Yuhara and his staff we extend our great thanks for their help and friendly cooperation. We would also like to thank Prof. Dr. Bambang Suhendro, Director of Academic Affairs, who patiently outlined the entire education system and recent changes to us and set us on the right track.

Dr. Boediono, Head of the Bureau of Planning of the Ministry of Education and Culture, and staff members of the Center for Informatics, especially Reta Hendrati Dewi and Bambang S. Joko, were always generous with their time when we were searching for Ministry publications and trying to make sense of contradictory statistics. Dr. Sumadi Suryabrata of the Overseas Training Office (OTO) of the National Planning Agency (BAPPENAS) deserves our sincere thanks for contributing the results of his research on grading practices in Indonesian universities and for sharing with us his vast experience with grading and evaluation practices.

Achmad Ali, Director of Secondary Education and members of his staff, especially Ahmad Riyanto and Maria Widiani, helped us with our research in secondary education. A. Wana Bise, assistant director of the Directorate of Primary Education, as well as Drs. H. Mudjito and Husaini Wardi were very helpful in the area of primary education. Thanks, too, to Dr. Rosjid Rosjan for explanations and statistics on preprimary education in Indonesia. Messrs. Muhammad, Cojim Siswa Adi, Mathias Daeli, and Samsudin of the Department of Technical Teacher Training brought us up to date on teacher training at the primary and secondary levels. Andadari of the Directorate of Vocational Education was helpful in gathering data on vocational education.

Officials of the Ministry of Religious Affairs, Jakarta, assisted us in our research on Islamic education: Dr. Agustiar, Director of Islamic Higher Education; Hasbullah Mursyid, Head of the Center for Research and Development; as well as Dr. Zamakhsyari Dhofier, Director of Islamic Educational Guidance; and Husni Rahim, Head of the Sub-Directorate of State Islamic Institute Guidance; H. Nasrun Rusli, Head of the Sub-Directorate of Pesantren Guidance; and Hamdun, Head of the Sub-Directorate of Madrasah Aliyah Guidance. All were generous with their time and data.

During the data collection phase of the project the authors visited educational institutions throughout Indonesia. Space prevents us from acknowledging individually the kindness and cooperation we received from very busy education officials and their staffs. Their willing collaboration contributed greatly to the breadth of information in this book.

In September 1991, Pamela Smith, the new Executive Director of the American Indonesian Exchange Foundation, Jakarta, took an active interest in the project and helped coordinate USAID and USIA (United States Information Agency) involvement. Her efforts were crucial not only in helping us find additional funding for the project from USIA, but also in moving the project along. On the American side Rebecca Dixon, then chair of the Projects for International Education Research (PIER) committee of AACRAO and NAFSA: Association of International Educators, was the first person in the United States to become involved in the project. At that early stage her trust and cooperation were of immense value. Our monitor, Ann Fletcher of Stanford University, was a godsend. Ann's previous WES experience and her editorial and organizational skills helped us turn our draft into a professional product.

Many scholars and specialists in Indonesia and the United States took the time to read various sections of the manuscript and provide us with valuable criticism. Dr. M. Makin Ibnu Hadjar, Dr. Tony Ungerer, John Paterson, Toenggoel Siagian, Dr. Patricia Whittier, Nancy Gong, Bonnie Leigland, Dr. A. Dahana, Yanti Wijaja, Claire Wilbur, Supangkat, Dr. Timothy Behrend, Dr. Mely Tan, Dr. Onghokham and Soetrisno Moertiyoso all deserve our special thanks.

Lastly, we would like to thank Oskar Simanjorang, who had the thankless but vital task of entering our survey data into the database and whose efforts were essential in generating the appendices of the book.

We gratefully acknowledge the help of all the above. Any errors or omissions that appear, however, are the responsibility of the authors alone.

Republic of Indonesia

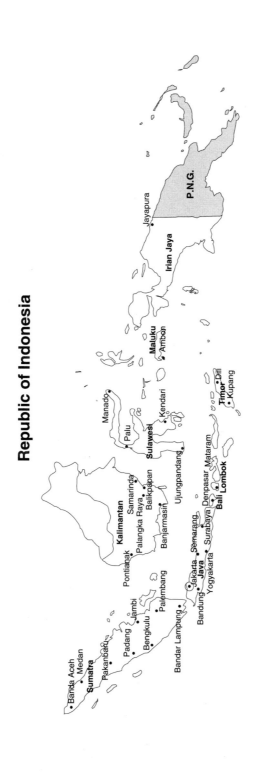

Educational Structure in Indonesia

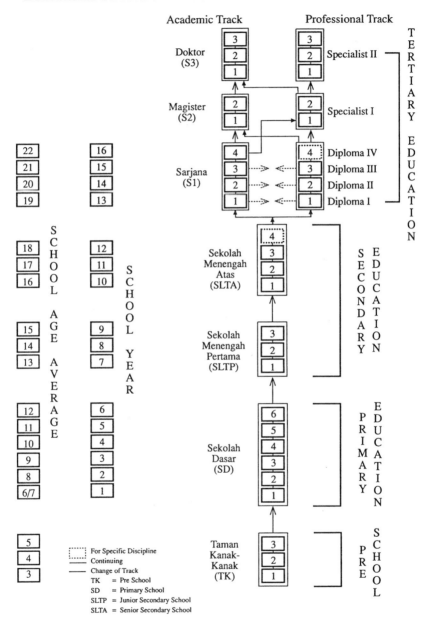

SOURCE: Adapted from "Education in Indonesia," Center for Informatics, Office of Educational and Cultural Research and Development, Ministry of Education and Culture.

I. Overview

Background

The unique geography of Indonesia, the world's largest archipelagic nation, helps explain its rich cultural diversity and provides an insight into its special problems. The 17,000 islands that make up the nation of Indonesia today stretch 3,200 miles east to west. Its population of approximately 185 million is scattered among 6,000 islands but is concentrated on the six main islands of Java, Sumatra, Sulawesi, Kalimantan, Bali, and Madura. Java, which is nearly the same size as New York state, is home to almost 60% of the population, although it comprises only 7% of the country's land area. On the other hand, the Indonesian portions of the islands of Borneo (Kalimantan) and New Guinea (Irian Jaya) comprise 50% of Indonesia's total land area but are home to only 5% of its population. In addition, there are 300 ethnic groups speaking distinct languages. Indonesia's unique geography has posed a challenge to communication and the equitable distribution of goods and services, including education, throughout Indonesian history. Administratively, the country has been divided into 27 provinces, each with its own regional government offices, including education, but the system is very much a centralized one.

Early Development of Education

The earliest documentary evidence of literacy in Indonesia is found on stones bearing Sanskrit inscriptions in Palla script, dating from the third or fourth century A.D. Hindu and Buddhist kingdoms located on the east coast of Borneo and in West Java near present-day Jakarta. Almost no other physical evidence of these civilizations remains and nothing is known about education in this period. In 671 A.D., in perhaps the earliest reference to education in Indonesia, the Chinese Buddhist pilgrim, I-Tsing, while on a voyage to India, spent six months studying Sanskrit grammar in the monastic academies of the kingdom of Sriwijaya, an important center of Mahayana Buddhist learning located on the east coast of Sumatra near the present-day city of Palembang and already well known in Tang Dynasty China. He returned to Sriwijaya in 685 A.D. to spend more than 10 years there writing his memoirs and translating religious texts from Sanskrit into Chinese.

Although indigenous literary forms, a variety of scripts, and adaptations of classical Indian epics testify to the existence of a literate elite, and later court literature (thirteenth to fifteenth century) records the history of Hindu and Buddhist kingdoms in Java, there is little evidence of formal education during this long period.

1

By the early sixteenth century, with the political power of the Hindu-Buddhist kingdoms on the wane, parts of the archipelago, especially the coastal regions, came under the ever increasing influence of proselytizing Muslim merchants from western India and the Middle East. Their religion, Islam, was the first sociocultural phenomenon in Indonesian history that required at least a minimal degree of literacy (in Arabic) for full participation in ritual life. The Islamic educational system they introduced represents the oldest surviving educational tradition in Indonesia. Long before the arrival of the European colonial powers in Southeast Asia, Islamic educational institutions were already well established on a number of islands in the archipelago, especially Sumatra and Java but extending as far east as the island of Ambon. The curriculum in those schools served the traditional aims of an Islamic education, i.e., to maintain orthodoxy by teaching students to read Arabic and analyze scripture well enough to gain an understanding of Islamic doctrine.

European Schools

The first European schools were also religious institutions, established after 1511 by the Jesuits in the Portuguese enclave of Malacca on the southwest coast of the Malay Peninsula and in the Molucca islands in eastern Indonesia. These schools were closed after the Dutch gained the upper hand in the area in 1641.

The first Dutch school in Jakarta was established in 1617, but enrollment was always small; in 1779 only 639 students were enrolled in three Dutch schools in Jakarta. On the island of Ambon, however, Dutch schools expanded more rapidly; by 1645 there were 33 schools enrolling 1,300 students and by 1708 the Ambon schools enrolled 3,996 students.

The growth of the educational system was negligible during the period of the Dutch East India Company. Only after the demise of the Company in 1799, the end of the four-year British interregnum in 1816, and the introduction in the 1820s of the *cultuurstelsel*, a system of forced cultivation, did the Dutch turn their attention to the development of a civil administration in their colonies. An educational system, however, was not established until the late 1840s. This system was two-tiered: one for children of the Dutch and one for Indonesian children. The Indonesian system was further subdivided into a seven-year upper track for the children of local aristocrats and a five-year lower track for the general population.

The colonial government established a Department of Education in 1867 and school enrollment grew to 52,000 pupils by 1892. Enrollment in missionary schools, especially in the Moluccas and North Sulawesi, grew from about 8,400 in 1871 to 15,750 in 1892. Although Dutch primary schools, Europeesche Lagere School/ELS, were opened to qualified Indonesians in 1864, Indonesians never made up more than a tiny fraction of the total enrollment. In 1893 a new two-tiered system was established for Indonesians: first class (*eerste klasse*) schools were established for the children of local aristocrats and second class (*tweede klasse*) schools for the general public.

Education to the Mid 1900s

In 1907 a different system of primary education for the general public was established: village schools (Volksschool) with three-year programs taught in Malay (the term then used to designate the Indonesian language) or other local languages, followed by a two-year continuation school (Vervolgschool). In some cases this led to a five-year Dutch-medium program in "link schools."

Although Indonesian enrollment in any kind of school was never more than a small fraction of the school-aged population, the expansion of educational opportunities at the beginning of the twentieth century reflected a growing need for Dutch-speaking Indonesians in the lower ranks of the government bureaucracy and in the expanding commercial sector. This led to the establishment of the Hollandsche-Inlandsche School/HIS. These schools offered a curriculum similar to the Dutch primary schools (ELS), but instruction, similar to the village school, was in Malay or another local language in the lower grades and in Dutch in the higher grades. Students who successfully completed HIS could continue in the Dutch secondary system or, after successfully completing the Lower Civil Service Examination, join the junior ranks of the colonial administration.

The success of the HIS led educators to recognize the need for other forms of schooling especially adapted to the particular needs of the colonies, and in 1914 a special version of the Dutch lower secondary system was established, the More Comprehensive Elementary School (Meer Uitgebreid Lager Onderwijs/MULO). The MULO differed from the other Dutch schools principally in its foreign language requirements; Dutch, German, and English were still required but French was optional and Malay was an additional choice. MULO graduates could seek admission to various trade schools or specialized schools, including two medical schools established to train Indonesian doctors. The latter were known by their acronyms, NIAS (Nederlandse-Indische Artsenschool) in Surabaya and STOVIA (School tot Opleiding van Inlandsche Artsen) in Jakarta. Their graduates, popularly known as *dokter Jawa*, achieved positions of prominence in colonial Indonesia.

After 1918 MULO graduates could also enter a special type of secondary school, the general secondary school (Algemeere Middelbare School/AMS). The AMS curriculum, at least in the "Eastern Classics" stream, was oriented towards Indonesian history, geography, and culture. English was the only compulsory European language. These schools were intended for ethnic Indonesians as well as the Dutch and the large Eurasian population permanently settled in Indonesia.

In the exclusively Dutch-medium system, in which Indonesian enrollment never exceeded 20%, the continental Dutch educational system was transferred to the colonies. Pupils began in the ELS or primary school. After completion of primary school, academic streaming began and students entered one of the types of secondary school designed to prepare them for tertiary studies: the Gymnasium; the Lyceum, which offered a traditional curriculum emphasizing classical languages; or the Hoogere Burger School (HBS). The system was extraordinarily elitist; selection was competitive and the failure rate was high among all students.

The resultant small number of secondary school graduates prepared to undertake tertiary studies explains in part why the Dutch had developed only the barest beginnings of a tertiary education system in Indonesia by the outbreak of World War II. An additional constraint on the development of tertiary education was the Dutch view that tertiary institutions developed in Indonesia should meet the same standards as continental Dutch institutions. The first tertiary institution in Indonesia, the Technical Higher School (Technische Hoogeschool), later to become the Bandung Institute of Technology (Institut Teknologi Bandung/ITB), was founded in 1921. In Jakarta a faculty of law was founded in 1924, a faculty of medicine in 1927, and a faculty of letters in 1940. An agricultural faculty was set up in Bogor in 1940.

Chinese Schools

The Dutch were not specifically concerned with education for the Chinese population, so the Chinese in Jakarta opened a Chinese-medium school in 1901. Similar schools were soon opened in other cities in Java and on other islands. In response to this development in 1908 the Dutch opened the Hollandsch-Chineesche Schools (HCS), the first schools in Indonesia to offer a Dutch-medium education to the Chinese. Although the Indonesian-born Chinese were quick to realize the advantages of Dutch-medium education, most Chinese were still educated in Chinese-medium schools. These schools were culturally and politically oriented towards China, an orientation induced by the civil status of the Chinses population as foreign orientals (*vreemde Oosterlingan*).

Japanese Occupation

With the Japanese occupation of Indonesia from 1942 to 1945 came the dismantling of the Dutch educational system. The use of Dutch was forbidden and the medium of instruction, if not Japanese, was Indonesian. After the declaration of independence in 1945, Indonesia struggled against the restoration of Dutch rule until 1949 when, under international pressure, the Dutch finally agreed to transfer sovereignty to an independent Indonesia. Indonesians then found themselves facing the difficult task, for which they had been ill-prepared by the Dutch, of establishing a civil administration in a country devastated by the wartime Japanese occupation.

Early Years of Independence

The development of an educational system in Indonesia was shaped by the country's first constitution, promulgated in 1945, and also by a number of education laws enacted in the early years of independence. The first national education law, National Law No.

4, enacted in a spirit of revolutionary optimism in 1950, declared the right of every Indonesian to an education, and the early 1950s saw the first attempts at coordinated large-scale expansion of the educational system. At the same time, attention was given to nonformal education and adult literacy programs.

The first new tertiary institution to be established in post-war Indonesia was Gadjah Mada University, founded in 1949 in Yogyakarta. A year later, the University of Indonesia was founded in Jakarta. Although this was a new university, it was also to some extent the result of an amalgamation of the medicine, law, and arts faculties established by the Dutch before the war.

In practical terms, even though Indonesia achieved independence in 1949, there were very few resources available for the development of a tertiary education system. Nonetheless, university expansion began in the 1950s and the pace increased in the early 1960s, when it was felt that each of the then 26 provinces (27 today, with the integration of East Timor in 1976) should have at least one university. Thirty of the present 49 state tertiary institutions were established during this period. In some cases these institutions were the result of the "nationalization" of formerly private institutions.

Consistency and quality of development were problematic in the late 1950s and early 1960s, as the country entered a period of political instability and economic decline. Sovereignty was threatened by secessionist rebellions and the economy deteriorated as international trade and domestic capital investment declined and hyper-inflation developed. In the wake of an unsuccessful coup attempt in 1965, the initial moves towards political change began; in 1966 executive power was transferred to then General Suharto. In the early years of what has come to be known as the "New Order," Indonesia reoriented itself towards the West and adopted western economic models as the basis for its development planning strategies.

The New Order

In 1969 President Suharto began the first of the Repelita five-year development cycles. The second cycle (1974-75 to 1978-79) saw primary education enrollments rise from 13 to 19 million, increasing the proportion of children educated in primary schools from 65% to 89%. During this period, teaching staff from the major state tertiary institutions on Java began receiving training in the United States and other western nations.

The huge oil price increases and resultant windfall profits of the late 1970s provided unforeseen funds for the Indonesian state budget. For the first time in its history, Indonesia had the fiscal capacity to formulate and implement long-term development plans. In addition, the role played by a group of western-trained planners and fiscal managers who rose to prominence in the early years of the New Order was a significant factor in enabling the government to deal authoritatively and coherently with fiscal, educational, and development policy issues.

Since the late 1960s, educational achievements have been remarkable. Progress towards universal primary education has been especially noteworthy, from only 50% of primary-aged children with access to schools in 1968 to a 91% net enrollment in 1992. At the same time, secondary enrollment has risen from only 10% in 1968 to 41% today.

Tertiary education also entered a period of sustained systematic expansion. State tertiary institutions not only expanded their enrollments but began the first systematic development of their facilities and strengthening of their faculties. Hundreds of lecturers were sent abroad to pursue postgraduate degrees under foreign scholarship programs. In addition, Indonesian state institutions initiated their own graduate programs, beginning at the Bogor Institute of Agriculture (Institut Pertanian Bogor/IPB) in 1975. Today 12 state tertiary institutions award graduate degrees.

In response to the increasing demand for tertiary education that the state system cannot fulfill, private tertiary institutions have grown dramatically. Although quality is an issue, the approximately 1,000 private institutions clearly play a vital role in Indonesian higher education.

Indonesia has made great strides in all areas of education. Numerous challenges must still be met, however, if the country is to achieve the ambitious economic and development goals it has set for itself. The National Education Law of 1989 set standards for all educational levels and for state and private educational institutions. This law also redefined basic education as comprising nine years, up from six. The planned curriculum changes of 1994 will implement this law, meaning that many new secondary schools will be needed in the coming years.

Indonesia must also make substantial improvements in the quality of its teachers as well as its educational facilities. In 1991 almost one third of primary and lower secondary students had no textbooks. The bottom 25% of primary schools had teacher-student ratios ranging from 1:45 to 1:100. The most noteworthy of the special teacher-training projects attempting to correct these problems is the Open University distance learning program aimed at upgrading primary and lower secondary teachers.

Achievement of high (at least 80%) secondary enrollment and improvement of vocational education is vital if Indonesia is to meet the challenges posed by the increasingly competitive economies of Southeast Asia.

II. Preprimary, Primary, and Secondary Education

Kindergarten

The majority of the 36,190 kindergartens (*taman kanak-kanak*) listed in 1988 by the Ministry of Education and Culture's Directorate of Primary Education (Direktorat Pendidikan Dasar/Dikdas) are privately run. In fact only 61 are state schools, 27 of which are designated as "model" kindergartens, one in each province. In 1988 the 81,500 kindergarten teachers (99% female) catered to over 1.5 million children aged 3-6, with an average teacher-student ratio of 1:19. Private kindergartens meeting government criteria for qualified staff, adequate facilities, certified enrollment, financial soundness, systematic administration and management, use of government curriculum, and general neatness and cleanliness are eligible for government subsidies in the form of teachers seconded from state schools, teacher training programs, and classroom and library materials.

Approximately 25% of kindergarten teachers have only a lower or upper secondary school diploma. The majority are graduates of teacher training high schools, Sekolah Pendidikan Guru/SPG (see chapter V, Teacher Training). The Ministry of Education and Culture (Departemen Pendidikan dan Kebudayaan/Depdikbud) ran special upgrading courses from 1979 to 1985 for these underqualified teachers. However, all SPGs closed in 1992, when the last students were graduated, raising the question of where future kindergarten teachers will be trained. To date, no regulation specifies kindergarten teacher qualifications, although a two-year postsecondary requirement (Diploma II) from either a teacher training institute (IKIP) or a university department of teacher training (FKIP) has been considered.

The Directorate of Primary Education in 1976 provided a national curriculum for kindergartens that attempts to develop the "Pancasila person,"[1] in addition to language ability, cognitive skills, motor/physical skills, creativity, social skills, moral/religious attitudes, and health and body awareness. Students attend school six days a week and are divided into three groups according to age (see Table 2.1).

Table 2.1. Kindergarten Age Grouping

Class	Age	Hours/Day	Hours/Week
A	3-4	2	12
B	4-5	2.5	15
C	5-6	2.75	16

[1]Pancasila is the five-point national ideology whose tenets are belief in one supreme God, justice and civility among peoples, the unity of Indonesia, democracy through deliberation and consensus among representatives, and social justice for all.

Primary Education

The government of Indonesia has significantly expanded primary education (*pendidikan dasar*) through the Repelita, or the Five-Year Development Plans that began in 1969. Indeed, a recent World Bank study called the achievement "one of the most successful cases of large-scale school system expansion on record." Aanenson's World Education Series volume on *Indonesia* (1979) listed 80,261 primary schools (*sekolah dasar*/SD) in 1976; by 1991 the number had almost doubled to some 147,000 primary schools (roughly 7% private) with an enrollment of 23,500,000 students (1,900,000 private). These figures do not include students enrolled in the Ministry of Religious Affairs schools (see chapter VI, Islamic Education). State primary schools graduated 3,100,000 students in 1990.

Six years of primary education are now compulsory and nearly universal. Grade 1 enrollment in 1991 reached 97.71% of the age cohort. Government programs have been instituted to reach the remaining 2.29%, who are classified as "underprivileged" because of a combination of economic and demographic factors (homelessness, isolation, nomadic lifestyle, and poverty). Dropout rates during the first three years average 10%. A World Bank review in 1989 found that, of 100 students enrolled in grade 1, 42 will graduate in 6 years, 42 will repeat the year, and 16 will drop out.

Administration and Finance

Two ministries oversee primary education: the Ministry of Education and Culture/MOEC is responsible for the training, certification, and evaluation of teachers as well as the curriculum; the Ministry of Home Affairs/MOHA (Departemen Dalam Negeri) is responsible for land, physical facilities, salary disbursement, school operating budgets, and teacher hiring and placement. Both ministries operate through regional and local offices.

Primary education funds come from three basic sources. The development budget pays for books, supplies, and teaching materials. In 1988-89, approximately U.S. $2.45 was allocated per student per year. In addition, a government subsidy for education, Subsudi Bantuan Pembiayaan Penyelenggaraan/SBPP, was instituted when primary fees were abolished in 1978 to pay for nonsalary operating and maintenance costs. In 1988-89 this averaged $1.50 per pupil. The third source, the routine budget, provides teachers' salaries, which in 1989 was approximately $67 per primary teacher per month. Additional funds are provided by the Presidential Instruction Fund (Inpres SD), which initially financed the construction of primary school buildings but today provides funds mainly for school renovation and housing for teachers.

Because of the inadequacy of these funds, primary schools depend heavily on parents' association contributions (Badan Pembinaan dan Penyelenggaraan Pendidikan/BP3) for books, supplies, and supplements to teachers' salaries. Primary schools often depend on BP3 contributions to make up the difference between school budgets as estimated by the headmasters and the funds provided by local and central government. Poorer areas thus receive poorer quality education. Moreover, the inability of poor families to pay the BP3 contributions sometimes discourages parents from enrolling their children.

Curriculum

The Directorate General of Primary and Secondary Education (Direktorat Jenderal Pendidikan Dasar dan Menengah/Dikdasmen) under MOEC sets the primary school curriculum (see Table 2.2), which must be followed by all schools (except those under the Ministry of Religion).

Table 2.2. Primary School Curriculum

Subjects	Grade/Hours per Week					
	I	II	III	IV	V	VI
Religion	2	2	2	3	3	3
Pancasila/Civics	2	2	2	2	2	2
History of the Struggle of the Nation*	1	1	1	1	1	1
Indonesian Language**	8/7	8/7	8/7	8/7	8/7	8/7
Social Studies	-	-	2	3	3	3
Mathematics	6	6	6	6	6	6
Physical Sciences	2	2	3	4	4	4
Physical Education and Health	2	2	3	3	3	3
Art	2	2	3	3	3	3
Handicrafts	2	2	4	4	4	4
Local Language***	(2)	(2)	(2)	(2)	(2)	(2)
Total Hours per Week	26	26	33	36	36	36
	(28)	(28)	(35)	(38)	(38)	(38)

SOURCE: Departemen Pendidikan dan Kebudayaan, *Garis-Garis Besar Program Pengajaran*, Direktorat Pendidikan Dasar, Dikdasmen, Jakarta. 1987.
*Given only every third term.
**8 hours/week, terms 1 and 2; 7 hours/week, term 3.
***Only offered in certain schools; increases total study hours.

The primary school year runs for 254 days, from July to June, and is divided into three terms. Students attend either morning or afternoon school six days a week, with students in grades 1 and 2 receiving instruction in 30-minute periods over three hours. Those in grades 3 through 6 attend for five hours. Only Indonesian and mathematics are taught every day. A single class teacher teaches all subjects except religion, art, and physical education. Religious instruction must be provided for students in their professed religion.

A national curriculum introduced in 1968 has since gone through two revisions, a major one in 1976 that set "mastery levels" for student achievement, followed by supplements to the curriculum in 1984. The 1984 curriculum (see Table 2.2) emphasizes "patriotism, the affective domain, and the spirit of independence." The teaching approach is based on active learning, the outcome of a pilot project begun in 1980 in selected West Java primary schools. The method (known as Cara Belajar Secara Aktif/CBSA, or Student Active Learning Project/SALP) proved so popular that its use spread rapidly, and in 1987 MOEC decided that preservice primary and secondary teachers and teachers receiving inservice training should be taught active learning methods. However, implementation of the system has not been easy. It requires close cooperation between supervisors, principals, and teachers, as well as use of materials not easily obtained by students in isolated areas. Because of its prestige, many schools claim to use the method, but they in fact emphasize rote learning and memorization. And teacher effectiveness has been limited by the government's inability to distribute enough curriculum manuals.

A new curriculum is planned for 1994 when nine years of basic education become a single unit and compulsory. Also planned are curricular consolidations at the primary level to avoid overlap of subjects and to simplify what critics say is a crowded curriculum.

Teachers and Supervision

Until 1989, primary teachers were certified after successfully completing three years in an upper secondary teacher training school. Since 1989, however, primary teachers must hold a two-year, tertiary-level qualification, a Diploma II (DII). Because an estimated 97% of state and 94% of private teachers have less than a DII qualification, the Directorate of Primary Education has been working with the Open University to upgrade primary teachers to the DII level in an inservice distance learning program. A total of 48,000 students were enrolled in 1992 (see chapter V, Teacher Training).

Nationally, there are 1.14 teachers per class, with a teacher-student ratio ranging from 1:6 to 1:50. The variation is due to the government's tendency to supply a full contingent of teachers to schools in isolated areas and to respond slowly to population shifts to industrializing areas (usually at the outskirts of cities).

Five thousand MOEC supervisors oversee 1,150,000 teachers. Each is responsible for an average of 26 primary schools, 12 principals, and 200 teachers.

Tests and Grading

Primary school students receive a report card at the end of each term, or three times a year. At the end of each term, students take an exam in each subject set by the local

Ministry of Education office. The final grade is based on work done during the term and a final examination. A grade of 4 or below is considered failing. The last report passes a student to the next grade or fails a student, who then must repeat the grade or drop out. The grading scale used at the secondary level (see p. 19) is also used in primary schools.

At the end of the sixth year, all students sit the national final examination, Evaluasi Belajar Tahap Akhir Nasional Sekolah Dasar/EBTANAS SD, a comprehensive examination in five subject areas: Pancasila/civics, Indonesian language, social studies, mathematics, and physical/natural science. The result, *nilai* EBTANAS *murni*/NEM, is given twice the weight of the school's own final examination and the student's report card grade in determining whether the student will pass or fail. The formula is as follows:

$$\frac{P + Q + nR}{2 + n}$$

P = the grade report from first two terms of Grade 6
Q = the end-of-year exam by the school
R = the EBTANAS score
n = the weight for primary school; the usual weight is 2, indicating that the EBTANAS score is given twice the importance of the other two scores. These weights may vary by region.[2]

The usefulness of EBTANAS SD has often been questioned in light of the anticipated nine-year compulsory education and because of the unevenness in the five versions of each test. Test items among versions are not weighted equally in difficulty, so comparisons among regions cannot be made. The pass rate is generally in the 90 percentile range.

Students are awarded an EBTANAS SD certificate used to select those moving on to the lower secondary level, but many students must also take an entrance examination to gain admission to their chosen school. Graduating students also receive a Surat Tanda Tamat Belajar Sekolah Dasar/STTB SD, the primary school certificate of completion, signed by the school principal.

Secondary Education

The Indonesian secondary education system is a six-year unit divided into three years of lower secondary school and three years of upper secondary school. At both levels the system is further divided into general secondary/academic education (*pendidikan menengah umum*) and secondary vocational education (*pendidikan menengah kejuruan*); however, the plethora of terms used to refer to educational levels and the types of schools

---

[2]SOURCE: Florida State University, et al. *Indonesia: Education and Human Resources Sector Review,* April 1986, Vol. 2, chapter 5, p. 44.

is confusing. The term Sekolah Lanjutan Tingkat Pertama/SLTP refers to all types of lower secondary schools, academic and vocational. The term Sekolah Menengah Pertama/SMP refers specifically to general academic lower secondary schools. Almost all lower secondary schools are general academic schools; vocational school enrollments at this level are very small. The term Sekolah Lanjutan Tingkat Atas/SLTA refers to all types of upper secondary schools. General academic upper secondary schools are known as Sekolah Menengah Atas/SMA. Vocational upper secondary schools (see pp. 17, 18) are of different types. Approximately 35% of all upper secondary students are enrolled in vocational schools.

In the last 25 years, secondary education has undergone significant change, particularly in the areas of curriculum, testing and evaluation, vocational education, and upgrading of teachers. Not only has the secondary school-aged population expanded but the definition of educational needs has broadened as well.

The secondary education system has grown dramatically. In 1979, 4 million students were enrolled in lower and upper secondary schools; by 1989 this figure had increased to 10 million. The number of lower and upper secondary schools had almost tripled, from 13,000 in 1979 to 32,000 in 1989 and the number of teachers had grown from 235,000 to 815,000. Although quantitative expansion of the system has been impressive, in 1988 only 40% of the secondary school-aged population was enrolled in secondary school. Indonesia must also reckon with the fact that as of 1987 only 10.5% of the population had graduated from either lower or upper secondary school.

With rising secondary enrollment and nine-year compulsory education on the horizon, the government has turned its attention to the renovation of more than 11,000 existing secondary classrooms and the construction of 12,450 new classrooms. Facilities vary greatly within the country. Although urban schools may be less disadvantaged than their rural counterparts, the contrast in educational quality is often more apparent in urban areas where the most selective state secondary schools and the best private secondary schools offer adequate facilities and qualified teachers. Private urban secondary schools with only lower accreditation status (see Private Secondary Education, below) very often have poor facilities, especially for teaching science, mathematics, and languages.

Administration and Finance

State and private secondary schools under MOEC supervision, both general academic and vocational, are administered by the Directorate General of Primary and Secondary Education (Direktorat Jendral Pendidikan Dasar dan Menengah/Dikdasmen). Administrative responsibility is further delegated to a number of directorates, three of which—the Directorate of General Secondary Education (Direktorat Pendidikan Menengah Umum), the Directorate of Secondary Vocational Education (Direktorat Pendidikan Menengah Kejuruan), and the Directorate of Private Schools (Direktorat Sekolah Swasta)—share principal responsibility for school administration. At the provincial level supervision and school inspections are carried out through MOEC district offices (*kantor wilayah* or *kanwil*).

State secondary education is financed through three main sources: the Anggaran Belanja Rutin Negara/ABRN, the routine government budget; the Dana Penunjang Pendidikan/DPP, funds for supporting education; and the Badan Penyelenggaraan Program Pendidikan/BP3, a parents' organization that funds school activities. The routine government budget generally provides the largest share, between 70% and 85%, of total costs, of which about 75% is spent on teacher's salaries. The DPP, primarily student fees, are collected and distributed in a rather complex manner. MOEC applies a sliding scale to provinces and individual secondary schools to determine the amount an individual student pays. The student fees are collected at each school and deposited in a local bank before being sent to Jakarta for national redistribution. In 1987, 75% of these funds were allocated to secondary schools; 25% went to local and district-level MOEC offices. Of the funds distributed to individual secondary schools, 50% was allocated to teacher salaries. The remainder was used for teacher upgrading, materials, and maintenance.

The third source of funding, BP3 contributions, consist solely of parental contributions, which vary widely from school to school and from province to province. Although in theory parents may determine how these funds will be spent, school officials are very influential in their allocation. Some schools use these funds to defray the costs of routine expenses, such as tests; in fewer cases, they are used to purchase additional teaching equipment. Like the supporting fund, however, parental contributions are in most cases used to supplement teachers' salaries.

Private Secondary Education

Private secondary schools enroll a considerable proportion of Indonesia's secondary student population: 35% of the total enrollment at the lower secondary level (SMP) and 65% at the upper secondary level (SMA) in 1989-90. Especially at the upper secondary level, private schools satisfy a demand for secondary education which MOEC cannot fill. In 1989-90, of the 11,550 upper secondary schools in Indonesia, 9,100 were private. General academic secondary schools comprise about 70% of this figure; vocational schools about 30%.

Accreditation. MOEC monitors and evaluates educational programs in the private system. It accredits private lower and upper secondary schools as equalized (*disamakan*), recognized (*diakui*), or registered (*terdaftar*) on the basis of their curriculum, teacher qualifications, physical plant, administrative capability, institutional development, and student body composition. The first three factors are considered the most important. Equalized schools are officially considered equal to state schools in terms of curriculum and facilities. In 1990-91 only 524 of the almost 14,000 lower secondary schools were equalized. Over 11,000 were recognized or registered and almost 2,000 were "listed" or unaccredited. Of the total 9,200 private upper secondary schools, only 455, mostly elite urban institutions, held equalized status. An equalized private upper secondary school is authorized to conduct its own end-of-year examinations (Evaluasi Belajar Tahap Akhir/EBTA) and may be asked by MOEC to conduct the EBTA examinations for other schools with a lower accreditation status.

The vast majority of upper secondary schools, over 6,800, were either recognized or registered; almost 2,000 were merely "listed" or unaccredited. A recognized private upper secondary school is authorized to conduct its own EBTA examinations while the students of a registered private upper secondary school must sit the EBTA examinations at a secondary school authorized by the local MOEC office.

The small number of private general academic secondary schools that are highly selective and equal in prestige to the best state secondary schools are often run by Catholic, Protestant, or Islamic religious foundations. The majority of private general academic secondary schools are generally inferior to the state secondary schools and were established to offer secondary education to students not selected by the more competitive state schools.

Many private secondary schools operate in cooperation with state secondary schools. For example, a state secondary school may operate in the morning and rent its premises to a private school to hold its classes in the afternoons. Some private schools own their own buildings while many others operate from rented premises. Teachers from state secondary schools often teach after hours in private secondary schools.

Lower Secondary Education

In 1989-90, 2,009,000 students (60%) out of a total of 3,355,000 primary school students who had graduated in 1988-89 entered the first year of lower secondary school (SMP or SLTP, state and private). In the same year total enrollment in state and private lower secondary schools was 5,850,000. Most students (98.3%) enrolled in general academic lower secondary schools. Vocational lower secondary schools enrolled less than 2% of the students at this level in 1989-90. These schools will be phased out with the introduction of a new curriculum in 1994 that defines basic education as a unitary nine-year program (see below, 1994 Curriculum Reform). Currently, the three types of lower secondary vocational schools are:

- lower secondary technical schools (Sekolah Teknik/ST)
- lower secondary home economics schools (Sekolah Kesejahteraan Keluarga Tingkat Pertama/SKKP)
- lower secondary commercial schools (Sekolah Menengah Ekonomi Tingkat Pertama/SMETP)

There are 20,000 lower secondary schools in Indonesia and a total of 467,000 teachers. In 1989 the average class size was 39. According to MOEC figures, 1,802,100 students completed lower secondary school in 1988-89 and 1,401,600 or 70% continued to upper secondary school in 1989-90.

Lower Secondary School Teachers

At the lower secondary level teachers must hold at least a Diploma II, representing two years of postsecondary education. MOEC reports that in 1989-90 only 28% of lower secondary teachers met this minimum requirement; 72% held no postsecondary qualification or held a one-year postsecondary diploma (DI) (see chapter V, Teacher Training).

Curriculum

The lower secondary school year runs 240 days and is divided into two semesters. Students attend either morning or afternoon schools six days a week. A typical school week is divided into 37 to 40 periods of 40 minutes each, as required by MOEC.

The lower secondary curriculum reflects the ideological priorities of the state. The present lower secondary curriculum was implemented in 1984 as a refinement of the 1976 curriculum reforms. In addition to the teaching of Pancasila (the official state ideology), mathematics, languages, science, social science, religion, and Indonesian history are also required. It should be noted that compulsory religious education classes in Indonesian schools, from the primary level up to and including the first semester of tertiary studies, are offered to students on the basis of their professed belief.

An official MOEC lower secondary curriculum is reproduced in Table 2.3. Except for the addition of local languages or other special subjects, the curriculum is standard throughout the country. However, many schools are unable to complete the full scope of the curriculum. A number of factors contribute to this: overall teacher shortages; a shortage of qualified subject teachers especially in the physical sciences, mathematics, and languages; and an inadequate supply of instructional materials, especially textbooks.

Testing and Evaluation

Students sit national school leaving examinations, Evaluasi Belajar Tingkat Akhir Nasional/EBTANAS, at the primary, lower secondary, and upper secondary levels. These examinations have three goals: to certify successful school completion, to provide a basis of selection for the next educational level, and to provide a quality control check on the effectiveness of the system. Examination results are weighted differentially to allow school administrators more flexibility in determining whether or not a student passes.

The result of the lower secondary school leavers' exam, EBTANAS SMP, is called NEM (*nilai* EBTANAS *murni*), and it is given twice the weight of the school's own final examination and the student's report card grade in determining whether the student will receive a Surat Tanda Tamat Belajar Sekolah Menengah Umum Tingkat Pertama/STTB SMP, the lower secondary school certificate of completion. The formula is as follows:

$$\frac{P + Q + nR}{2 + n}$$

P = the grade report from the 4th and 5th semesters
Q = the end-of-year exam by the school
R = the EBTANAS score
n = the weight for primary school; the usual weight is 2, indicating that the EBTANAS score is given twice the importance of the other two scores. These weights may vary by region.[3]

Table 2.3. Lower Secondary School Curriculum

Subject	Year Sem.	I 1	2	II 3	4	III 5	6	Periods/ Week
Religion		2	2	2	2	2	2	12
Pancasila/Civics		2	2	2	2	2	2	12
History of the Struggle of the Nation		-	2	-	2	-	2	6
Physical Education and Health		3	3	3	3	3	3	18
Art		2	2	2	2	2	2	12
Indonesian Language		5	5	5	5	5	5	30
Local Language*		(2)	(2)	(2)	(2)	(2)	(2)	(12)
English		4	4	4	4	4	4	24
Social Science		4	4	4	4	4	4	24
Mathematics		6	4	6	4	6	4	30
Natural Sciences								
Biology		3	3	2	2	2	2	14
Physics		3	3	3	3	3	3	18
Vocational Education**		4	4	4	4	4	4	24
Total Hours per Week		38	38	37	37	37	37	224
		(40)	(40)	(39)	(39)	(39)	(39)	(236)

SOURCE: Department of Primary and Secondary Education, and *An Analysis of the Status of Curriculum Reform and Textbook Production in Indonesia*, Florida State University, et al. April 1990, p. 10.
    *For areas or schools that offer local language.
    **Each semester one study packet is chosen.

---

[3]SOURCE: Florida State University, et al. *Indonesia: Education and Human Resources Sector Review*, April 1986, Vol. 2, chapter 5, p. 44.

Although 90% of lower secondary school leavers passed the EBTANAS examination in 1989, only 74% continued to upper secondary school. The 24% drop in the transition rate reflects a number of socioeconomic factors, such as longer distance from home to upper secondary school and increased school expenses.

EBTANAS results are the most important determinants of an SMP leaver's upper secondary school placement, acting as a filtering device for entrance to either general academic upper secondary schools or nonacademic vocational upper secondary schools. General academic upper secondary schools known for quality set higher minimum EBTANAS scores and almost always have many more applicants than available places. Less prestigious schools set lower standards in order to ensure full enrollment.

Upper Secondary Education

Upper secondary education in Indonesia is offered by two types of schools: general academic upper secondary schools and a variety of vocational upper secondary schools. General academic education *(pendidikan menengah umum)* at the upper secondary level is administered by the Directorate of General Secondary Education (Direktorat Pendidikan Menengah Umum).

Vocational education *(pendidikan kejuruan)* is organized under the Directorate of Vocational Secondary Education (Direktorat Pendidikan Menengah Kejuruan). The principal types of vocational upper secondary school are:

- technical upper secondary school (Sekolah Teknik Menengah/STM)
- commercial upper secondary school (Sekolah Menengah Ekonomi Atas/SMEA)
- home economics upper secondary school (Sekolah Menengah Kesejahteraan Keluarga/SMKK).

There are also several other types of vocational upper secondary schools with very small enrollments, fewer than 5,000 in 1989-90. These schools include the following:

- home technology vocational upper secondary school (Sekolah Mengenah Teknologi Kerumahtanggaan/SMTK)
- handicraft industry vocational upper secondary school (Sekolah Menengah Industri Kerajinan/SMIK)
- traditional dance vocational upper secondary school (Sekolah Menengah Karawitan Indonesia/SMKI)
- music vocational upper secondary school (Sekolah Menengah Musik/SMM)
- art vocational upper secondary school (Sekolah Menengah Seni Rupa/SMSR)
- graphic arts vocational upper secondary school (Sekolah Menengah Teknologi Grafika/SMT Grafika)
- shipbuilding vocational upper secondary school (Sekolah Menengah Teknologi Perkapalan/SMT Perkapalan)

- agriculture vocational upper secondary school (Sekolah Teknologi Menengah Pertanian/STM Pertanian)
- aviation technology vocational upper secondary school (Sekolah Menengah Teknologi Penerbangan/STM Penerbangan)
- chemistry vocational upper secondary school (Sekolah Menengah Teknologi Kimia/SMT Kimia)

In addition, there are a small number of vocational upper secondary schools which offer an intensive four-year curriculum and are referred to as development vocational upper secondary schools (Sekolah Teknologi Menengah Pembangunan/STM Pembangunan). An accounting curriculum from a commercial upper secondary school is given in Table 2.4.

One of the most salient features of the upper secondary system since 1977 has been the growth of general academic secondary education. Enrollment in vocational upper secondary schools has declined from over 55% of the total enrollment in 1977 to less than 35% in 1989-90. This decline reflects the increased value attached to general academic secondary education because of the access it provides to tertiary studies. On the other hand, development trends in the Indonesian economy indicate an increasing need for larger numbers of skilled workers and technicians.

In 1989-90 upper secondary schools enrolled 4,030,000 students and employed 347,000 teachers. The teacher-student ratio is thus 1:12. Although this ratio appears at first glance to be quite favorable, it should be noted that the teacher spends less time in the classroom per week than the student and that a secondary school may employ a number of part-time or nonpermanent staff. These teachers contribute to the low ratio although they do not necessarily teach every day. Therefore, average class size, 39 students per classroom in 1989, is a more realistic indicator.

Teachers

The minimum qualification for upper secondary teachers is a Diploma III (DIII), representing three years of postsecondary education. In 1989-90, 32% held a DIII, 41% held a *sarjana* degree (the first academic degree), 1% held a postgraduate degree, and the remaining 26% held less than a DIII.

Curriculum

The upper secondary school year runs 240 days and is divided into two semesters. Students attend either morning or afternoon schools six days a week. A typical school week is divided into 38 to 40 periods of 40 or 45 minutes each. This is a basic MOEC requirement. In practice, many of the better general academic upper secondary schools, both state and private, offer additional instruction, e.g., foreign languages or computer skills, in excess of this requirement.

Streaming in general academic upper secondary schools begins in the second year. The four streams are physics (A1), biology (A2), social science (A3), and language and culture (A4). In practice this last stream is seldom offered, except occasionally in urban upper secondary schools. The division of the curriculum into these four streams is an organizational remnant of the Dutch educational system. The mandatory curriculum is the same for all streams, i.e., Pancasila/civics, religion, history, and Indonesian language (see Table 2.5).

The stream students enter in the second year of upper secondary school effectively determines which university departments they may apply to upon completion of upper secondary school. The absence of advanced mathematics and the physical sciences from the social science and language and culture curricula means that graduates of these streams are limited to certain fields of study when they apply to tertiary institutions. However, science stream graduates may apply to any university department. Thus the actual function of secondary streaming appears to be selection based on competitive ranking of academic ability in mathematics and natural sciences, not selection based on aptitude or interest.

Testing and Evaluation

Upper secondary school students are tested and reports are issued each semester. The grading scale is given below.

Grade	Meaning
10	*istimewa*/excellent
9	*baik sekali*/very good
8	*baik*/good
7	*lebih dari cukup*/above average
6	*cukup*/average
5	*hampir cukup*/below average
4	*kurang*/fail
3	*kurang sekali*/fail
2	*buruk*/fail
1	*buruk sekali*/fail

The upper secondary leaving examination, EBTANAS SMA, taken in the final semester of upper secondary school, covers most subjects taught in the three years of upper secondary school, with particular emphasis on the later semesters. Students in all four streams are tested on three subjects: Pancasila/civics, Indonesian language and literature, and English language. In addition, students in the physics and biology streams are tested on mathematics, physics, biology, and chemistry. Students in the social sciences stream are tested on mathematics, economics, public administration, and

Table 2.4.   Accounting Curriculum, Commercial Upper Secondary School, 1984

Year	I		II		III		Total
Sem.	1	2	3	4	5	6	Credits
Subject							
Religion	2	2	2	2	2	2	12
Pancasila/Civics	2	2	2	2	2	2	12
History of the Struggle of the Nation	2	-	2	-	2	-	6
Indonesian and World History	-	2	-	2	-	2	6
Indonesian Language and Literature	2	2	2	2	2	2	12
Physical Education and Health	2	2	2	2	2	-	10
Mathematics	4	4	4	4	-	-	16
English Language	3	3	4	4	4	4	22*
Introduction to Management	2	2	-	-	-	-	4
Economics	2	2	2	2	-	-	8
Cooperatives	2	2	2	2	-	-	8
Introduction to Business	4	4	-	-	-	-	8
Introduction to Accounting	4	4	-	-	-	-	8
Civil Law and Trade	2	2	2	2	-	-	8
Corresponding in Indonesian	3	3	-	-	-	-	6
Higher Financial Accounting	-	-	7	7	5	5	24
Cost Accounting	-	-	4	4	5	5	18
Financial Report Analysis	-	-	-	-	2	4	6
Internship	-	-	-	-	2	2	4
Data Management Technology	-	-	-	-	4	4	8
Taxes	-	-	-	-	4	4	8
Statistics	-	-	2	2	2	2	8
Business Economics	-	-	2	2	2	2	8

Source: Depdikbud. 1987. *Panduan Belajar ke Sekolah Menengah Kejuruan Tingkat Atas* (SMKTA) (Guide to Study in Upper Secondary Vocational Schools).

*10 credits in basic English Language, 12 in Business English = 22 credits.

Table 2.5. Upper Secondary Core Curriculum for All Streams and A1-A4 Core Curricula

Year	I		II		III		Study
Sem.	1	2	3	4	5	6	Load
Subject							
Religious Education	2	2	2	2	2	2	12
Pancasila/Civics	2	2	2	2	2	2	12
History of the Struggle of the Nation	2	-	2	-	2	-	6
Indonesian Language and Literature	4	4	3	3	2	2	18
Indonesian and World History	3	3	2	2	2	2	14
Economics	3	3	-	-	-	-	6
Geography	-	-	2	2	3	3	10
Physical Education	2	2	2	2	-	-	8
Art	3	3	2	2	-	-	10
Handicrafts	2	4	2	2	-	-	10
Mathematics	4	4	-	-	-	-	8
Biology	3	3	-	-	-	-	6
Physics	2	2	-	-	-	-	4
Chemistry	2	2	-	-	-	-	4
English	3	3	-	-	-	-	6
Total Credits							134 (60%)
A1/Physics Subjects							
Mathematics	-	-	6	6	8	6	26
Biology	-	-	2	2	3	3	10
Physics	-	-	4	6	6	6	22
English	-	-	3	3	3	3	12
Chemistry	-	-	4	4	5	5	18
Total Credits							88 (40%)
Total Credit Load							222 (100%)
A2/Biology Subjects							
Mathematics	-	-	4	4	6	6	20

(continued)

Biology	-	-	4	6	7	5	22
Physics	-	-	4	4	4	4	16
Chemistry	-	-	4	4	5	5	18
English	-	-	3	3	3	3	12
Total Credits							88 (40%)
Total Credit Load							222 (100%)
A3/Social Science Subjects							
Economics	-	-	5	5	5	5	20
Sociology and Anthropology	-	-	3	3	3	3	12
Civics	-	-	2	2	3	3	10
Mathematics	-	-	3	4	4	3	14
English	-	-	3	5	6	6	20
Other Foreign Languages	-	-	3	2	4	3	12
Total Credits							88 (40%)
Total Credit Load							222 (100%)
A4/Language and Culture							
Cultural History	-	-	4	4	4	4	16
Literature	-	-	3	3	6	4	16
Sociology and Anthropology	-	-	2	4	4	4	14
English	-	-	5	5	7	7	24
Regional/Other Foreign Languages	-	-	3	3	4	4	14
Mathematics	-	-	2	2	-	-	4
Total Credits							88 (40%)
Total Credit Load							222 (100%)

SOURCE: "Secondary Education in Indonesia In Brief," Ministry of Education and Culture, Directorate General of Primary and Secondary Education, Directorate of Secondary Education, Jakarta. August 22, 1991.

sociology and anthropology. Students in the language and culture stream are tested on cultural history, literature, other foreign or local languages (depending on the school), and sociology and anthropology.

Passing the EBTANAS SMA (see Document 2.1) is a prerequisite to receiving an upper secondary certificate of completion, Surat Tanda Tamat Belajar Sekolah

Menengah Umum Tingkat Atas/STTB SMA (see Document 2.2). The results are weighted according to the same formula as that used for the primary level EBTANAS. The result, NEM (*nilai* EBTANAS *murni*), is given twice the weight of the school's own final examination and the student's report card grade. The formula is as follows:

$$\frac{P + Q + nR}{2 + n}$$

P = the grade report from 4th and 5th semesters
Q = the end-of-year exam by the school
R = the EBTANAS score
n = the weight for upper secondary school; the usual weight is 2, indicating that the EB-TANAS score is given twice the importance of the other two scores. These weightings may vary by region.[4]

Overall, this examination is less important than the lower secondary EBTANAS since it is not used to determine admission to tertiary education. The overall upper secondary pass rate in 1989 was over 90%. Graduates of state upper secondary schools or MOEC-accredited private upper secondary schools receive the STTB SMA, which is signed by the head of the school. On the back of the certificate is a list of grades for all subjects tested in the EBTANAS as well as other subjects not tested in the EBTANAS.

Secondary Education: Quality Indicators

In determining an Indonesian secondary school graduate's suitability for admission to a U.S. undergraduate program, a number of factors should be considered. Is the applicant coming from a state school (*sekolah negeri*) or a private school (*sekolah swasta*) with equalized (*dismakan*) accreditation status? Although a graduate of a private upper secondary school with recognized or registered accreditation status is not necessarily less able than graduates of state or equalized private schools, state and equalized private schools are more selective in admissions requirements and very often offer more challenging educational programs and better facilities.

In evaluating an applicant's academic record, the following factors are important. Is the applicant a graduate of a science stream (A1, A2) or a nonscience stream (A3, A4)? The science streams set higher entry standards, especially in mathematics and the natural sciences.

Class rank in Indonesian upper secondary schools is generally calculated on a "homeroom" basis (a comparison of approximately 40 students) and is not a ranking of all graduates of a particular year, as in U.S. upper secondary schools. Applicants should indicate on which basis their upper secondary school calculates class rank. If calculated on a "homeroom" basis, applicants should indicate how many such classes make up their academic stream (whether A1, A2, A3, or A4) for the year of graduation.

[4]SOURCE: Florida State University, et al. *Indonesia: Education and Human Resources Sector Review*, April 1986, Vol. 2, chapter 5, p. 44

1994 Curriculum Reform

The definition of universal basic education in Indonesia as a unitary nine-year program has significant implications for the organization and structure of the educational system at the lower and upper secondary levels. The 1994 curriculum proposes to eliminate the vocational lower secondary schools. At the upper secondary level, the present system of formal streaming will be replaced by an unstreamed system that will allow students a greater range of subject options based on their academic or career goals. This should result in an expansion of opportunities for upper secondary graduates at the tertiary level since admission to university departments will no longer be tied to completion of a particular upper secondary stream. This model is similar to the U.S. secondary education model. It is an attempt to overcome the rigidity and university preparation orientation of the present system and to expand educational opportunity in response to market demand for accountants, junior managers, and technicians.

III. Tertiary Education

Introduction

Tertiary education in Indonesia is offered by state, state religious, and private institutions. The number of tertiary institutions has grown from only two institutions with approximately 10,000 students in 1950 to 970 state and private institutions with approximately 2.5 million students in the early 1990s. The growth in the education system began approximately a decade after Indonesian independence with an expansion of the state education system followed by a rapid expansion in the private education sector.

The Growth of State Education

The development of state education can be divided into three distinct periods. At the time of independence in 1945 the only institutions of higher education the Dutch had established were the precursors of the Bandung Institute of Technology/ITB, Bogor Institute of Agriculture/IPB[1], and the faculties of medicine, law, and letters which later became the University of Indonesia/UI. Growth began in the 1950s, with the passage of Law No. 4/1950: Concerning the Bases of Education and Instruction in Schools, and was rapid but undirected, with 30 of the current 49 state tertiary institutions established in the 1960s. The 1975-85 decade and its unforeseen oil profits led to more systematic development at all educational levels. But it has been during the third and current period, with the ratification of National Education Law No. 2/1989, that a national system of education, encompassing private and public institutions at all levels, has been established.

Resources and tertiary institutions have traditionally been centered on the island of Java, but government efforts to decentralize development have led to increasing support for provincial universities and other tertiary institutions outside Java. Twenty-six of the 27 provinces have at least one state institution of higher education. (East Timor has no state tertiary institutions.)

Article 16 of Law No. 2/1989 stipulates that an "education unit which conducts higher education . . . may be in the form of an academy (*akademi*), polytechnic (*politeknik*), advanced school (*sekolah tinggi*), institute (*institut*), or university (*universitas*)." The function of each unit has been set out in Government Regulation No. 30/1990 Concerning Higher Education, which also stipulates two streams of education

---

[1] Also translated as the Bogor Agricultural University by IPB; the Bogor Institute of Agriculture is the MOEC translation.

(academic and professional) and instructs all tertiary institutions to carry out the threefold aims of education, research, and community service.

The Growth of Private Education

Private tertiary institutions have increased in number from 384 to 911 between 1979 and the early 1990s (see Appendix B). These institutions have been established by educational foundations run by religious, academic, business, or other groups. They range in quality from excellent to deplorable and in size from large multifaculty universities to small, single-subject institutions located above the local supermarket. (See also Accreditation of Institutions in this chapter.)

Two factors prompted the rapid expansion of private tertiary education over the past decade. First, with more secondary school graduates, the demand for tertiary education has increased. The implementation of a national university entrance exam for the major state universities and teacher training institutes resulted in extremely large numbers of applicants, over 700,000 at the peak in the mid-1980s, most of whom were unsuccessful yet were set on postsecondary education. Secondly, as the Indonesian economy grew, demand for qualified manpower by the private sector supported the growth of private tertiary institutions. Graduates could find jobs outside the civil service, traditionally one of the largest employers of tertiary degree holders.

What attracts students to private institutions? A small number of programs are competitive and are the first choice of applicants. In general, these applicants graduate at the top of their upper secondary school classes in the physics or biology streams. Other programs exist to absorb those who are not qualified to enter a competitive state or private program, and these institutions advertise aggressively at the time state university entrance exam results are announced. Tuition fees at private institutions are higher than at state institutions, so a competitive institution will attract students who can afford to pay.

Table 3.1 shows that enrollment at state institutions is nearly half that of private institutions, although the number of graduates is comparable. The number of lecturers in state institutions is nearly double that of private institutions.

Table 3.1. State and Private Undergraduate (S1) Programs, 1991-92

	Total State	Total Private
Total Enrollment	553,800	1,094,800
Total # of Graduates	75,800	74,600
Total # of Lecturers	51,300	27,100

SOURCE: Toisuta, Willi. "Private Higher Education in Indonesia" in Hill. *Indonesia Assessment 1991*, p. 71.

Organization of Tertiary Institutions

All tertiary institutions are made up of one or more faculties. A faculty consists of one or more departments, and departments comprise one or more study programs. Thus, a faculty of economics may consist of three departments: management, accounting, and economics and development. Within the departments further specialization is available through programs of study.

The following are the main types of state and private tertiary institutions:

Academies (*akademi*). These offer professional nondegree diploma programs of one, two, and three years. There are currently two state arts academies. The 288 private academies offer programs in areas such as secretarial studies, banking and finance, management and computer skills, agriculture, and industrial technology. Each is headed by a director.

Polytechnics (*politeknik*). The 25 state and two private polytechnics offer professional nondegree diploma programs (mostly two- and three-year programs) to meet the skilled manpower needs of the industrial and business sectors in six fields: engineering (*rekayasa*), commerce (*tata niaga*), agriculture (*pertanian*), shipbuilding (*perkapalan*), tourism (*pariwisata*), and graphics (*grafika*). Each is headed by a director (see Polytechnics, below).

Advanced schools (*sekolah tinggi*). These offer both professional nondegree diploma programs and academic degree programs, but specialize in a single field of study. They may award both nondegree diplomas and academic *sarjana* (S1) degrees. An advanced school can become an institute or university only when it has at least three faculties and meets other educational and physical MOEC requirements. There are currently two state and 348 private advanced schools, each headed by a rector.

Institutes and universities (*institut, universitas*). These offer both professional nondegree diploma programs and academic degree programs. Some also offer graduate degree programs. A university or institute consists of at least three faculties and is headed by a rector. There are 35 state institutes and universities as well as the 10 teacher training institutes (Institut Keguruan dan Ilmu Pendidikan/IKIPs, discussed in chapter V, Teacher Training). There are also 270 private universities and institutes.

Organization, Administration, and Finance

In 1992 there were 49 state tertiary institutions overseen by the Directorate General of Higher Education (Direktorat Jenderal Pendidikan Tinggi/Dikti) of the Ministry of Education and Culture/MOEC: 30 universities, 10 teacher training institutes, three institutes of technology, five arts institutions (two advanced schools, one institute, and two academies), and the huge Open University for distance education. Twenty-five polytechnics currently attached to state universities or institutes are scheduled to become independent institutions by 1994.

Over 100 other tertiary institutions are run by government ministries other than the MOEC. Ministries operate a variety of educational institutions, *kedinasan* (government service) schools, that fall outside the domain of MOEC, although the curricula of these institutions must be endorsed by MOEC. Most of these programs offer nondegree diplomas (DI-DIV); a few award academic S1 degree programs. Often inter-institutional agreements allow students from these institutions to transfer to state universities or institutes to complete their S1 degrees. Applicants are usually civil servants, and all must be secondary school graduates with a minimum 6.5 grade point average. Most programs now use the credit system. Many are being privatized and thus will come under the private tertiary category. (See also chapter VI, Islamic Education.)

Private institutions, including universities, institutes, advanced schools, and academies, are administered by the MOEC through the Directorate of Private Tertiary Education (Direktorat Perguran Tinggi Swasta) under the Directorate General of Higher Education. Under the Directorate, 12 regional government offices comprise the Kopertis system (Koordinasi Perguruan Tinggi Swasta, Coordination of Private Tertiary Education) that coordinates private tertiary education throughout the country.

The Ministry of Education has 11 advisory consortia that determine core curricula for various disciplines as well as for the set of nationally required general courses (religion, Pancasila/civics, etc.). Both state and private institutions follow these guidelines.

Government expenditure on higher education as of 1991 was approximately $230 per student per year. State tertiary institutions are funded from three sources: the government's routine and development budgets, and, increasingly of late, student tuition fees. In 1990 tuition at state institutions ranged from $70-$100 per semester, although recent regulations have given institutions more financial autonomy. Consequently, state tuition fees have risen. Private tertiary education is highly dependent on tuition fees, which in 1991 ranged from $175-$350 per semester, plus fees for exams, contributions to building funds (the amount is often negotiable), and other miscellaneous costs.

Accreditation of Institutions

Until 1993 all state institutions had the same status. Private institutions have been accredited by the Ministry of Education and Culture at the level of the smallest unit of study, either department or program. A new national accreditation board responsible for accrediting all tertiary institutions, both state and private, as well as government service schools, is in the planning stages and is expected to start functioning in 1993. (State institutions are listed in Appendix A. Private institutions and their accreditation status are listed in Appendix B.)

Prior to 1993, each program of study at a private institution was assigned to one of the following three categories on the basis of facilities, staff, curriculum, number of graduates, research, and community service. The regional Kopertis representative oversees the private institutions, organizes state exams, and certifies all diplomas and certificates (*ijazah*).

Disamakan/**Equalized.** A degree awarded to a graduate of a program of study with this status is considered equivalent to a degree conferred by a state institution. In 1990, 8% of all private programs of study were equalized (*disamakan*). (See Document 3.1. for an example of an equalized degree certification.)

Diakui/**Recognized.** A degree awarded to a graduate of a program of study with *diakui* status is not considered equivalent to a degree from a state institution. Equivalency may be obtained after the student passes a state examination on 32-38 of the 144-160 credits required for the program. Twenty-five percent of the exam committee comes from state tertiary institutions and 75% from the private institution. The regional Kopertis official stamps the diplomas of graduates who have passed the state examination. Prior to 1990 a separate certificate was issued by the regional Kopertis office, certifying that the state examinations had been passed. In 1990, 11% of all private programs of study were recognized (*diakui*).

Terdaftar/**Registered.** A degree awarded to a graduate of a program of study with this status is not considered equivalent to a degree from a state institution. Equivalency may be obtained after the student passes a state examination on 32-38 of the total 144-160 credits. Fifty percent of the examination committee members are from state tertiary institutions; the rest are from the private institution offering the degree. The regional Kopertis official stamps the diplomas of graduates who have passed the state examination. Prior to 1990 a separate certificate was issued by the regional Kopertis office certifying that the state examination had been passed (see Document 3.2). In 1990, 81% of all private programs of study were registered (*terdaftar*).

Private tertiary institutions are generally small, with only a few large campus universities. Very few offer programs requiring a large investment in laboratories or equipment. For example, of the 12 private medical programs, none have the highest (equalized) accreditation status. Equalized accreditation has been awarded to two private dentistry programs, one architecture program, and six private engineering programs (see Appendix B).

Government efforts to integrate state and private education into one national system include the assignment of state lecturers to private institutions, assistance in establishing a credit/hour system, and provision of laboratory equipment. Most importantly, the administrative and coordination function of Kopertis continues to improve.

Students

In 1991 approximately 2.2 million students, or 5.77% of all 19- to 24-year-olds (and many over that age), were enrolled in state and private degree and nondegree programs at the tertiary level. These students represent approximately 52% of all secondary school graduates. Indonesia aims to increase net enrollment to 25% of all 19- to 24-year-olds by the year 2018.

Staff

Nationwide, approximately 5% of the teaching staff at tertiary institutions hold doctoral degrees. The proportion of faculty members who hold graduate degrees ranges from 50% at major urban state universities on Java to 5%-10% at many smaller institutions and those in regions off Java. (See Appendix A for staff with graduate degrees.)

Overall, the teacher-student ratio in tertiary institutions is expected to fall from 1:25 in 1993 to 1:15 in 2018. Already some state institutions meet the government target of 1:15 in the exact sciences and 1:20 in the social sciences. At Gadjah Mada University/UGM, all faculties except engineering, economics, law, and social sciences meet this target; at Bandung Institute of Technology the ratio is 1:9.5. However, private universities generally have higher teacher-student ratios: the economics faculty at Trisakti University has a 1:76 ratio and dentistry 1:11. The Indonesian Muslim University in South Sulawesi, the largest private university in eastern Indonesia, has a ratio of 1:85.

A major problem with tertiary lecturers is their widespread practice of holding two or three jobs to make enough money to survive. One study reported that faculty members at UI, IPB, and ITB spent 30% and at UGM 40% of their time working in their faculties. In the remaining time, many staff members were teaching part-time in other tertiary institutions or in other faculties within their own institutions.

Degrees and Diplomas

Based on National Education Law No. 2/1989, the national system for higher education is divided into academic degree programs and professional (including technical) nondegree programs (see Table 3.2). One credit hour is equal to one 50-minute lecture hour, one hour of self-study, and one hour of independent study, or three hours of a laboratory class. Each program stipulates the minimum and maximum amount of time required to complete the program. This new requirement was enacted to improve efficiency of student flow, as in the past only a small proportion of students completed their studies within the prescribed period of time. Students are allowed a maximum of 1 1/2 times the normal number of semesters specified for a program to complete their degrees. They are allowed to repeat courses failed within these time limits.

Academic Degrees

Prior to 1990 the following degrees were awarded:[2] *sarjana muda* (SM), after three years of study and a short thesis; *sarjana,* and often referred to as *sarjana lengkap* (Doctorandus, Drs., or Doctoranda, Dra.[3]), after five years of study (two years past the

---

[2]See Charles Aanenson, *Indonesia*, the World Education Series guide (1979) for more information on the degrees awarded in the old system.

[3] It should be noted, however, that diplomas from some institutions continue to state that an S1 graduate has the right to use the title Doctorandus/a. See Document 6.3a.

sarjana muda) and a thesis; *insinyur* (Ir.), the equivalent of the *sarjana* degree for engineering and agriculture graduates; *magister sains*, two years beyond the *sarjana*; and *doktor* (DR., no coursework, submission and defense of a dissertation). This system was gradually phased out beginning in the 1970s at some universities, and officially ended in 1990 as a result of Government Regulation No. 30/1990.

In the current system, three degrees are awarded in the academic stream: *sarjana* (*strata satu*, or S1) or first degree, *magister* (*strata dua* or S2) or first graduate degree, and *doktor* (*strata tiga* or S3), or second graduate degree. The *magister* and *doktor* degree programs are discussed in chapter IV, Graduate Education.

The change to the credit system and the implementation of a more guided program of education was made to improve efficiency and standardize the system. The establishment of credit requirements and definitions of a credit hour in terms of work for both student and lecturer, time limits for graduation, and the option to repeat only courses and not whole years of study allows institutions to make better use of facilities and faculty time and results in higher graduation rates.

Table 3.2. Tertiary-Level Degree and Nondegree Programs, Credits, and Periods of Study

Academic Degree Program	Professional Nondegree (S0) Program	Credits (cum.)	Semesters in Curric. (cum.)	Min.-Max. Semesters (cum.)
	DI	40-50	2	2-4
	DII	80-90	4	4-6
	DIII	110-120	6	6-10
S1	DIV	144-160	8	8-14
S2	Sp.I	180-194	12	12-18
S3	Sp.II	228-233	16	16-22

SOURCE: Keputusan Menteri Pendidikan dan Kebudayaan, Nomor 0211/U/1982.
Note: S = *strata*, with S1, S2, and S3 representing the three levels of academic degrees. S1 programs in medicine, dentistry, and veterinary science require additional credits. S0 = nondegree programs; D = (nondegree) diploma; Sp. = Specialist, the nondegree graduate (*pasca sarjana*) certification.

Admission. A series of joint admissions examinations for state institutes, universities, and teacher training institutes was used prior to 1984. From 1984-88 a nation-wide examination, the SIPENMARU (Sistem Penerimaan Mahasiswa Baru), replaced these joint examinations, and applicants' results were reviewed centrally by a meeting of university rectors to determine admission to particular faculties and institutions. In 1989 the name of the examination was changed to Ujian Masuk Perguruan Tinggi Negeri/UMPTN, and institutions were given more autonomy in the use of scores to determine admission.

The UMPTN is given in three regions of the country, with equivalent forms of the test administered in each region. It may be taken by secondary school graduates from the current year or the previous two years. Students may select only two study programs, one of which must be in the region of the country where they take the test. The second may be in the same or another region. If they make only one selection, it may be in any region. Students must select either teacher training or nonteacher training programs. In the past, many students would select a teacher training program as a less competitive fallback, with no intention of entering the field of education, even though Indonesia is chronically short of teachers.

The UMPTN has two options: social sciences (Ilmu Pengetahuan Sosial/IPS) and sciences (Ilmu Pengetahuan Alam/IPA). Secondary school graduates from the physics (A1) and biology (A2) streams can apply to any department; social science (A3) and humanities (A4) graduates are restricted to nonscience and nontechnology fields. Students may elect to take one or both tests. A skills or talent test is also required for arts and physical education.

Of approximately 1.2 million secondary school graduates in 1991, 500,000 took the UMPTN and 80,000 were admitted to state institutions. The number taking the test is falling as universities develop other admissions methods and private universities, which are far more expensive, grow in number, and improve in quality. Each private university has its own admissions procedures, with its own criteria and entrance examinations.

The Open University (Universitas Terbuka/UT) admits anyone who has graduated from secondary school regardless of the year of graduation. There is no entrance examination and the degree is equivalent to those of other state tertiary institutions.

Merit-Based Admission Programs. Over the years selective state institutions have used a variety of national and institutional programs to identify talented secondary school graduates and admit them to tertiary institutions without their having taken the national entrance exams. The Bogor Institute of Agriculture/IPB was the pioneer in this program. IPB has consistently tried to identify students with academic potential rather than depend on the results of standardized tests.

As institutions become more autonomous, merit-based admissions become more important. The 1984-88 merit-based admission program, Penelusuran Minat Dan Kemampuan/PMDK, was stopped after 1988 because of widespread falsifying of secondary school transcripts. However, merit-based admissions programs are being reinstated by some institutions: IPB reinstated its merit-based program in 1989, Gadjah Mada University in 1990, and the University of Indonesia in 1992. Other well known universities have not yet instituted any sort of merit-based admissions program.

Programs vary, but in general secondary schools in each region with good reputations are invited to submit applications from students ranking in the top 10 in the first four semesters of secondary school. Schools that falsify documents and enable underqualified students to be admitted are not invited to participate in the program the following year. Up to 25% of the entering class at prestigious institutions are selected through merit-based admission, with over 50% of entering students at Bogor Institute of

Agriculture selected in this way. Efforts are being made to increase access for students from islands other than Java.

Transfers. In general, transfers are possible within institutions, between faculties or departments, and between state institutions. Transfers from private to state institutions are theoretically possible but rare; the transfer is more likely to be from the state to the private institution. Any transferring student must be in good academic standing, have a letter from the receiving institution as well as from the home institution, and have good reason for requesting a transfer. Courses are evaluated individually by the receiving institution.

Curriculum/Programs. At most institutions students are admitted directly into the faculty and study program in which they intend to major. Some institutions, including the Bogor Institute of Agriculture/IPB and the Bandung Institute of Technology/ITB, have a common first year in which most students take the same courses before entering a major field of study.

S1 programs have a set of basic compulsory courses established by the MOEC's consortia for the disciplines and are of three types: *mata kuliah dasar umum*/MKDU, institution-wide general core courses in religion, civics, history, and national ideology; *mata kuliah dasar keahlian*/MKDK, faculty-wide basic courses; and *mata kuliah keahlian*/MKK, departmental compulsory courses in the major field. Additional courses are determined by each student and institution to add up to 144-160 credits.

Considerable variation exists among disciplines in the number of credits required in the compulsory curriculum. For example, although 144-160 credits are needed for S1 degrees, geography and law require only 73 and 72 compulsory credits, respectively, while at the other extreme pharmacy requires 118 and psychology requires 158 compulsory credits.

The more compulsory credits a program requires, the less freedom an individual institution has to develop its own specialties or areas of excellence. Also, programs that require students to take a heavy load of compulsory courses and specialize in a major field beginning in the first semester do not allow students to investigate areas outside their own fields.

Table 3.3 lists S1 programs by faculty at state tertiary institutions. Note that programs may have faculty status at one institution, but only departmental status at another.

Graduation Requirements. All programs have a specified length and maximum amount of time in which requirements must be completed. Graduates of S1 programs must complete their degree requirements within a time limit of 1 1/2 times the number of semesters specified for the curriculum and obtain a minimum grade point average of 2.0 with no failing grades. Some programs require comprehensive exams. Most programs require the submission of a senior thesis (*skripsi*) and completion of community service.

Graduates of private institutions that do not have equalized accreditation status must take state exams before their degrees are considered equivalent to those from state

Table 3.3. S1 Program Offerings at State Tertiary Institutions, 1989*

Faculty	Philosophy	Psychology	Communications	Soc. & Poli. Sci.	Administration	Geography	Math & Science	Pharmacy	Biology	Teaching & Education	Education	Soc. Sci. Education	Language & Arts Ed.	Math & Science Ed.	Voc. & Technical Ed.	Sports & Health Ed.	Engineering	Industrial Engineering
	1	2	3	4	5	6	7	8	9	10	11	12	13	14	15	16	17	18
U. Indonesia (UI)		•		•			•										•	
IKIP Jakarta											•	•	•	•	•	•		
Bogor Inst. of Agriculture (IPB)							•											
Bandung Inst. of Technology (ITB)							•											•
Padjadjaran U. (UNPAD)		•	•	•			•											
IKIP Bandung											•	•	•	•	•	•		
Jenderal Sudirman U. (UNSOED)									•									
Diponegoro U. (UNDIP)				•													•	
IKIP Semarang											•	•	•	•	•	•		
Sebelas Maret U. (UNS)				•						•							•	
Gadjah Mada U. (UGM)	•	•		•		•	•	•	•								•	
IKIP Yogyakarta											•	•	•	•	•	•		
Airlangga U. (UNAIR)				•			•	•										
Sepuluh Nopember Inst. of Technology (ITS)							•											•
IKIP Surabaya											•	•	•	•	•	•		
Brawijaya U. (UNIBRAW)					•												•	
IKIP Malang											•	•	•	•	•			
Jember U. (UNEJ)				•						•								
Syiah Kuala U. (UNSYIAH)										•							•	
U. North Sumatra (USU)				•			•										•	
IKIP Medan											•	•	•	•	•	•		
Andalas U. (UNAND)								•										
IKIP Padang											•	•	•	•	•	•		
Riau U. (UNRI)				•			•			•								
Sub-total	1	3	1	9	1	1	9	3	2	4	8	8	8	8	8	7	7	2

*excluding IAINs

Faculty	Mineral Engineering	Civil Eng. & Planning	Marine Engineering	Medicine	Dentistry	Public Health	Law	Economics	Agriculture	Fisheries	Animal Science	Forestry	Agricultural Eng.	Veterinary Science	Arts & Letters	Art & Design	Fine Arts
	19	20	21	22	23	24	25	26	27	28	29	30	31	32	33	34	35
U. Indonesia (UI)				●	●	●	●	●							●		
IKIP Jakarta																	
Bogor Inst. of Agriculture (IPB)									●	●	●	●	●	●			
Bandung Inst. of Technology (ITB)	●	●														●	
Padjadjaran U. (UNPAD)				●	●		●	●	●		●				●		
IKIP Bandung																	
Jenderal Sudirman U. (UNSOED)							●	●	●		●						
Diponegoro U. (UNDIP)				●				●			●				●		
IKIP Semarang																	
Sebelas Maret U. (UNS)				●			●	●	●						●		
Gadjah Mada U. (UGM)				●	●		●	●	●		●	●	●	●	●		
IKIP Yogyakarta																	
Airlangga U. (UNAIR)				●	●		●	●						●			
Sepuluh Nopember Inst. of Technology (ITS)		●	●														
IKIP Surabaya																	
Brawijaya U. (UNIBRAW)				●			●	●	●	●	●						
IKIP Malang																	
Jember U. (UNEJ)							●	●	●						●		
Syiah Kuala U. (UNSYIAH)				●			●	●	●					●			
U. North Sumatra (USU)				●	●		●	●	●						●		
IKIP Medan																	
Andalas U. (UNAND)				●			●	●	●		●				●		
IKIP Padang																	
Riau U. (UNRI)								●		●							
Sub-total	1	2	1	10	5	1	11	13	10	3	7	2	2	4	8	1	0

*excluding IAINs

(continued)

Faculty	Philosophy	Psychology	Communications	Soc. & Poli. Sci.	Administration	Geography	Math & Science	Pharmacy	Biology	Teaching & Education	Education	Soc. Sci. Education	Language & Arts Ed.	Math & Science Ed.	Voc. & Technical Ed.	Sports & Health Ed.	Engineering	Industrial Engineering
	1	2	3	4	5	6	7	8	9	10	11	12	13	14	15	16	17	18
Jambi U. (UNJAM)										•								
Sriwijaya U. (UNSRI)										•							•	
Lampung U. (UNILA)										•								
Tanjungpura U. (UNTAN)				•						•							•	
Palangkaraya U. (UNPAR)										•								
Lambung Mangkurat U. (UNLAM)		•								•							•	
Mulawarman U. (UNMUL)		•								•								
Sam Ratulangi U. (UNSRAT)		•								•							•	
IKIP Manado											•	•	•	•	•	•		
Hasanuddin U. (UNHAS)		•					•										•	
IKIP Ujung Pandang											•	•	•	•	•	•		
Pattimura U. (UNPATTI)		•								•							•	
Udayana U. (UNUD)										•							•	
Mataram U. (UNRAM)										•								
Nusa Cendana U. (UNDANA)					•					•								
Cendrawasih U. (UNCEN)		•								•								
Haluoleo U. (UNHALU)		•								•								
Tadulako U. (UNTAD)		•								•								
Bengkulu U. (UNIB)		•								•								
Indonesian Institute of Arts (ISI)																		
Open U. (UT)		•				•				•								
Indonesian Advanced School of Arts, Surakarta																		
Indonesian Advanced School of Arts, Denpasar																		
Sub-total	0	0	0	11	1	0	2	0	0	17	2	2	2	2	2	2	7	0
Totals	1	3	1	20	2	1	11	3	2	21	10	10	10	10	10	9	14	2

Faculty	Mineral Engineering	Civil Engr. & Planning	Marine Engineering	Medicine	Dentistry	Public Health	Law	Economics	Agriculture	Fisheries	Animal Science	Forestry	Agricultural Eng.	Veterinary Science	Arts & Letters	Art & Design	Fine Arts
	19	20	21	22	23	24	25	26	27	28	29	30	31	32	33	34	35
Jambi U. (UNJAM)							•	•	•		•						
Sriwijaya U. (UNSRI)			•				•	•	•								
Lampung U. (UNILA)							•	•	•								
Tanjungpura U. (UNTAN)							•	•	•								
Palangkaraya U. (UNPAR)								•									
Lambung Mangkurat U. (UNLAM)							•	•	•	•		•					
Mulawarman U. (UNMUL)								•	•			•					
Sam Ratulangi U. (UNSRAT)				•			•	•	•	•	•				•		
IKIP Manado																	
Hasanuddin U. (UNHAS)				•	•	•	•	•	•		•				•		
IKIP Ujung Pandang																	
Pattimura U. (UNPATTI)							•	•	•	•							
Udayana U. (UNUD)				•			•	•	•		•				•		
Mataram U. (UNRAM)							•	•	•		•						
Nusa Cendana U. (UNDANA)							•		•		•						
Cendrawasih U. (UNCEN)							•		•								
Haluoleo U. (UNHALU)								•	•								
Tadulako U. (UNTAD)							•	•	•								
Bengkulu U. (UNIB)							•	•	•								
Indonesian Institute of Arts (ISI)																•	•
Open U. (UT)								•									
Indonesian Advanced School of Arts, Surakarta																	•
Indonesian Advanced School of Arts, Denpasar																	•
Sub-total	0	0	0	4	1	1	14	16	16	3	6	2	0	0	3	1	3
Total	1	2	1	14	6	2	26	29	26	6	13	4	2	4	11	2	3

institutions. This is particularly important when graduates apply for jobs in the civil service, traditionally a major employer of university graduates.

Academic Titles

Because tertiary graduates are entitled to place a title after their name and because titles are in widespread use in written communications, the Ministry of Education and Culture in February 1993 issued an official list of academic titles (listed below). Others may be added in the future.

- Sarjana Agama/S.Ag. (religion)
- Sarjana Ekonomi/S.E (economics)
- Sarjana Hukum/S.H (law)
- Sarjana Ilmu Politik/S.Ip (political science)
- Sarjana Ilmu Sosial/S.Sos (social sciences)
- Sarjana Kedokteran/S.Ked (medicine)
- Sarjana Kedokteran Gigi/S.KG (dentistry; see Document 3.3)
- Sarjana Kedokteran Hewan/S.KH (veterinary medicine)
- Sarjana Kehutanan/S.Hut (forestry)
- Sarjana Kesehatan Masyarakat/S.KM (public health)
- Sarjana Komputer dan Informatika/S.Kom (computer and informatics)
- Sarjana Matematika dan Ilmu Pengetahuan Alam/S.Si (mathematics and natural sciences)
- Sarjana Pendidikan/S.Pd (education)
- Sarjana Perikanan/S.Pi (fisheries)
- Sarjana Pertanian/S.P. (agriculture)
- Sarjana Peternakan/S.Pt (animal husbandry)
- Sarjana Psikologi/S.Psi (psychology)
- Sarjana Sastra/S.S. (arts and letters)
- Sarjana Seni/S.Sn (fine arts)
- Sarjana Teknik/S.T. (engineering)

Professional (Sarjana/S1) Degrees

Professional programs in law, medicine, nursing, pharmacy, and dentistry are S1 programs in the academic stream in Indonesia. Students enroll directly after secondary school. S1 degrees in medicine, pharmacy, dentistry, and veterinary science all require nine semesters of undergraduate work (155-160 credits). Two semesters of internships and/or externships yield an additional 36-40 credits. On completion of these first professional degrees (including relevant exams or practical work), graduates are awarded the *sarjana* (*strata satu*, S1) degree and are qualified to practice in their professions.

Medicine

Graduates of the 14 state medical faculties obtain an S1 medical degree (Sarjana Kedokteran) and are entitled to use the title *dokter* (dr.). Graduates of the 12 medical faculties of private universities must take state exams administered twice a year by the National Board of Evaluation, Consortium of Health Sciences (NB/CHS). There are five written exams in addition to exams in 12 clinical areas. Often there is a backlog of medical graduates who wait several years to take these exams to be eligible to practice medicine. Beginning in 1993 the NB/CHS will be replaced by the regional Kopertis in the administration of these exams.

Nursing

An S1 nursing degree (Sarjana Keperawatan) is conferred only by the University of Indonesia and requires eight to nine semesters of study. The curriculum was reportedly still undergoing changes in 1992.

Dentistry

Graduates of the six state dental faculties obtain an S1 dentistry degree (Sarjana Kedokteran Gigi) and are entitled to use the title *dokter gigi* (drg.). The same is true for graduates of the two private universities with dental faculties with equalized accreditation status, Dr. Moestopo University and Trisakti University. After February 1993 the title became S.KG, placed after the name. All graduates of other private dental faculties must take state exams, both written and clinical, prior to being certified to practice dentistry and use the title *dokter gigi* (S.KG after February 1993).

Veterinary Science

The five state veterinary faculties at the Bogor Institute of Agriculture, Airlangga University, Udayana University, Syiah Kuala University, and Gadjah Mada University award the S1 degree in veterinary medicine (Sarjana Kedokteran Hewan). Graduates are entitled to use the professional title *dokter hewan* (drh.). After February 1993, the title became S.KH, placed after the name.

Pharmacy

The eight state pharmacy programs (two faculties and six programs within faculties of mathematics and natural science) award the S1 degree in pharmacy, Sarjana Farmasi, after nine semesters of coursework. Graduates may take a further one-year professional qualification consisting of coursework in management and hospital pharmacy, lab work integrating information from earlier coursework, and a four- to six-month internship in a pharmacy or industry to become a registered pharmacist. On passing the state exam, graduates are entitled to use the professional title *apoteker* and to work as registered pharmacists.

Law

S1 programs in law require eight semesters and 144 credits to graduate with an S1 degree in law (Sarjana Hukum). Courses are divided into the same categories as other S1 programs, i.e., institution-wide general core courses, faculty-wide basic courses, departmental compulsory courses in the major field, and electives. In the 1993-94 academic year, law programs will be changed to eliminate majors in specialized fields. At the time of publication the exact form of these changes was not known.

Professional (Nondegree) Diplomas

Professional (nondegree/*strata nol*/S0) programs are offered at both undergraduate and graduate (*pasca sarjana*) levels. The undergraduate programs are primarily vocational/technical in nature and lead to one-, two-, three-, or four-year diplomas (DI through DIV). Post-S1 specialist programs (Sp.I and Sp.II) offered at the graduate level are a continuation of both professional and academic programs. Specialist diplomas are awarded for completion of training in specialized (mainly medical) fields. The specialist programs are discussed in chapter IV, Graduate Education.

Diploma programs are offered by academies, advanced schools, polytechnics, institutes, and universities to fill market demands for skilled employees. The diploma is thus considered a terminal degree in Indonesia, but graduates of diploma programs may continue to the next highest diploma level, depending on grade point average and work experience. At some institutions academically qualified DIII graduates may enter S1 programs.

The diploma is issued by the rector or director. The regional Kopertis representative of MOEC signs diplomas from private institutions.

Diploma I (DI)

The one-year DI programs are open to secondary school graduates. Admissions procedures vary by institution, but generally include an entrance examination.

The fewer than 10 DI programs in the country in the areas of agriculture, forestry, computer programming, English language, secretarial studies, and tourism will likely be phased out soon by MOEC. The DI program requires the completion of 40-50 credits over a period of two to four semesters. Graduates generally enter the work force.

Diploma II (DII)

The two-year DII programs are open to secondary school graduates. Admissions procedures vary, but requirements often include an admissions test or the national UMPTN admissions test. DII programs are offered primarily in education (see chapter V, Teacher Training, for information on the DII requirement for primary school teachers.).

Technical programs are offered in polytechnics. Programs are also offered in economics, secretarial studies, and forestry. Approximately 45%-80% of the DII program is practical training, with 20%-55% theory. The curriculum for a DII in Livestock Reproduction is provided in Table 3.4.

Table 3.4. Curriculum Leading to Diploma (DII) in Livestock Reproduction, Bogor Institute of Agriculture, 1992

Subject	Credits	Lecture	Practical
Semester 1			
Pancasila/Civics	3	3	0
Religion	2	3	0
Indonesian Language	3	3	0
Introduction to Agriculture	2	2	0
Introduction to Breed Improvement	2	2	0
Livestock Science	2	2	0
Livestock Extension	2	1	1-3
Livestock Management	3	2	1-3
Total	19	18	2-6
Semester 2			
Ruminant Feed Science	3	2	1-3
Livestock Policy	2	2	0
Reproductive Anatomy	3	2	1-3
Embryology	2	1	1-3
Reproductive Physiology	3	2	1-3
Semen Collection and Processing	4	2	4-6
Artificial Insemination	3	2	1-3
Total	20	13	9-12

(continued)

Semester 3

Estrus Synchronization/ Embryo Transfer	3	2	1-3
Obstetrics	4	2	4-6
Uterine Disorders	3	2	1-3
Infertility	4	2	4-6
Obstetrics and Infertility	5	0	5-15
Field Practice	0	0	0-3
Total	19	8	15-36
Semester 4			
Estrus Synchronization/ A.I. Field Practice	5	0	5-15
Pregnancy Examination/ Obstetrics Practice	6	0	6-18
Infertility Control Practice	8	0	8-24
Total	19	0	19-57

SOURCE: Lewin, Elizabeth. "Animal Health and Livestock Science Education," in *Integrated Animal Health Services Study*, Vol. 2. June 1991. CIDA-OMAF Yogyakarta Disease Investigation Project.
NOTE: Total credits needed for two-year program, 80-90; total required credits, 77 (3-13 credit options); theory to practice, 30:70.

The DII diploma requires the completion of 80-90 credits over a period of four to six semesters. Graduates of a DII program generally work in their fields but may also continue on to a DIII program in the same field if they fulfill the requirements (a minimum 1.97 GPA at many institutions).

Diploma III (DIII)

The three-year DIII programs are open to secondary school graduates. Admissions procedures vary depending on the institution, but often include an admissions test or the UMPTN or polytechnic entrance exam. Programs are offered in such areas as engineering, secretarials skills, foreign languages, banking and finance, and computer skills. Approximately 45%-80% of the program is practical training.

The DIII requires 110-120 credits and six to 10 semesters of work. Graduates may either work, apply for admission to DIV programs, or apply to S1 programs as transfer students. For example, the S1 nursing program at the University of Indonesia/UI admits DIII graduates of the Academy of Nursing and accepts 50 transfer credits. A DIII curriculum for River Engineering is provided in Table 3.5.

Table 3.5. Curriculum in River Engineering Leading to Diploma (DIII), Public Works Polytechnic, Diponegoro University

Subjects	Credits
General core courses (MKDU): 13 credits	
Pancasila/Civics	2
National Defense Training	2
Religion	2
Introduction to Humanities and Social Sciences	2
Indonesian Language	2
English Language	3
Faculty-wide basic courses (MKDK): 12 credits	
Mathematics	6
Physics	4
Computer	2
Departmental courses in major field (MKK)	
A. Basic specialization: 29 credits	
Engineering Mechanics	7
Engineering Geology	2
Fluid Mechanics	7
River Morphology	2
Hydrology	4
Coastal Engineering	1
Soil Mechanics	5
Engineering Drawing	1
B. Specialization: 38 credits	
Irrigation	4
Water Construction	4
River Engineering	6
Foundation Engineering	2
Reinforced Concrete Construction	6
Steel Construction	2
Wood Construction	2
Drainage	3
Engineering Implementation	2
River and Sediment Hydraulics Soil Removal	2

(continued)

Transport	2
Reclamation	1
Water Power Reservoirs and Construction	2
C. Supplementary courses: 19 credits	
Land Surveying	6
Road and Bridge Construction	2
Management and Planning	2
Operations and Maintenance	2
Water and Soil Conservation	2
Contracts	2
Engineering Economics	1
Environmental Impact	1
Duty Assignment (*kedinasan*)	1
Total	111

Diploma IV (DIV)

The four-year DIV programs are open to secondary school graduates. Admissions procedures vary but usually include an admission test or the UMPTN used for admission to universities or the polytechnic entrance examination (see Polytechnics later in this chapter). The very few DIV programs include tourism (*kepariwisataan*) at Udayana University, social science and politics (*ilmu sosial dan ilmu politik*) at Gadjah Mada University, river engineering (*teknik persungaian*) at the Ministry of Public Works' polytechnic at Diponegoro University (see river engineering curriculum, Table 3.6), and medical physics (*fisika kedokteran*) at Diponegoro University's polytechnic in Semarang. More DIV programs will be offered as the polytechnics become more established.

Students must successfully complete 144-160 credits over eight to 14 semesters in order to graduate. Some DIV graduates have applied and been admitted to master's degree programs outside Indonesia, with admission dependent on the background required for the field of study. Within Indonesia, however, the DIV is intended to be a terminal qualification and graduates enter the civil service at a lower grade than S1 graduates.

Table 3.6 lists the curriculum for the DIV in River Engineering. The DIV program consists of two semesters of study after the DIII and includes a final project, a practicum, and a field externship.

Polytechnics

Polytechnics are state institutions representing a major new government initiative. They were established to increase opportunities for practical training in technical fields needed in Indonesia. They offer two-, three-, and four-year professional nondegree programs in engineering, agriculture, and business that lead to DII, DIII, and DIV diplomas. Diplomas are signed by the director of the polytechnic.

Table 3.6. Curriculum in River Engineering Leading to Diploma (DIV), Public Works Polytechnic*, Diponegoro University

DIII program (111 credits) plus the following:	Credits
General core courses (MKDU): 2 credits	
Introduction to Humanities and Social Sciences	2
English Language I and II	0
Departmental courses in major field (MKK)	
A. Basic specialization: 5 credits	
Aerial Photo Interpretation	2
River Engineering	2
Engineering Economics	1
B. Specialization: 20 credits	
River Control	2
Watergate Design	2
River Basin Development	3
River Erosion and Sedimentation Control	3
Estuary and Coastal Control	3
Dam Design	2
Building Construction Implementation Engineering	2
River Exploitation and Preservation	3
C. Supplementary courses: 5 credits	
Water Resources Law and Implementation Regulations	2
Environmental Impact for Projects	2
Land Use and Soil Capacity	1
D. Practicum and final project: 12 credits	
Field Externship	2
Final Project	6
Practicum	4
Total	**44**

SOURCE: Buku Pedoman, Universitas Diponegoro, 1991-92.

    *A non-MOEC (*kedinasan*) polytechnic operated by the Ministry of Public Works.

The first state polytechnic was established with support from Switzerland at Bandung Institute of Technology in 1975. However, most of the 25 state polytechnics were established in the 1980s (see Table 3.7). The polytechnics are attached to universities and are headed by directors who are responsible to the university rector. The number of state tertiary institutions will increase nearly 50% when all polytechnics become independent institutions in 1994.

Admission. The system of national exams for admission to polytechnics, called the Polytechnic Entrance Examination (Ujian Masuk Politeknik/UM Politeknik), is similar to the UMPTN for S1 admission. Specialized polytechnic programs may have their own screening tests.

Table 3.7. Polytechnics Attached to State Universities/Institutes

Polytechnic	Programs Offered	Diploma Offered
Politeknik Lhokseumawe, Syiah Kuala University	Civil, Mechanical, Electrical, and Chemical Engineering	DIII
Politeknik Medan, University of North Sumatra	Civil, Mechanical, and Electrical Engineering; Accounting, Business Administration	DIII
Politeknik Padang, Andalas University	Civil, Mechanical, and Electrical Engineering	DIII
Politeknik Pertanian Payakumbuh, Andalas University	Food Crops, Plantation Crops, Agricultural Technology	DIII
Politeknik Palembang, Sriwijaya University	Civil, Mechanical, Electrical, and Chemical Engineering; Accounting, Business Administration	DIII
Politeknik Pertanian Bandar Lampung, Lampung University	Food Crops, Plantation Crops, Agricultural Technology	DIII
Politeknik Jakarta, University of Indonesia	Civil, Mechanical, and Electrical Engineering; Accounting, Business Administration; Graphics and Publishing	DIII
Politeknik Manufaktur (Politeknik Swiss), Bandung Institute of Technology	Mechanical Engineering; Illustration and Design; and Metal Casting Engineering	DII DIII

Politeknik Bandung, Bandung Institute of Technology	Civil, Mechanical, Electrical, Computer, and Chemical Engineering; Accounting, Business Administration	DIII
Politeknik Semarang, Diponegoro University	Civil, Mechanical, and Electrical Engineering; Accounting, Administration	DIII
Politeknik Elektronika Surabaya, Sepuluh Nopember Institute of Technology	Electrical and Telecommunications Engineering	DIII
Politeknik Perkapalan Surabaya, Sepuluh Nopember Institute of Technology	Shipbuilding, Marine Electrical Engineering	DIII
Politeknik Malang, Brawijaya University	Civil, Mechanical, Electrical, and Chemical Engineering; Accounting, Business Administration	DIII
Politeknik Pertanian Jember, Jember University	Food Crops, Plantation Crops, Agricultural Technology	DIII
Politeknik Denpasar, Udayana University	Civil, Mechanical, and Electrical Engineering; Accounting, Business Administration; Tourism	DII, DIII, DIV
Politeknik Pontianak, Tanjungpura University	Civil, Mechanical, and Electrical Engineering	DII
Politeknik Banjarmasin, Lambung Mangkurat University	Civil, Mechanical, and Electrical Engineering	DII
Politeknik Samarinda, Mulawarman University	Civil, Mechanical, and Electrical Engineering; Accounting, Business Administration	DII
Politeknik Pertanian Samarinda, Mulawarman University	Forest Management, Forest Product Processing	DIII
Politeknik Manado, Sam Ratulangi University	Civil, Mechanical, and Electrical Engineering; Accounting, Business Administration	DII

(continued)

Politeknik Ujung Pandang, Hasanuddin University	Civil, Mechanical, Electrical, and Chemical Engineering	DIII
Politeknik Pertanian Pangkajene Kepulauan, Hasanuddin University	Fisheries, Fish Cultivation	DIII
Politeknik Pertanian Kupang, Nusa Cendana University	Food Crops, Plantation Crops Dryland Farming Management, Cattle Breeding	DIII
Politeknik Kupang, Nusa Cendana University	Civil, Mechanical, and Electrical Engineering	DII
Politeknik Ambon, Pattimura University	Civil, Mechanical, and Electrical Engineering	DII

Curriculum. The curriculum is composed of 45%-80% practical work in workshops, laboratories, or practical training, and 20%-45% theory. The academic year is composed of two 22-week semesters with one week equal to 38-42 hours. There is little choice in the selection of courses within a study program.

The polytechnic curricula are divided into four areas: MKK (*mata kuliah umum*)—general core courses, including subjects such as religion, Pancasila/civics, basic management, Indonesian, English, mathematics, physics, and chemistry; MKTD (*mata kuliah teknik dasar*)—basic core courses in the major field; MKTT (*mata kuliah teknik terapan*)—applied or specialized technical courses in the major field; and KPK (*kegiatan praktek kejuruan*)—a one-semester practicum.

Graduation Requirements. Polytechnic graduates must satisfactorily fulfill all requirements for the DII, DIII, or DIV diplomas, generally including a one-semester practicum.

Grading

In state institutions both the academic and the professional streams use the credit system as the basis for calculating study units. However, most polytechnics continue to use a module system, which requires that students repeat the whole year's program if they fail a single course.

Some private institutions also continue to use courses or programs as the unit of study, but most have already begun to provide a grade point average (GPA), even if the students are required to follow a prescribed program with no electives or to repeat a whole year or semester rather than a single course.

One credit is considered equivalent to one 50-minute lecture hour plus one hour of guided self-study and one hour of independent study, or three contact hours of laboratory or practical work. Most programs now use the grading system established by the Ministry of Education and Culture shown below.

Grade	Credit Weighting	Meaning
A	4	Excellent (*Istimewa/sangat baik/baik sekali/bagus sekali*)
B	3	Good (*Baik*)
C	2	Fair/Passed with credit (*Cukup/sedang*)
D	1	Poor/Passed (*Kurang/lulus bersyarat*)
E/F	0	Fail (*Gagal/tidak lulus*)

An exception to the above grading scale is that used by the Bandung Institute of Technology, which grades on a scale of 1-5, with 5=A and 1=E. Thus, GPAs from ITB must be converted by subtracting 1 point to make them equivalent to other 4-point scales.

Although the Indonesian 4-point scale appears to be similar to the U.S. grading system, in practice there are wide variations in grading practices among institutions and among faculties and departments within institutions (see Appendix C). In general, grade point averages are lower than their U.S. equivalents and tend to cluster around the average grade, rather than being evenly distributed along a bell curve.

For example, although only the very top Indonesian secondary school graduates enter the Bogor Institute of Agriculture, between 1975 and 1988 just 1% of graduates of the faculties of Forestry and Animal Husbandry earned GPAs of 3.0. However, differences in grading practices within this institution could be seen, as approximately 18% of graduates of the Faculty of Agricultural Technology had GPAs of 3.0.

At the Bandung Institute of Technology, between 1985 and 1988 few graduates earned GPAs over 3.0 (after grades are converted from a 5-point to a 4-point scale) except in the Faculty of Information Technology, which awarded GPAs of 3.0 to approximately 10% of its graduates. Some departments have awarded the same GPA to all students in a graduating class. Additional information on grading practices is presented in Appendix C.

Until the late 1960s, many institutions used either a 10-point or 100-point grading system. Transcripts of students who graduated when these systems were in use may show grades converted to the new 4-point scale. Thus, original transcripts from the year of graduation may look different from a recently requested copy of the same transcript. Alternatively, the institution may provide the original 10- or 100-point grades, but give an explanation equating these grades with the 4-point scale or with letter grades. Table 3.8 gives comparisons for the various scales.

Table 3.8. Comparison of Grading Scales Used in Tertiary Institutions

Number Grades				Letter Grade	Meaning
10 *(sepuluh)*	100	4	5	A+	Superior
9 *(sembilan)*	90	4	5	A	Excellent
8 *(delapan)*	80	4	5	B+	Very Good
7 *(tujuh)*	70	3	4	B	Good
6 *(enam)*	60	2	3	C	Fair
5 *(lima)*	50	1	2	D	Poor
1-4 *(satu, dua, tiga, empat)*	1-40	0	1	E	Fail

SOURCE: Based on information from Sumadi Suryabrata, 1992; and Aanenson, 1979.

Quality Indicators

The quality of an institution or applicant may be indicated by the following factors:

The institution

1. is a state institution under the control of the MOEC;
2. offers graduate degrees (see Tables 4.1 and 4.3, and p. 61);
3. offers graduate programs in conjunction with one of the institutions above in no. 2 (see Table 4.4 in chapter IV);
4. has been in operation for 20-30 years and has therefore benefitted from significant input in facilities, resources, and staff training overseas;
5. has a significant number of faculty members with graduate degrees;
6. is a private institution offering programs with equalized (*disamakan*) status.

The applicant

1. has a GPA above the average for the particular faculty, university, and year (see Appendix C). A GPA of one standard deviation ($\overline{X} + 1.0$ s) above the average puts a student into the top 15% of the group; one-half a standard deviation above average ($\overline{X} + .5$ s) places a student in the top 30% of the group;
2. has completed a tertiary program of study within the standard period of time. Good students often finish on time, although it is not true that those who take longer are not good students. Delays may be due to the absence of advisors or other reasons beyond the control of the student;

3. has written an undergraduate thesis (*skripsi*) on a relevant topic. Some programs, though by no means all, allow students to write a thesis or complete only coursework. A *skripsi* is required for admission to an advanced degree program;
4. has graduated from one of the most competitive faculties: engineering or economics for students from the A1 (physics) stream in secondary school; medicine, engineering, or agriculture for students from the A2 (biology) stream;[4]
5. has come from one of the major urban universities on Java which offers graduate programs. These institutions admit the top 5% of all students nationwide;
6. was admitted through the merit-based admissions process and not through the national university entrance exam. These students ranked near the top of their upper secondary school graduating classes. They may have poor grades in the early years of university because of the relatively poor quality of the upper secondary school, but are usually able to overcome this disadvantage. However, good students are admitted through the standard procedures, since merit-based admissions programs have not been in effect for all universities, for all secondary schools, nor for all years in which students may have entered tertiary-level study;
7. comes from a secondary school outside Java and was admitted to a major urban institution on Java.

---

[4]From Nasoetion in Hill, p. 71.

IV. Graduate Education

Graduate education (*pendidikan pasca sarjana*) in Indonesian tertiary institutions has been variously organized under a graduate school (Sekolah Pasca Sarjana, 1975-80), a graduate faculty (Fakultas Pasca Sarjana, 1981-89), and, as of 1990, under a graduate program (Program Pasca Sarjana) headed by a director. In 1992, 24 state and two private institutions offered graduate programs; of these, 12 state institutions were authorized to award graduate degrees.

Under the Dutch system, graduate education was limited to doctoral degrees (DR.; see Academic Degrees, chapter III, Tertiary Education), which were awarded after the writing of a dissertation; no coursework was required. This practice continued into the 1970s, producing very few graduates. In 1975 the Director General of Higher Education established a committee to study existing graduate degree programs and to formulate a new, uniform structure for graduate programs. *Magister* and *doktor* degree programs were the outcome, followed by the promulgation of Government Regulation No. 27/1981 Regarding the Structure of University/Institute Departments.

The Bogor Institute of Agriculture pioneered the new *magister* and *doktor* programs beginning in 1975. Eight other state tertiary institutions were authorized to begin their own graduate programs in 1979: University of Indonesia; Gadjah Mada University; Padjadjaran University; Airlangga University; Bandung Institute of Technology; and the teacher training institutes (Institut Keguruan dan Ilmu Pendidikan/IKIP) in Jakarta, Bandung, and Malang. Hasanuddin University joined this group in 1986, and in 1987 Satya Wacana Christian University became the first private university to offer a graduate program (not a degree) through a credit-earning agreement with the University of Indonesia.

More recently, Law No. 2/1989 on the National Education System further strengthened the organization of graduate education and eliminated most of the remaining Dutch educational practices. This law gave rise to a quartet of government regulations, one of which, Government Regulation No. 30/1990, sets out regulations for higher education, including graduate education.

Only universities, institutes, and advanced schools may offer graduate programs, and as in the undergraduate system two educational streams are offered, academic and professional. The academic degrees are four-semester/two-year magister (strata dua/S2) degrees followed by six-semester/three-year doktor (strata tiga/S3) degrees. Professional diplomas are the Specialist I (Spesialis I/Sp.I) and Specialist II (Spesialis II/Sp.II), although the latter is not yet offered, as of 1993. Professional programs are intended to be at the same level as S2 and S3 degrees in terms of required credits and length of program, but their content is more practically oriented in contrast to the research orientation of magister and doktor programs. Indeed, the majority of Sp.I programs are designed to enable medical doctors to gain professional training and experience in a specialized area (surgery, pediatrics, etc.). Specialist I programs are also offered in law and dentistry.

The *Magister* (S2)

The *magister* degree (S2) is awarded by 12 state tertiary institutions (see Table 4.1; see also Document 4.1), including three teacher training institutes (discussed in chapter V, Teacher Training) and two state Islamic institutes (Institut Agama Islam Negeri/IAIN, discussed in chapter VI, Islamic Education). The program length is four semesters or two years of study. Admission is competitive and requires an S1 (*skripsi*/thesis option) in the same or related field as the intended graduate program from one of three sources: 1) a state tertiary institution, 2) an equalized (*disamakan*) study program in a private tertiary institution, or 3) a non-equalized (*diakui* or *terdaftar*) study program in a private institution where the degree holder has passed the state examination (see Accreditation in chapter III, Tertiary Education). Other requirements include a GPA of 2.50 to 2.75, two letters of recommendation (preferably one from the S1 academic advisor and another from one of the applicant's S1 lecturers), and sometimes a prequalification test if the applicant's background lacks certain prerequisites. Some programs require English proficiency (400-450 TOEFL score or equivalent) before entry; others require English proficiency by the time the thesis is finished.

The role of the academic advisor is much more important in graduate study, whether the advisor acts alone in guiding the student's coursework and thesis or as part of an advisory committee.

All students are required to take 36-50 credits of coursework, including 8-12 credits for the thesis, research methodology, and English, and to review the literature of the field. Some institutions require a computer skills course. All require a semester course of English for Research. Students must also attend and give seminars and colloquia, submit a research proposal for approval by the advisor or advisory committee, conduct research, and write a thesis on which they are tested orally in an open forum. The Bogor Institute of Agriculture requires unanimous advisory committee approval for graduation. Students may repeat the oral examination once if they fail. Fulltime study requires at least 9 credits per semester, and all students must finish within eight semesters or four years. No E grades (fail) are allowed, and students must maintain a GPA of at least a 2.75 or 3.0, depending on the institution.

Grading at the postgraduate level follows the same system used at the undergraduate (S1) level. (See Grading in chapter III, Tertiary Education.)

Master in Business Administration (MBA) Programs

Outside the MOEC-accredited system, private sector management institutions have been offering a Master in Business Administration (MBA) since the early 1980s; one school has been offering the MBA since the 1960s. These courses come under the umbrella of the Directorate General for Nonformal Education, Youth, and Sports (Direktorat Jenderal Pendidikan Luar Sekolah, Pemuda, dan Olahraga/Ditjen PLSPO) and have the same status as a short course in computer science or French conversation.

The MBA degree programs offered by these private management institutions are not accredited by the Directorate General of Higher Education, the degrees are not recognized by the government, and their graduates are not eligible to enter state S3 programs.

The well established MBA institutions have already begun conforming, to a certain extent, to the criteria set by Law No. 2/1989 and Government Regulation No. 30/1990 Concerning Higher Education. For example, some have changed their names from "School of . . ." to "Institute of . . .," thereby conforming to one of the five state-approved units of higher education. The better management institutions have admission requirements at least as stringent as state S2 academic programs, and fulfill or exceed the minimum criteria for physical facilities set by the Directorate General of Higher Education. None, however, has (as of 1992) fulfilled curriculum requirements, preferring to maintain a flexibility of course content that MOEC accreditation does not allow. An even more basic problem is that the degree, called a "Master in Business Administration," does not officially exist in Indonesian educational nomenclature.

The older and more respected MBA institutions produce graduates who easily find jobs in the management-hungry Indonesian business world. These institutions—including the Institute of Management Development and Education (Institut Pendidikan dan Pembinaan Manajemen/IPPM, founded in the mid-1960s), Indonesian Institute for Management Development (Institut Pengembangan Manajemen Indonesia/IPMI, founded in 1983), and the Prasetiya Mulya Management Institute (Institut Manajemen Prasetiya Mulya/IMPM, founded in 1982)—require an S1 for admission, a GPA of 2.5 to 2.7, and a TOEFL score of between 400 and 500. Most have a modular curriculum that allows students to complete their programs within varying time frames. Diplomas are issued by the institution and signed by its director.

Other "MBA" institutions often require only a high school diploma for admission and thus cannot be considered graduate level institutions. Indeed, MBA schools are problematic for MOEC, given their varying admissions standards and quality of facilities and instruction.

Master in Management (MM) Programs

Realizing that the large demand for graduate business education was being filled by private MBA programs, four state tertiary institutions took their cue from these successful private institutions and developed their own graduate management programs. These programs have been approved by the Directorate General of Higher Education and are considerably more expensive (U.S. $6,000 to $10,000 per year) than other state S2 academic programs. Gadjah Mada University/UGM in 1988 was the first to offer the S2 management degree, called Magister Manajemen/MM (Master in Management) to distinguish the state degrees from the MBAs offered by the private sector. The University of Indonesia/UI, the Bogor Institute of Agriculture/IPB, and the Bandung Institute of Technology/ITB followed shortly with new MM programs.

Table 4.1.   State Tertiary Institutions Authorized to Confer *Magister*
and *Doktor* Degrees, 1992

Institution	Study Programs (S2/S3)
Bogor Institute of Agriculture (Institut Pertanian Bogor/IPB)	Agricultural and Rural Development Communications, Agricultural Economics, Agricultural Engineering, Agro-industrial Technology, Agrobusiness Management, Agroclimatology, Agronomy, Animal Science, Applied Statistics, Aquatic Science, Biology, Community Nutrition and Family Resources, Development Communications, Entomology and Plant Pathology, Food Science, Forestry, Medical Entomology, Natural and Environmental Resource Management, Postharvest Technology, Regional and Rural Development Planning, Reproductive Biology, Rural Sociology, Soil Science, Veterinary Public Health, Veterinary Science, Watershed Management
Bandung Institute of Technology (Institut Teknologi Bandung/ITB)	Analytical Chemistry, Architectural Design, Biochemistry, Business and Administration for Technology, Construction Engineering and Management, Control Systems, Corrosion Engineering, Developmental Biology, Drilling Engineering, Earth Physics, Electrical Information Systems, Electrical Power, Energy Conversion, Environmental Biology, Environmental Engineering, Exploration Geophysics, Fine Arts, Formation Evaluation Engineering, Functional Biology, Geodynamics, Geology, Geophysical Data Management, Geophysical Engineering, Geotechnics, Highway Engineering, Hydrogeology, Industrial Management, Industrial Engineering, Instrumentation and Control, Machine Manufacturing, Machine Construction and Design, Materials Science and Engineering, Mathematics, Microelectronics, Mineral Resource Management, Mineral and Metallurgical Engineering, Mining Exploration, Nuclear Science and Technology, Nuclear Physics, Nuclear Chemistry, Nuclear Control and Instrumentation, Organic Chemistry, Pharmaceutical Chemistry, Pharmaceutics,

(continued)

Table 4.1 *continued*

	Pharmacognosy, Pharmacology, Physical Chemistry, Physical Properties of Earth Materials, Physics of Materials, Phytochemistry, Process Engineering, Product Design, Production Engineering, Production Techniques and Materials, Quantitative Geodynamics, Radiobiology, Radiochemistry, Regional Planning, Reservoir Engineering, Road Systems and Engineering, Solid State Physics, Structural Engineering, Survey and Mapping, Transport Planning, Transportation, Transportation Engineering, Urban Planning, Water Resource Management, Water and Waste Water Management
Airlangga University (Universitas Airlangga/ UNAIR)	Basic Medicine, Dental Health, Immunology, Law, Management, Mathematics and Science, Pharmacy, Public Health, Reproductive Health, Sports Medicine
Gadjah Mada University (Universitas Gadjah Mada/UGM)	Accounting, Agribusiness, Agricultural Economics, Agricultural Mechanization, Agronomy, American Studies, Architectural Engineering, Basic Medicine, Biology, Chemical Engineering, Chemistry, Civil Engineering, Defense Studies, Dentistry, Economics and Development Studies, Environmental Science, Epidemiology, Food Science and Technology, Forestry, Geography, History, Hospital Management, Indonesian and Javanese Literature, Law, Livestock Science, Management, Occupational Health and Safety, Pharmacy, Physics, Plant Pathology, Plant Pest Control, Plantation Yield Technology, Political Science, Population Studies, Psychology, Public Health, Remote Sensing, Sociology, Soil Science, State Administration, Veterinary Science
Hasanuddin University (Universitas Hasanuddin/ UNHAS)	Development Studies, Environmental Studies, Farming Systems, Health Science, Language Studies, Regional Studies, Resource Economics, Science and Technology

University of Indonesia (Universitas Indonesia/UI)	Accounting, American Studies, Anthropology, Chemistry, Computer Science, Defense Studies, Demography and Human Resources, Economics, Electronic Optics and Laser Applications, Environmental Science, History, Japanese Studies, Law, Library Science, Linguistics, Literature, Management, Materials Science, Medical Sciences, Physics, Psychology, Public Health, Sociology and Politics, Women's Studies
Padjadjaran University (Universitas Padjadjaran/ UNPAD)	Accounting, Administrative Science, Agriculture, Anatomy, Anthropology, Cattle Production and Nutrition, Communications, Conservation and Land Reclamation, Constitutional Law, Dentistry, Economics of Agricultural Development, Economics of Cooperatives, Economics of Agribusiness, Health Biochemistry, International Law, Linguistics, Literature, Mathematics and Science, Microbiology and Parasitology, Pathobiology, Pharmacology, Philology, Physiology and Physical Education Health, Plant Ecophysiology, Social Psychology, Social and Political Science, Sociology, Soil Fertility and Plant Nutrition, Weed Science
IKIP Bandung	Curriculum Development, Educational Administration, Extracurricular Education, General Education, Guidance and Counseling, Indonesian, Science Education, Social Science
IKIP Jakarta	Chemistry Education, Demography and Environmental Education, Educational Research and Evaluation, Educational Technology, Educational Administration, History Education, Language Education, Physics Education, Sports Education, Vocational and Technical Education
IKIP Malang	Biology, Economics, Educational Management, Educational Technology, English, Guidance and Counselling, Indonesian, Mathematics, Nonformal Education
IAIN Syarif Hidayatullah	Interdisciplinary Islamic Studies
IAIN Sunan Kalijaga	Education, Theology

The MM programs are academic study programs usually offered by an economics faculty. Program length varies from one year (ITB and UI) to 14 months (IPB). UGM's program takes 13 months. According to the head of UI's MM program, the course content of the state programs differs from that of the better established private MBA programs in the amount of business theory taught. Case studies take up at least 50% of both the state and better-established MBA curricula. (See Table 4.2 for UI's MM curriculum.)

Admission to MM programs is exceptionally competitive: in 1989-90 UI took only seven out of 174 applicants; at UGM, 5% of the applicants were admitted. Applicants must fulfill more stringent requirements than those required for admission to other state S2 programs; in addition to an S1 degree, applicants must prove their English proficiency with a TOEFL score of at least 550, score 500 on the GMAT, and pass the Tes Potensi Akademik/Academic Potential Test (an Indonesian academic aptitude test usually used to select civil servants for overseas training). Some institutions also require an interview and/or a psychological test.

Graduation requires completion of 50 to 61 credits, a final project rather than a thesis, and a GPA of 3.0. UGM and IPB require an internship as well. Graduates are eligible for S3 programs.

The *Doktor* (S3)

The same 12 state institutions awarding *magister* degrees are also authorized to award *doktor* degrees, which require between six to ten semesters, or three to five years beyond the *magister*. Applicants must have an S2 or an Sp.I in the same or similar field from a state tertiary institution, and a GPA of at least 3.25 to be admitted. Two letters of recommendation are required, plus a statement of purpose and proof of English proficiency equivalent to a TOEFL score of 450-500.

Forty to 53 credits are required to graduate, 12 of which are research credits for the dissertation. Core coursework includes philosophy of science, special topics, and research methodology (and sometimes computer skills). Students attend and give seminars and colloquia, and defend their dissertation twice, once in a closed forum and again in an open forum.

Academic Titles

Because tertiary graduates are entitled to place a title after their names, and because of the widespread use of titles in written communications (and perhaps the problem regarding the legality and legitimacy of the title MBA), the Ministry of Education and Culture in February 1993 issued an official list of graduate titles that may be placed before (in the case of *doktor* degree holders) or after the graduate's name (for *magister* degree holders). Other titles may be added in the future.

- Magister Humaniora/M.Hum (literature, law, women's studies)
- Magister Manajemen/M.M. (management, economics)
- Magister Sains/M.Si (economics, social and political sciences, area studies, environmental studies, library science, national defense studies, sociology, psychology, mathematics and natural sciences)
- Magister Kesehatan/M.Kes (health, public health, dentistry)
- Magister Pertanian/M.P. (agriculture, animal science, veterinary medicine, development education, forestry, fisheries)
- Magister Teknik/M.T (engineering)
- Magister Komputer/M.Kom (computer science and informatics)
- Magister Seni/M.Sn (fine arts)
- Magister Pendidikan/M.Pd. (education)
- Magister Agama/M.Ag. (religious studies)
- Doktor/Dr

Credit-Earning (KPK) Programs

The 26 institutions offering graduate programs in 1992 had similar admission and graduation requirements. However, only 12 of these institutions (including three IKIPs and two IAINs) were authorized to confer the *magister* or *doktor* degree (see Table 4.1). The other 14 tertiary institutions have offered credit-earning programs (*kegiatan pengumpulan kredit*, KPK) since 1982. These institutions (listed in Table 4.3) do not yet meet the criteria necessary to award graduate degrees. They work in conjunction with state degree-granting institutions to provide graduate programs to students outside Java, where only one graduate degree-granting institution (Hasanuddin University) exists. Credit-earning programs also allow two private tertiary institutions, Parahyangan Catholic University and Satya Wacana Christian University, to offer graduate programs. Teaching responsibilities are shared by the institution offering the graduate program and the institution conferring the degree. Academic criteria and regulations follow those of the degree-granting institution.

New Graduate Program Authorizations

At the end of 1992 and in early 1993, four private universities (three located in Jakarta, one in Surabaya) were given permission by the Directorate General of Higher Education (Dikti) to offer S2 programs, starting in 1993, without engaging in a KPK arrangement—that is, these new graduate programs stand on their own. The graduate degree is awarded by the private institution and not by a state institution, as was the case until 1993. Satya Wacana Christian University prides itself on being the first private tertiary institution to confer its own *pasca sarjana* degree. The status Dikti gives these new S2 programs is *diakreditasi* or accredited, a status new to Indonesian education, and

Table 4.2. Master in Management Curriculum, University of Indonesia, 1992

Subject	Credits	
	International Management	Management Accounting
Semester 1		
Accounting	4	4
Quantitative Methods for Business	3	3
Management Information Systems	3	3
Statistics for Business	3	3
Organizational Behavior and Structure	3	3
Semester 2		
Macroeconomics for Managers	2	2
Microeconomics for Managers	3	3
Financial Management	3	3
Marketing Management	3	3
Human Resource Management	2	2
International Business	3	-
Accounting Information Systems	-	3
Semester 3		
Business and Law	3	3
Production Management	3	3
International Finance	3	-
International Marketing	3	-
Advanced Management Accounting	-	3
Audit Management	-	3
Final Project	2	2
Semester 4		
Analysis of Business Environments	3	3
Strategic Management	3	3
International Trade	3	-
Management Accounting	-	3
Final Project	6	6
Total Credits	61	61

hints at an accreditation board at work (see Accreditation in chapter III, Tertiary Education). But at the time of this book's publication, the accreditation board existed only as a report to the Director General of Higher Education.

Whatever the case, as of 1993 the following four institutions offer *magister* (S2) programs and award the degrees. The *ijazah*/certificate of completion must be signed and stamped by the appropriate Kopertis official.

University	New *Magister* Programs
Atma Jaya University/ Universitas Atma Jaya	Law; Applied Linguistics
Trisakti University/ Universitas Trisakta	Management
Tarumanagara University/ Universitas Tarumanagara	Law
Surabaya University/ Universitas Surabaya	Management; Law

Specialist Programs

As of 1992, Specialist (Spesialis/Sp.) programs are offered almost exclusively in medical fields (Table 4.4). An exception is the Sp.I program in law, which is 80% practical work and 20% theory (see Sp.I Law Curriculum, Table 4.5). Admission requirements for Sp.I programs are the same as for admission to S2 academic programs. Although no Sp.II programs are now offered, the admission requirements are to be similar to those required for admission to S3 academic programs, except that an Sp.I diploma can be substituted for the *magister* degree requirement. Medical doctors must have several years of experience before applying to Specialist programs. Students complete 40 to 75 credits and write a final report or thesis, as well as present papers in seminars. The degree conferred is a professional diploma, Spesialis I or Spesialis II. (See Document 4.2 in Appendix D for a Specialist I diploma in public health.)

Staff and Students

Indonesian graduate programs have become increasingly important as the state tertiary system works to strengthen the quality of its teaching staff. These programs are particularly important to the universities outside Java, whose staff members make up the majority of graduate enrollment in Indonesia. The older institutions generally send their faculty overseas for graduate education.

Table 4.3.　Institutions Offering Credit-Earning Graduate Programs

Offering Institution	Conferring Institution	Study Programs
Andalas University (Universitas Andalas/UNAN)	Bogor Institute of Agriculture (Institut Pertanian Bogor/IPB)	Agronomy, Animal Science, Regional and Rural Development Planning, Soil Science
Brawijaya University (Universitas Brawijaya/UNIBRAW)	Gadjah Mada University (Universitas Gadjah Mada/UGM)	Earth Science, Social Science and Economics
Diponegoro University (Universitas Diponegoro/UNDIP)	University of Indonesia (Universitas Indonesia/UI)	Law
IKIP Padang	IKIP Jakarta	Educational Administration
IKIP Yogyakarta	IKIP Jakarta	Educational Administration
Mulawarman University (Universitas Mulawarman/UNMUL)	Bogor Institute of Agriculture (Institut Pertanian Bogor/IPB)	Forestry
Sam Ratulangi University (Universitas Sam Ratulangi/UNSRAT)	Bogor Institute of Agriculture (Institut Pertanian Bogor/IPB)	Agricultural Entomology, Development and Mobilization of Economic Resources and Social Commodities, Development of Plant Science, Plant Science
Sepuluh Nopember Institute of Technology, also called Surabaya Institute of Technology (Institut Teknologi Surabaya/ITS)	Bandung Institute of Technology (Institut Teknologi Bandung/ITB)	Electrical Engineering, Mechanical Engineering, Chemical Engineering
University of North Sumatra (Universitas Sumatera Utara/USU)	Bogor Institute of Agriculture (Institut Pertanian Bogor/IPB)	Agronomy, Soil Science, Regional and Rural Development Planning, Natural Resource and Environmental Management

	Gadjah Mada University (Universitas Gadjah Mada/UGM)	Civil Law
Hasanuddin University (Universitas Hasanuddin/UNHAS)	Bogor Institute of Agriculture (Institut Pertanian Bogor/IPB)	Agricultural Science, Environmental Management, Livestock Science, Regional Development, Resource Economics
Satya Wacana Christian University (private; Universitas Kristen Satya Wacana/UKSW)	Bogor Institute of Agriculture (Institut Pertanian Bogor/IPB)	Development Studies
Parahyangan Catholic University (private; Universitas Katolic Parahyangan/UNPAR)	University of Indonesia (Universitas Indonesia/UI)	Management, Economic Planning
IAIN Ar-Raniry (Bandah Aceh)	IAIN Syarif Hidayatullah (Ciputat)	Islamic Law
IAIN Alauddin (Ujung Pandang)	IAIN Syarif Hidayatullah (Ciputat)	Interdisciplinary Islamic Studies

Research

To strengthen tertiary institutions—i.e., by strengthening research capabilities and physical facilities—and increase the number of *pasca sarjana* graduates, the Directorate General of Higher Education, with the aid of the World Bank, established 16 Inter-University Centers (Pusat Antar Universitas) in 1986 at five well-established state institutions on Java: Gadjah Mada University, Bandung Institute of Technology, Bogor Institute of Agriculture, University of Indonesia, and the Open University. Each has up to five "centers of excellence" designed to provide graduate-level training, research facilities, and support to university teachers and researchers in biotechnology, economics, engineering, food and nutrition, social studies, life sciences, microelectronics, computer science, and instructional media.

Table 4.4. State Universities Awarding Specialist I Diplomas, 1992

Institution	Study Programs
Airlangga University (Universitas Airlangga/UNAIR)	Medicine
Bandung Institute of Technology (Institut Teknologi Bandung/ITB)	Highway Engineering
University of Indonesia (Universitas Indonesia/UI)	Medicine, Dentistry, Law
Sam Ratulangi University (Universitas Sam Ratulangi/UNSRAT)	Medicine
Andalas University (Universitas Andalas/UNAND)	Medicine
Brawijaya University (Universitas Brawijaya/UNIBRAW)	Medicine
Sebelas Maret University (Universitas Sebelas Maret/UNS)	Medicine
Hasanuddin University (Universitas Hasanuddin/UNHAS)	Medicine
Padjadjaran University (Universitas Padjadjaran/UNPAD)	Medicine
Sriwijaya University (Universitas Sriwijaya/UNSRI)	Medicine
University of North Sumatra (Universitas Sumatera Utara/USU)	Medicine
Diponegoro University (Universitas Diponegoro/UNDIP)	Medicine, Law
Gadjah Mada University (Universitas Gadjah Mada/UGM)	Medicine, Dentistry

Table 4.5. Specialist I in Law Curriculum, Diponegoro University, 1992

Subject	Credits
Pancasila/Civics	2
Ethics and Codes of Ethics	2
Regulations for Notarial Duties/Functions I	3
Title and Deed Writing I	2
Dowries	2
Inheritance Law I	2
Contract Law	2
Securities Law	2
Fiscal Law I	2
Tax Stamp Regulations	2
Agrarian Law I	3
Preparation of Wills I	2
Preparation of Basic Legal Documents I	4
Notarial Regulations II	3
Preparation of Titles and Deeds II	2
Inheritance Law II (Customary Law and Islamic Law)	2
Fiscal Law II	2
Agrarian Law II	3
Preparation of Wills II	2
Preparation of Basic Legal Documents II	4
Practicum (in notarial office)	2
Total	50

SOURCE: Departemen Pendidikan dan Kebudayaan, Universitas Diponegoro, Semarang: *Buku Pedoman Universtas Diponegoro, 1991-92*, p. 103.

V. Teacher Training

Training for primary and secondary teachers takes place at the tertiary level in 10 state teacher training institutes, Institut Keguruan dan Ilmu Pendidikan/IKIP, or in the teacher training faculties, Fakultas Keguruan dan Ilmu Pendidikan/FKIP, located in 23 of the 31 state universities under the direction of the Directorate General of Higher Education. In general, where no state IKIP exists to train teachers, the provincial state university has an FKIP. Six of the 10 state IKIPs are located in Java, two in Sulawesi, and two in Sumatra. In addition, there are private IKIP and FKIP as well as advanced schools (*sekolah tinggi*) specializing in teacher training that use the acronym STKIP (Sekolah Tinggi Keguruan dan Ilmu Pendidikan). These schools are discussed in the last section of this chapter.

All IKIP and FKIP offer the following programs: Diploma II Kependidikan (Diploma II in Education, DII) for primary school teachers; Diploma III Kependidikan (Diploma III in Education, DIII) for primary or secondary teachers; and a Sarjana Kependidikan (*strata satu*/S1), a first degree in education. The DII and DIII are considered professional diplomas, the *sarjana* an academic degree. Only IKIPs Jakarta, Bandung, and Malang award the graduate (*pasca sarjana*) degrees S2 and S3 in education.

Primary Teacher Training

The tertiary-level qualification for primary school teachers has only been in effect since 1989. Since Indonesia's independence in 1945, the minimum qualification for a primary teacher has gradually risen from a six-year primary school diploma (STTB SD) to the STTB plus a two-year teacher training program in a lower secondary school, to nine years of basic education plus three years of teacher training in an upper secondary teacher training school. These upper secondary teacher training schools were of three types—Sekolah Pendidikan Guru/SPG, Teacher Education School, for class teachers teaching the range of subjects; Sekolah Guru Olahraga/SGO, Physical Education and Health Teachers School, for sports and health subject teachers; and Sekolah Guru Pendidikan Luar Biasa/SGPLB, Special Education Teachers School for teachers of physically or mentally handicapped students.

Teacher Training at the Upper Secondary Level (SPG, SGO, and SGPLB)

Admission. Admission to the SPGs, SGOs, and SGPLB upper secondary programs required a Certificate of Completion of Lower Secondary School (an STTB SMP). Selection was based on the student's leaving examination score, the NEM (*nilai EBTANAS murni*). (See also chapter II, Preprimary, Primary, and Secondary Education.)

Curriculum. All three schools required 240-252 credits earned over six semesters or three years, or an average of 40-42 credits a semester. The curriculum was in three parts. Basic courses (*program dasar umum*/PDU) were taught in the first two semesters and included religion, Pancasila/civics, History of the Struggle of the Nation, mathematics, and science. The basic teacher training courses (*program dasar keguruan*/PDK), and the teacher training courses (*program keguruan*/PK) in years two and three included courses on pedagogy, psychology, special education, materials and methods, evaluation, and a practicum (see Table 5.1).

The 1989 ministerial decision (Keputusan Menteri 0342/1989) specified that beginning in 1992 primary school teachers would be required to hold at least a Diploma II (DII) from a tertiary-level teacher training institution. Thus, the nearly 50,000 students who graduated from the SPGs and SGOs in 1990 were underqualified when they entered the job market, as were those who graduated after them. The SPGs and the SGOs graduated their last students in 1992. The Directorate General of Higher Education has organized courses to upgrade primary school teachers to the DII level through the Primary School Teacher Training Program (Pendidikan Guru Sekolah Dasar/PGSD) at selected state and private IKIP and FKIP and through inservice training programs offered through the Open University.

Lower Secondary Teacher Training

The government decree requiring primary school teachers to have at least a DII means that primary and lower secondary teachers hold the same qualification. However, most lower secondary teachers (estimated at 72% in 1989) hold only a Diploma I or an SPG/SGO/SPGLB certificate of completion. And although the Directorate General of Higher Education is providing inservice upgrading for primary teachers at government expense through the Open University, no similar upgrading program has been made available to lower secondary teachers since the 1989 closure of the Directorate General of Primary and Secondary Education's Pendidikan Guru Sekolah Menengah Tingkat Pertama/PGSMTP program. The PGSMTP program upgraded lower secondary teacher qualifications from the upper secondary level to DI. This situation has prompted complaints from lower secondary teachers who must pay for DII programs at an IKIP, FKIP, or STKIP. In addition, lower secondary teachers who generally prefer to take a second or third job do not want to sacrifice this income from outside employment to enroll in a Diploma II program. This is a problem for the Indonesian government in view of the 1994 curriculum changes making primary and lower secondary education a single unit of schooling.

Table 5.1. Primary Teacher Training School (SPG) Curriculum, 1986

		Subject/Credits					
	Year	I		II		III	
Basic Program	Sem.	1	2	3	4	5	6
Religious Education		2	2	2	2	2	2
Pancasila/Civics		2	2	2	2	2	2
History of the Struggle of the Nation		2	-	2	-	2	-
Indonesian Language		2	2	2	2	2	2
Social Studies		3	3	3	3	-	-
Physical Education and Health		2	2	2	2	2	-
Art		2	2	-	-	-	-
Handicrafts		2	2	-	-	-	-
Mathematics		4	4	2	-	-	-
Science		4	4	-	-	-	-
English Language		4	4	-	-	-	-
Basic Teacher Training							
Pedagogy		6	8	4	2	-	-
Psychology		3	3	2	4	-	-
Basics of Special Education		2	2	-	-	-	-
Teacher Training							
Materials, Methods, and Evaluation for Pancasila/Civics and History of the Struggle of the Nation		-	-	4	4	2	4
Materials, Methods, and Evaluation for Indonesian Language		-	-	4	4	4	2
Materials, Methods, and Evaluation for Social Studies		-	-	4	4	2	4
Materials, Methods, and Evaluation for Science		-	-	2	2	4	6
Materials, Methods, and Evaluation for Mathematics		-	-	2	2	4	6
Materials, Methods, and Evaluation for Art and Handicrafts		-	-	3	5	4	6
Materials, Methods, and Evaluation for Local Language*		(2)	(2)	(2)	(2)	(2)	(2)
Practicum		-	-	-	2	10	6

Total	40	40	40	40	40	40
	(42)	(42)	(42)	(42)	(42)	(42)
Grand Total	240	(252)				

*For areas or schools that offer Local Language study.

The Diploma Programs

The Diploma I (DI) teaching qualification was phased out along with the SPG, SGO, and SGPLB qualifications in 1989 and replaced by the DII. The three-year Diploma III (DIII) qualification is for primary and lower and upper secondary school teachers, although theoretically all upper secondary school teachers should hold a *sarjana* (S1) degree. Ministry of Education data for 1989-90 show that about 41% of upper secondary teachers hold a *sarjana*, 1% hold a *pasca sarjana*, 32% hold a DIII, 14% hold a DII, and 12% hold a lesser qualification (i.e., a teaching qualification granted by an SPG or an SGO, etc.).

Admission. Admission to state IKIP and FKIP diploma and degree programs is gained through one of three methods: the Entrance Examination for State Tertiary Institutions (Ujian Masuk Perguruan Tinggi Negeri/UMPTN), National Entrance Examination for Primary Teacher Training Program (Ujian Masuk Pendidikan Guru Sekolah Dasar/UMPGSD), or a merit-based selection process that assesses the interests and abilities of upper secondary school graduates. This last option is not a test but a search for promising students whose admission is determined on the basis of the first four semesters of upper secondary school. (See chapter III, Tertiary Education). Nationwide, 75% of IKIP applicants are admitted via UMPTN and UMPGSD, and 25% through merit selection. This proportion is likely to change as state tertiary institutions are given more autonomy in determining admission requirements and use merit-based programs.

In 1988-89 approximately 49,000 students applied to IKIPs and FKIPs for admission to nondegree diploma programs; 25%, or 12,000, were admitted. Approximately 64,000 students applied for *sarjana* (S1) degree programs, and 30%, or 19,400, were admitted. Most students were from general academic upper secondary schools, but graduates of upper secondary vocational schools could also apply. Also eligible were graduates of the SPGs and SGOs. In 1990-91 approximately 24,500 diploma students and 13,000 S1 degree students were graduated from state teacher training institutes.

Before 1986 when students could apply for both teacher training and non-teacher training programs, the bulk of new IKIP and FKIP students had selected teacher training as a second choice. Since 1986, however, students must choose either an IKIP/FKIP or a non-teacher training tertiary program. On Java, this regulation has resulted in a decrease in the number of state IKIP and FKIP science applicants, as many students in Java prefer to apply for a place at a more prestigious state university or institute. Off Java, however, the number of state IKIP/FKIP science applicants has increased. In 1988-89 nearly 40% of all tertiary-level science students were studying in teacher training programs.

Graduation Requirements. Diploma students must pass all coursework; no failing grades are allowed. Failed courses may be repeated. Diploma II students are given a maximum of three years to finish the two-year/four-semester program and must have a 1.76 GPA (grade point average) to graduate. Diploma III students are given a maximum of five years to finish the three-year/six-semester program and must have at least a 1.9 GPA. Some diploma programs require a short paper on the practicum experience.

Upon graduation, students receive a diploma certification, Diploma II (see Document 5.1 in Appendix D) or Diploma III, as well as an Akta certification, a teaching certificate commensurate with their level of study (see below). Both the diploma and Akta are signed by the rector of the IKIP and the dean of the faculty.

Although diploma programs are considered terminal programs in Indonesia, graduates of DIII programs may enter an S1 program provided they meet the S1 program requirements, have worked as teachers for a certain number of years, and understand that many of their 120 credits are not transferrable.

The Sarjana (S1)

IKIP and FKIP students have two study options for the S1: thesis (*skripsi*) or non-thesis (non-*skripsi*). The thesis option requires 144-160 credits, a 2.5 GPA with no failures, a seminar presentation, and an oral thesis examination. The non-thesis option requires 144 credits of coursework, no failing grades, and, depending on the institution, a comprehensive examination (usually oral) at the end of the program. Sarjana programs theoretically require between four and four-and-a-half years, but because of difficulties in finishing the thesis, six years are usually required to complete the thesis option program[1]. The time limit for an S1 is seven years.

Upon graduation, students receive a degree certification, Sarjana Pendidikan (education degree) (see Document 5.2 in Appendix D), listing the study program and faculty and signed by the rector of the university and the dean of the faculty. Students also receive a teaching certification, the Akta , also signed by the rector and the dean.

Curriculum

Most well-established IKIPs have six faculties: teaching and education; language and arts education; mathematics and natural science education; social sciences education; vocational and technical education; and sports and health education. The FKIPs follow the same organization at the departmental level, although program offerings are less comprehensive. As of 1988-89, eight provinces had no S1 or DIII physics program, seven had no chemistry program, one had no mathematics program, and one had no biology program.

---

[1]At IKIP Jakarta, between 1975-84, the thesis requirement was suspended because of the bottleneck of students who had not finished their thesis. Graduates of those years may enter an S2 program after passing a special test.

All IKIP and FKIP curricula are divided into four basic components, shown in Table 5.2 with the required courses for each diploma and degree program. Thirty percent of the courses are in general subjects and 70% are in subject area specialization subjects. One credit hour is equal to 50 minutes of class time and one hour of out-of-class work per week. One class hour is also equal to four to five hours of field work or two to three hours of practicum. Both diploma and degree students must fulfill the requirements of the curriculum as set out in Table 5.2.

Table 5.2. Components of the Teacher Training Curriculum

Components	DI*	DII	DIII**	S1+
	Program Levels and Credits Required			
General Coursework	9	8-13	8-15	14-16
General Education Courses	2	12	10	10-14
Teaching-learning Process	4-6	12-18	12-22	12-22
Subject Area Specialization	26-36	48-62	80-87	100-116

*The DI qualification for primary and lower secondary school teachers was phased out and replaced in 1989 by DII.
**The DIII qualification is for lower and upper secondary school teachers.
+The S1 is for upper secondary school teachers and may also be the only qualification held by many tertiary teachers.

General courses include Pancasila/civics, religion, Indonesian, and an introduction to the social or natural sciences. General education coursework comprises pedagogy, educational psychology, administration and supervision, and guidance and counselling. The teaching-learning process requirement was added in 1989 and includes teaching technologies (course planning, management, and evaluation), micro teaching, remedial teaching, educational research, and a teaching practicum that is worth 4 credits and involves teaching in a nearby state or private primary or secondary school for one to three months, depending on the IKIP/FKIP. Four to six subject area specialization credits in the S1 program count toward the undergraduate thesis.

Akta: Teacher Certification

The Akta teacher certification has been required for all teachers since 1982 by the National Civil Service Administration. In effect, the policy protects the teaching profession from graduates of non-teacher training institutions by requiring that all teachers have the appropriate Akta in order to teach. The teacher certification for each level is as follows:

DI   Akta I, (until 1989) may teach at the primary level (Sekolah Dasar/SD);

DII   Akta II (see Document 5.3), may teach at the primary or lower secondary level (Sekolah Menengah Pertama/SMP);

DIII   Akta III, may teach at the lower or upper secondary level (Sekolah Menengah
        Atas/SMA);

S1   Akta IV, may teach at the upper secondary level (Sekolah Menengah
        Atas/SMA);

S1   Akta V, for non-teacher training S1 graduates who wish to teach in a tertiary
        institution. In reality very few tertiary teachers hold the Akta.

IKIP and FKIP graduates receive the Akta commensurate with their level of study.
Diploma and degree holders of non-teacher training institutions may enroll in an Akta
program which requires 20 credits in education methodology and a teaching practicum.
For example, an S1 history graduate of the University of Indonesia who wishes to teach
in an upper secondary school would enroll in an Akta V program in order to earn the
appropriate teaching certification.

Graduate Degrees

Three state IKIPs—Jakarta, Bandung, and Malang—offer graduate degrees: the
Magister Kependidikan (Master of Education) at the *strata dua*/S2 level, and the Doktor
Kependidikan (Doctor of Education) at the *strata tiga*/S3 level. IKIP Yogyakarta and
IKIP Padang offer S2 and S3 credit-earning programs (see Credit-Earning Programs,
chapter IV, Graduate Education) with IKIP Jakarta, which confers the degree. *Magister*
and *doktor* degrees are not offered at FKIPs.

Magister Kependidikan (S2)

Admission. To be admitted to an S2 program, a student must have successfully
completed the S1 *skripsi* option with a GPA of at least 2.75 and pass an entrance exam
set by the IKIP offering the S2.

Graduation. A *magister* requires approximately 50 credits of coursework beyond
the S1 degree, 8-12 of which count towards a thesis (*tesis*). S2 students must defend their
theses in a closed forum. Upon graduation, a student receives a degree certification
(*ijazah*) signed by the faculty director and the rector of the IKIP.

Doktor Kependidikan (S3)

Admission. To be admitted to an S3 program, a student must have successfully
completed the S2 program with a 3.0 GPA and have written a thesis. "Honor" students
from the S2 program (GPA of 3.3 in the subject specialization) may enter the S3 program
directly without a thesis.

Graduation. The S3 requires approximately another 50 credits beyond the S2 degree, 15-23 of which count towards a dissertation (*disertasi*). Coursework, with equal credit loads for S2 and S3, is required in foundations of knowledge (8 credits), basic education (9 credits), and a specialization area (33 credits). Doctoral students must defend their dissertations twice, once in a closed forum and again in an open forum.

Upon graduation, students receive a degree certification (*ijazah*) signed by the director of the graduate program and by the rector of the institution.

Staff

Approximately 90% of all lecturers in IKIPs and FKIPs are graduates of teacher training programs. The majority of them (85%) hold a *sarjana* degree, although the minimum requirement for teaching at the tertiary level is a graduate degree (S2 or S3). There are two frequent complaints about teacher training graduates in Indonesia. First, because of the attention to teaching methodology in a subject area like mathematics or engineering, the teaching of subject-specific content in IKIPs and FKIPs is considered to be about one year behind the equivalent subject area in universities and non-teacher training institutions; and as most IKIP and FKIP teachers are recruited directly from their IKIP/FKIP alma mater, subject content courses continue to lag behind the same subject courses in universities and non-teacher training institutions. Secondly, the majority of IKIP and FKIP teachers have never taught in a primary or secondary school, although they are training new teachers to do so.

In an effort to upgrade teaching staff at IKIPs and FKIPs, a correspondence program for the Akta IV certification is offered by the Open University (see Akta: Teacher Certification, above). In addition, more IKIP and FKIP staff are being sponsored for graduate studies both in Indonesia and abroad, in education as well as in non-education fields.

Grading and Evaluation

Grading and evaluation follows the same system used in universities and other institutes. (See Grading, chapter III, Tertiary Education.)

Special Programs/Projects

Because of rapid increases in secondary enrollment over the years, a variety of emergency training programs have been developed to train secondary school teachers.

Pemantapan Kerja Guru/PKG Sanggar (literally, Strengthening the Work of Teachers). This very successful program uses an inservice/onservice approach; lower secondary school teachers receive two weeks of intensive training in a workshop followed by six weeks of supervised training at their school. The project was initially intended for lower secondary school science teachers, but its success has led to the inclusion of math, English, social studies, and Indonesian language teachers and to its becoming a permanent part of inservice teacher training.

Diploma III Program. Special government projects are sometimes instituted to fill shortages, such as the Diploma III program begun in 1985 to train math and science teachers in nine leading non-teacher training institutions (University of Indonesia, Bogor Institute of Agriculture, Bandung Institute of Technology, Padjadjaran University, Surabaya Institute of Technology, Gadjah Mada University, University of North Sumatra, Airlangga University, and Hasanuddin University). This DIII program was scheduled to end in 1992, although a definite decision had not yet been made at the time of publication. In general, special projects to train teachers continue until the shortage is filled.

Primary Teacher Upgrading. The Directorate General of Primary and Secondary Education and the Curriculum Development Center in conjunction with the Open University (Universitas Terbuka/UT) have developed a huge distance learning project to upgrade primary teachers to the DII level. Begun in 1990, UT has enrolled 48,000 of the 330,000 primary teachers scheduled to be upgraded during Repelita V (1989-94). Students receive modular study programs through the mail, study in groups, and meet with a local tutor once a week. Three years of part-time study are normally required to complete the two-year program. The DII curriculum is followed, with credit given to teachers with five or more years of teaching experience.

Private Teacher Training Institutions

Approximately 100 private teacher training institutions are open to upper secondary school graduates, each with its own admission procedures. These institutions range from the respected IKIP Sanata Dharma with 12 equalized study programs to the widespread IKIP Muhammadiyah (with only the Jakarta IKIP Muhammadiyah offering equalized study programs) and Persatuan Guru Republik Indonesia/PGRI (Indonesian Teachers' Association) IKIPs to numerous advanced schools of teacher training bearing the acryonym STKIP (Sekolah Tinggi Keguruan dan Ilmu Pendidikan). Few of these institutions have equalized study programs (see Appendix B). In 1991 these schools graduated approximately 2,500 diploma students and 10,000 S1 students.

VI. Islamic Education

Islamic education in Indonesia is the responsibility of the Ministry of Religious Affairs/MOR (Departemen Agama) which operates an extensive educational system that in many aspects parallels the national Ministry of Education and Culture/MOEC system. Like MOEC, MOR operates at the primary, secondary, and tertiary levels and is responsible for state institutions as well as a large system of private education.

State Islamic educational institutions, including primary, secondary, and tertiary institutions, are directly supervised by the ministry. Those private Islamic institutions that choose to follow MOR regulations and meet MOR standards are accredited by it in much the same way MOEC accredits private nonreligious schools. (See Private Secondary Education in chapter II, Preprimary, Primary, and Secondary Education.)

The current organization of Islamic education in Indonesia is based on the National Educational Law No. 2/1989 which provided the legal basis for the integration of the Islamic educational system into the national educational system. The administration and development of Islamic education is carried out by MOR under the authority of MOEC. The 1989 law also set the broad outlines of the curriculum for Islamic primary and secondary schools. Subjects are taught in an 80:20 proportion: 80% nonreligious and 20% religious subjects.

MOEC-Accredited Religious Schools

In addition to MOR-accredited private religious schools, private primary, secondary, and tertiary institutions in Indonesia offer educational programs in an Islamic atmosphere. Primary and secondary schools of this type offer the national curriculum and are accredited by MOEC, as are nonreligious faculties in private tertiary institutions. Faculties of Islamic subjects in these same private tertiary institutions, however, are accredited by MOR and are discussed below (see Islamic Tertiary Education).

Islamic Primary and Secondary Education

Schools under the direct control of MOR or MOR-accredited private schools are known as *madrasah*. *Madrasah* are organized along the same 6-3-3 lines as MOEC schools and include Islamic primary schools known as *madrasah ibtidyah*, Islamic lower secondary schools known as *madrasah tsanawiyah*, and Islamic upper secondary schools known as *madrasah aliyah*. Like MOEC schools, these schools are generally coeducational.

Islamic schools may also choose to remain outside the MOR accreditation system and still receive assistance from MOR in planning and development. These schools are organized either along the same lines as other private *madrasah* or operate as residential schools known as *pondok pesantren*. *Pesantren* students are called *santri*. *Pesantren* education represents the oldest tradition of Islamic education in Indonesia. Although today relatively few *pesantren* are completely traditional, many have nonetheless chosen to remain outside the MOR accreditation system. Independent Islamic schools outside the MOR accreditation system are not obliged to offer any part of the state curriculum. Their graduates do not receive a state-recognized upper secondary certificate of completion, a prerequisite for admission to all state tertiary institutions and most private tertiary institutions, whether religious or nonreligious.

Almost all Islamic primary education (over 98% in 1989) is private. In the same year, total enrollment in Islamic primary schools was 3,056,000 or almost 8% of the total primary enrollment. At the lower secondary level in 1989, 8% or 1,006,000 students were enrolled in Islamic schools. Of that total, 93% were enrolled in private Islamic schools. In 1989 Islamic upper secondary schools enrolled a total of 339,000 students (nearly 3% of the total upper secondary enrollment), 12% in MOR schools and 88% in private schools.

Secondary Curriculum

The curriculum of a MOR Islamic upper secondary school (*madrasah aliyah negeri*/MAN) differs from that of a nonreligious state school principally in the amount of time devoted to the teaching of religious subjects. Classes meet for an average of 38-44 periods a week, each period lasting 45 minutes. The academic streams of the *madrasah aliyah negeri* are similar to those in the national MOEC system but offer a religious studies stream. The five streams include religious studies (A1), physics (A2), biology (A3), social science (A4), and language and culture (A5).

Table 6.1 shows that, except for religious subjects, the social science (A4) stream curriculum of a *madrasah aliyah negeri* is the same as an MOEC upper secondary school, social science (A3) stream curriculum (see Table 2.4).

Testing and Evaluation

At the end of the third year, *madrasah aliyah* students sit for an examination called Evaluasi Belajar Tahap Akhir Nasional/EBTAN (see Document 6.1). The content of this examination, prepared in Jakarta by MOR, is similar to the state (MOEC) EBTANAS examination (see Testing and Evaluation in chapter II, Preprimary, Primary, and Secondary Education).

Upon graduation from a *madrasah aliyah*, a student receives a certificate (*ijazah*) called a Surat Tanda Tamat Belajar – Madrasah Aliyah (Madrasah Menengah Tingkat Atas)/certificate of completion of upper secondary school, signed by the head of the *madrasah* (see Document 6.2). This certificate bears the same name (STTB) as a state (MOEC) upper secondary certificate of completion.

Table. 6.1. Social Science Curriculum (A4), Madrasah Aliyah

Year	I		II		III	
Sem.	1	2	3	4	5	6
Core Program						
The Koran and Sayings of the Prophet	2	2	2	2	2	2
Theology and Moral Theology	2	2	2	2	2	2
Islamic Law	2	2	2	2	2	2
History and Islamic Civilization	-	-	-	-	2	2
Arabic Language	3	3	3	3	2	2
Pancasila/Civics	2	2	2	2	2	2
History and Struggle of the Nation	-	2	-	2	-	2
Indonesian Language and Literature	2	2	2	2	4	4
Indonesian and World History	4	3	2	2	-	-
Economics	2	2	-	-	-	-
Geography	4	3	-	-	-	-
Biology	2	2	-	-	-	-
Physics	2	2	-	-	-	-
Chemistry	2	2	-	-	-	-
Mathematics	3	3	-	-	-	-
English Language	3	3	-	-	-	-
Physical Education and Health	2	2	2	2	-	-
Art	3	3	2	-	-	-
Handicrafts	-	-	2	2	2	2
Specialization Courses						
Economics	-	-	5	5	5	5
Sociology and Anthropology	-	-	3	3	3	3
Public Administration	-	-	2	2	3	3
Mathematics	-	-	3	3	3	3
Elective Foreign Language	-	-	2	2	2	2
English Language	-	-	4	4	6	4
Total Credits	240					

SOURCE: Ministry of Religious Affairs, 1992.

Islamic Tertiary Education

The first Islamic tertiary institution in the country, the Islamic Advanced School, was established in Jakarta on July 8, 1945, by Muhammad Hatta—later to become the first vice-president—and Muhammad Natsir, a prominent pro-independence political figure. Shortly thereafter, independence was declared. In 1948 the school moved to the central Javanese city of Yogyakarta, provisional capital of the Republic. In Yogyakarta it became the nucleus of the Islamic University of Indonesia (Universitas Islam Indonesia), a private tertiary institution (see Appendix B). In 1950 the Islamic Studies faculty of the new Islamic University was reorganized as the first state tertiary Islamic institution.

A system of 14 state Islamic institutes (Institut Agama Islam Negeri/IAIN) now exists throughout the country (see Appendix A). Some of the IAINs operate additional faculties, particularly education and law, on branch campuses in other provincial cities. All IAINs have at least three faculties: theology (*ushuluddin*), law (*syari'ah*), and education (*tarbiyah*). In addition, three IAINs (Antasari, Walisongo, and North Sumatra) have faculties of Islamic propagation (*da'wah*), and six IAINs (Sunan Kalijaga, Syarif Hidayatullah, Ar-Raniry, Sunan Ampel, Alauddin, and Imam Bonjol) have both Islamic propagation faculties and faculties of Arabic language and Islamic civilization (*adab*).

In 1989-90, 84,000 students were enrolled in the 14 IAINs. The largest proportion, 55.2%, was enrolled in the faculties of education followed by 20.9% in Islamic law. Overall, Arabic language and Islamic civilization had the smallest enrollment, 3.3%.

The organization of degree programs in the IAINs is identical to that of degree programs in tertiary institutions under MOEC. The *sarjana* (*strata satu*/S1) degree, offered by all IAINs, is awarded after successful completion of 150 to 160 semester credits, including an undergraduate thesis, with a minimum GPA of 2.0. Courses in undergraduate programs are divided into three groups: general basic subjects (*mata kuliah dasar umum*/MKDU) required of all students in all faculties; subjects required of all students in a particular faculty (*mata kuliah dasar keahlian*/MKDK); and the required and elective courses that comprise a specific study program within a faculty (*mata kuliah keahlian profesi*/MKKP).

The grading system used in the IAINs is identical to that of other state tertiary institutions. (See Grading, chapter III, Tertiary Education.) Upon graduation from an IAIN, an undergraduate student receives a diploma written in Indonesian or Arabic or an official English translation signed by the rector stating that the student has been awarded the degree *sarjana* (*strata satu*/S1). (See Document 6.3 in Appendix D.)

Graduate degrees, both the S2 (*strata dua*) and S3 (*strata tiga*), are offered by IAIN Syarif Hidayatullah and IAIN Sunan Kalijaga. The S2 requires 50 to 60 credits beyond the S1, including a thesis; and the S3 requires 40 to 50 credits beyond the S2, including a dissertation. At IAIN Sunan Kalijaga, the S2 and S3 degrees are offered by the faculties of theology and education, while at IAIN Syarif Hidayatullah, the graduate program is not specialized by faculty but consists of a common program of Islamic subjects and interdisciplinary subjects, particularly philosophy, social sciences, and research methodology. Specialization is reflected in the particular focus of the thesis research. IAIN Alauddin and IAIN Ar-Raniry offer S2 programs through a credit-earning activity program (see Credit-Earning Programs, chapter IV, Graduate Education) in conjunction with IAIN Syarif Hidayatullah, which awards the degree.

Admission

Undergraduate admission to the IAINs is determined by an IAIN entrance examination, which is written by individual IAINs. In 1989-90, for example, IAIN Sunan Kalijaga tested applicants in social science, Islamic subjects, and languages (Indonesian, Arabic, and English). In 1989-90, 18,540 new students, out of a total of 35,893 applicants, were accepted by the 14 IAINs. Most of the successful applicants, 81%, were graduates of state Islamic upper secondary schools.

A *sarjana* degree is the formal prerequisite for admission to both the S2 and S3 programs. Admission is determined by the results of an examination that tests the candidate's knowledge of Arabic, English, Indonesian, and specialized Islamic subjects. Graduate programs appear to serve faculty development needs: in 1989-90 almost all of the 54 candidates enrolled in the S2 and S3 programs were themselves IAIN lecturers.

Faculty

Staff development in the IAINs has received considerable attention since 1972, when MOR decided to support the training of IAIN teaching staff in western methods of scholarship. In 1992 a total of 57 lecturers were enrolled in graduate programs in Australia, the United States, Canada, the Netherlands, and Britain. Of this number, 35 were pursuing degrees in Islamic or Middle Eastern studies, and 22 were enrolled in fields such as education, women's studies, and anthropology.

Enrollment

Faculties of Islamic subjects in private tertiary institutions enrolled 34,600 students in 1989-90. Of the 243 faculties offering Islamic subjects, 164 were registered and 79 were recognized; none had been granted equalized status by MOR (see Accreditation of Institutions, chapter III, Tertiary Education). The high undergraduate enrollment in the faculties of Islamic education and Islamic law reflect postgraduation, job-market reality. Given the demographic origin and socioeconomic background of much of the student body—often rural or small town, agricultural or small trader—the faculty of education in an IAIN functions much like an FKIP in a regional university (see chapter V, Teacher Training). It offers graduates occupational mobility and provides teachers of Arabic and religious subjects for MOEC, MOR and private Islamic schools. The relatively high enrollment in the Islamic law faculty reflects the opportunities in government service, particularly in local MOR offices and the religious courts that have jurisdiction over Muslims in matters of marriage, divorce, and inheritance.

VII. Placement Recommendations

The Role of the National Council on the Evaluation of Foreign Educational Credentials

The National Council on the Evaluation of Foreign Educational Credentials is an interassociational group that provides guidelines for interpreting foreign educational credentials for the placement of holders of these credentials in U.S. educational institutions. Its main purpose is to review, modify, and approve placement recommendations drafted for publications used by the U.S. admissions community. The Council also helps establish priorities, research guidelines, and review procedures for international admissions publications. The Council participates in international meetings that involve foreign educational credentials for the purpose of international exchanges of students and scholars. The membership of the Council reflects the diversity of U.S. educational institutions for which recommendations are made. For detailed information on the Council and its membership, see pages v-vi.

The placement recommendations approved by the Council identify the level or stage of education represented by an educational credential and thus the appropriate placement of the holder of the credential in U.S. educational institutions. Council recommendations are not directives, nor do they make judgments about the quality of programs and schools. Quality indicators may be provided by the author in the text. The effective use of placement recommendations depends on careful review of the supporting text in the publication and consideration of individual institutional placement policies and practices.

The Council suggests that institutions apply the same standards for a foreign applicant as for a U.S. applicant with a similar educational background. Recommendations reflect U.S. philosophy and structure of education and may differ from the practices of the educational system being reviewed.

Guide to the Understanding of Placement Recommendations

The National Council on the Evaluation of Foreign Educational Credentials (referred to as "the Council") has approved the placement recommendations published in this PIER full-country study in consultation with its authors. See pages v-vi for a listing of the Council member organizations and their representatives.

Over the years, certain phrases used repeatedly in the recommendations have acquired specific meanings within Council usage. To assist the reader in understanding the intent of these phrases, the Council has prepared this "Guide to the Understanding of Placement Recommendations." It provides an index to the meanings of the placement recommendations that appear specifically in this full-country study.

Questions or comments about Council placement recommendations should be sent to this address: Chair, National Council on the Evaluation of Foreign Educational Credentials, c/o AACRAO, One Dupont Circle, NW, Suite 330, Washington, DC 20036-1171.

Primary and Lower Secondary

May be placed in grade . . .

This recommendation is based on a year-for-year placement of students at this level.

Upper Secondary

May be placed in grade . . .

This recommendation is used if freshman admission cannot be recommended, but specific secondary school placement is suggested by the total years of primary and secondary school studies represented by the credential.

May be considered for freshman admission if a vocational (technical, specialized) program is appropriate preparation.

This recommendation suggests the specialized nature of the curriculum followed. The wording further suggests that within the foreign educational system the educational opportunities open to holders of the credential in question may be limited to some postsecondary, usually nonuniversity, options.

May be considered for freshman admission.

This recommendation is for graduates of academic, university-preparatory secondary school programs and other programs that can be considered for freshman admission without reservations or qualifiers.

Undergraduate

May be considered for undergraduate admission with up to . . . year(s) of transfer credit, determined through a course-by-course analysis.

This recommendation sets the maximum amount of credit, depending on the length of study, for a university program. The phrasing "course-by-course analysis" asks the evaluator to look carefully at course contents, such as course descriptions from catalogues, in order to determine the appropriateness of transfer credit.

May be considered for undergraduate admission with up to . . . year(s) of transfer credit determined through a course-by-course analysis. Because of the specialized nature of the program, the syllabus should be carefully reviewed.

This recommendation asks the evaluator to look very closely at the course contents because of the specialized nature of this nonuniversity program. Given this precautionary statement, the evaluator should try to get additional information on the program, e.g., course content, program requirements, time allocated for practical training, and profile of the school attended.

Graduate or Advanced Professional Admission

May be considered for graduate admission.

This recommendation is used if the program of study is considered to provide adequate preparation for graduate study, without reservation or qualifiers. Normally such a program represents a total of 16 years of education and gives access to graduate education within the foreign system. This recommendation may be used for programs requiring more than 16 years of study if no graduate transfer credit is recommended.

May be considered for graduate admission in a related field if the specialized nature of the program followed is appropriate preparation.

This recommendation is used for programs that are generally comparable to U.S. bachelor's degrees but the curriculum is specialized in nature and provides limited or no access to more advanced study in the home country.

May be considered for graduate transfer credit determined through a course-by-course analysis.

The phrasing "course-by-course analysis" asks the evaluator to look carefully at course contents, such as course descriptions from catalogues, in order to determine the appropriateness of transfer credit at the graduate level.

May be considered comparable to a U.S. master's degree.

This recommendation is used if the program of study is considered comparable to that of a U.S. master's program. This recommendation is usually not used for first degrees that may represent a level of academic attainment comparable to that of a master's degree but that are different in program structure.

May be considered comparable to an earned U.S. doctorate.

This recommendation is used if the program of study is considered comparable to a U.S. doctoral program. There may be differences in the structure and requirements of the program, but the credential represents advanced research and dissertation work of a sufficiently high level to recommend doctoral comparability.

A first professional degree in . . . (medicine, dentistry, veterinary medicine, law, architecture). May be considered for graduate admission.

This statement is used to point out the first professional degrees awarded in a particular field. No graduate transfer credit is awarded. While preparation for the profession occurs at the graduate level in the U.S., it occurs at the undergraduate level in many foreign educational systems.

Represents the completion of a specialization in . . . (medicine, dentistry, veterinary medicine).

This statement is used for credentials awarded for completion of a medical or dental specialization, following the first professional degree in the field.

A professional qualification (. . . in teaching). May be considered for academic placement on the basis of other credentials.

This recommendation is used for credentials that represent advanced training, primarily nonacademic in nature, and that are not appropriate for placement determination.

No Recommendation

Because this credential had not been awarded at the time the research on this educational system was conducted, no placement recommendation was made.

This statement is used for credentials for which there is not yet a history; the credentials are to be awarded in the future. Textual information should guide the user to understand as fully as possible the role and value of the credentials.

Placement Recommendations

Note: The first entry in column 1 for credentials 1-3 is a certificate of completion for MOEC and other schools; the second entry is for Islamic schools.

Primary and Secondary Education

Name of Credential	Entrance Requirements	Length of Study	Gives Access in Indonesia to	Placement Recommendations
1. Surat Tanda Tamat Belajar–Sekolah Dasar (STTB SD)/Surat Tanda Tamat Belajar –Madrasah Ibtidayah (STTB MI) (Certificate of Completion of Primary School) (pp. 10-11)	Age 6	6 years	Lower secondary school	May be placed in grade 7.
2. Surat Tanda Tamat Belajar–Sekolah Lanjutan Tingkat Pertama (STTB SMP)/–Madrasah Tsanawiyah (STTB MT) (Certificate of Completion of Lower Secondary School) (pp. 15-17)	STTB SD/STTB MI; Certificate of Completion of Primary School	3 years	Upper secondary school	May be placed in grade 10.
3. Surat Tanda Tamat Belajar–Sekolah Menengah Umum Tingkat Atas (STTB SMA)/–Madrasah Aliyah (STTB MA) (Certificate of Completion of General/ Academic Upper Secondary School) (pp. 17-24)	STTB SMP/STTB MT; Certificate of Completion of Lower Secondary School	3 years	Tertiary education	May be considered for freshman admission.
4a. Surat Tanda Tamat Belajar–Sekolah Teknik Menengah (STTB STM) (Certificate of Completion of Vocational Technical Upper Secondary School) (pp. 17-24)	STTB SMP/STTB MT; Certificate of Completion of Lower Secondary School	3 years	Tertiary education	May be considered for freshman admission if the specialized program is appropriate preparation.

4b.	Surat Tanda Tamat Belajar–Sekolah Menengah Ekonomi Atas (STTB SMEA) (Certificate of Completion of Commercial Secondary School) (pp. 17-24)	STTB SMP/STTB MT; Certificate of Completion of Lower Secondary School	3 years	Tertiary education	May be considered for freshman admission if the specialized program is appropriate preparation.
4c.	Surat Tanda Tamat Belajar–Sekolah Menengah Kesejahteraan Keluarga (STTB SMKK) (Certificate of Completion of Home Economics Secondary School) (pp. 17-24)	STTB SMP/STTB MT; Certificate of Completion of Lower Secondary School	3 years	Tertiary education	See 4b.
4d.	Surat Tanda Tamat Belajar–Sekolah Pendidikan Guru (STTB SPG)–Sekolah Guru Olahraga (STTB SGO) (Certificate of Completion of Teacher Training Upper Secondary School) (discontinued after 1992) (pp. 66-69)	STTB SMP/STTB MT; Certificate of Completion of Lower Secondary School	3 years	Tertiary education	See 4b.

Tertiary Education

Former Credentials

The following academic degrees were phased out and discontinued completely in 1990. These placement recommendations were approved by the Council in 1978 based on the Aanenson WES volume.

Sarjana Muda (p. 30)	Certificate of Completion of Upper Secondary School and entrance exam	3 years	Sarjana programs	May be considered for undergraduate admission with up to three years of transfer credit.
Sarjana, Sarjana Lengkap, Insinyur (p. 30)	Sarjana Muda	2 years	Graduate programs	May be considered for graduate admission.
Magister Sains (Master of Science) (p. 52)	Sarjana	2 years	Doctoral programs	May be considered comparable to a U.S. master's degree.
Doktor (p. 30)	Sarjana	Unspecified	-	Not considered comparable to a U.S. doctoral degree.

Current Undergraduate Credentials

The following placement recommendations are for credentials awarded by public institutions, by private institutions for equalized programs, and by private institutions where the holder of the credential has passed the state Kopertis examination.
For credentials listed below that have been awarded by private institutions where the program is not equalized and where the holder has not passed the state Kopertis examination, the placement recommendation is: May be considered for admission and placement in accordance with institutional policies for students/graduates of U.S. institutions that do not have regional accreditation.

Academic Degrees

Students who have completed some coursework for any of the programs listed below may be considered for undergraduate admission with up to one year of transfer credit for each year studied, determined through a course-by-course analysis. If length of study is cited, it refers to the standard length of the program when pursued on a fulltime basis. The actual period of attendance may be longer.

5a.	Sarjana *strata satu* (S1) (Sarjana first academic degree I) (pp. 31-34; 70-71)	Certificate of Completion of Upper Secondary School and entrance exam or merit-based admissions program	4 years	Graduate programs	May be considered for graduate admission.
5b.	Sarjana *strata satu* (S1), *hukum* (law) (pp. 31-34; 40)	See 5a	4 years	Graduate programs	A first professional degree in law; may be considered for graduate admission.
5c.	Sarjana *strata satu* (S1), Farmasi (pharmacy) (p. 39)	See 5a	4 1/2 years	Graduate programs	A first professional degree in pharmacy; may be considered for graduate admission.
5d.	Sarjana *strata satu* (S1), Kedokteran (medicine), Kedokteran Gigi (dentistry), Kedokteran Hewan (veterinary medicine) (pp. 34; 39-40)	See 5a	5 1/2 years	Graduate programs	A first professional degree in medicine, dentistry, veterinary medicine; may be considered for graduate admission.

Professional Nondegree Diplomas

6.	Diploma I (DI) (pp. 40; 46; 48; 69; 71)	Certificate of Completion of Upper Secondary School and entrance exam	1 year	Employment, DII programs	May be considered for undergraduate admission with up to one year of transfer credit determined through a course-by- course analysis. Because of the specialized nature of the program, the syllabus should be carefully reviewed.
7.	Diploma II (DII) (pp. 41-42; 46; 48; 69-70; 71)	Certificate of Completion of Upper Secondary School and entrance exam	2 years	Employment, DIII programs	May be considered for undergraduate admission with up to two years of transfer credit determined through a course-by-course analysis. Because of the specialized nature of the program, the syllabus should be carefully reviewed.
8.	Diploma III (DIII) (pp. 42; 44; 46; 48; 69-70; 71)	Certificate of Completion of Upper Secondary School and entrance exam	3 years	Employment, DIV, or S1 programs	May be considered for undergraduate admission with up to three years of transfer credit determined through a course-by-course analysis. Because of the specialized nature of the program, the syllabus should be carefully reviewed.
9.	Diploma IV (DIV) (pp. 44; 46; 48)	Certificate of Completion of Upper Secondary School and entrance exam	4 years	Employment, S1 programs	May be considered for up graduate admission in a related field if the specialized nature of the program is appropriate preparation

Current Graduate Credentials

Academic Degrees

Credential		Length	Gives access to	Recommendation
10.	Magister/*strata dua* (S2) (Level II) (pp. 52; 72)	S1	2 years	S3 programs	May be considered comparable to a U.S. master's degree.
11.	Magister Manajemen (MM) (Master in Management) (pp. 54; 58; 60)	S1	12-14 months	S3 programs	May be considered comparable to a U.S. master's degree.
12.	Doktor (DR)/*strata tiga* (S3) (Level III) (pp. 58; 72)	S2, Sp.I	3 years	-	May be considered comparable to an earned U.S. doctorate.

Professional Nondegree Diplomas

13a.	Spesialis I (Sp.I) (Specialist I) in medical fields (pp. 52; 58; 61; 64)	S1 and appropriate professional experience	2 years	Employment, Sp.2 or S3 program	Represents the completion of a specialization in the medical field.
13b.	Spesialis I (Sp.I) in other fields (pp. 52; 61; 64; 65)	S1 and appropriate professional experience	2 years	Employment, Sp.2 or S3 program	May be considered for graduate transfer credit determined through a course-by-course analysis.
13c.	Spesialis II (Sp.II) (Specialist II) (pp. 52; 61)	S2 or Sp.I	3 years	Employment	Because this credential had not been awarded at the time the research on this educational system was conducted, no placement recommendation was made.

Teacher Training Certificates

14.	Akta I (Teacher certification I) (Discontinued in 1992) (pp. 71-72)	Completion of DI	20 credits	Employment as a primary school teacher	A professional qualification for teaching. May be considered for academic placement on the basis of other credentials.
15.	Akta II (Teacher certification II) (pp. 71-72)	Completion of DII	20 credits	Employment as a primary or lower secondary school teacher	A professional qualification for teaching. May be considered for academic placement on the basis of other credentials.
16.	Akta III (Teacher certification III) (pp. 71-72)	Completion of DIII	20 credits	Employment as a lower or uppper secondary school teacher	A professional qualification for teaching. May be considered for academic placement on the basis of other credentials.
17.	Akta IV (Teacher certification IV) (pp. 71-72)	Completion of DIV or S1	20 credits	Employment as an upper secondary school teacher	A professional qualification for teaching. May be considered for academic placement on the basis of other credentials.

Appendix A. State Tertiary Institutions

The following list includes all tertiary institutions operated by the Ministry of Education and Culture and the Ministry of Religion. Each entry includes: 1) name of the institution in Indonesian, 2) Indonesian acronym/abbreviation, 3) name in English, 4) address, 5) year founded [YF], 6) 1990 total enrollment [EN], 7) number of fulltime teaching staff [FT], 8) number of fulltime teaching staff holding graduate degrees [(S2, S3)], and 9) diplomas [Dip.] and degrees [S1, S2, S3] offered by the institution. S2* and S3* indicate credit-earning activity programs. "Indonesia" must be added to all addresses.

Akademi Seni Karawitan Indonesia Padang Panjang/ASKI Padang Panjang/Indonesian Academy of Art and Music, Padang Panjang; Jl. Putri Bungsu No. 35, Padang Panjang, 27128, Sumatera Barat; YF 1965; EN 596; FT 107 (S2 0, S3 0); Dip.

Akademi Seni Tari Indonesia Bandung/ASTI Bandung/Indonesian Academy of Dance, Bandung; Jl. Buah Batu 212, Bandung, Jawa Barat; YF 1970; EN 461; FT 98 (S2 0, S3 0); Dip.

Institut Agama Islam Negeri Alauddin/IAIN Alauddin/Alauddin State Institute for Islamic Studies; Jl. Sultan Alauddin, Kotak Pos 225, Ujung Pandang, Sulawesi Selatan; YF 1965; EN 12,566; FT 203 (S2 10, S3 5); Dip., S1, S2*

Institut Agama Islam Negeri Antasari/IAIN Antasari/Antasari State Institute for Islamic Studies; Jl. Jend. Ahmad Yani Km. 4.5, Banjarmasin, Kalimantan Selatan; YF 1964; EN 3056; FT 119 (S2 4, S3 1); S1

Institut Agama Islam Negeri Ar-Raniry/IAIN Ar-Raniry/Ar-Raniry State Institute for Islamic Studies; Darussalam, Kotak Pos 76, Banda Aceh, DI Aceh, Sumatera; YF 1963; EN 4795; FT 115 (S2 10, S3 5); S1, S2*

Institut Agama Islam Negeri Imam Bonjol/IAIN Imam Bonjol/Imam Bonjol State Institute for Islamic Studies; Jl. Jend. Sudirman No. 15, Padang, Sumatera Barat; YF 1966; EN 3753; FT 185 (S2 10, S3 8); S1

Institut Agama Islam Negeri Raden Fatah/IAIN Raden Fatah/Raden Fatah State Institute for Islamic Studies; Jl. Jend. Sudirman Km. 3, Kotak Pos 54, Palembang, Sumatera Selatan; YF 1964; EN 4696; FT 129 (S2 8, S3 0); S1

Institut Agama Islam Negeri Raden Intan/IAIN Raden Intan/Raden Intan State Institute for Islamic Studies; Jl. Teuku Umar Labuhan Ratu Km. 9.5 Kedaton, Bandar Lampung, Lampung; YF 1968; EN 3331; FT 101 (S2 8, S3 0); S1

Institut Agama Islam Negeri Sultan Syarif Qasim/IAIN Sultan Syarif Qasim/Sultan Syarif Qasim State Institute for Islamic Studies; Jl. Ahmad Dahlan No. 94, Pekanbaru, Riau, Sumatera; YF 1970; EN 2456; FT 70 (S2 5, S3 1); S1

Institut Agama Islam Negeri Sultan Thaha Saifuddin/IAIN Sultan Thaha Saifuddin/Sultan Thaha Saifuddin State Institute for Islamic Studies; Jl. Telanaipura, Jambi, Sumatera; YF 1967; EN 2900; FT 115 (S2 24, S3 1); S1

Institut Agama Islam Negeri Sumatera Utara/ IAIN Sumatera Utara/North Sumatra State Institute for Islamic Studies; Jl. IAIN Medan, Sumatera Utara; YF 1973; EN 4848; FT 131 (S2 7, S3 3); S1

Institut Agama Islam Negeri Sunan Ampel/IAIN Sunan Ampel/Sunan Ampel State Institute for Islamic Studies; Jl. Jend. Ahmad Yani No. 117, Wonocolo, Surabaya, Jawa Timur; YF 1965; EN 11,034; FT 309 (S2 19, S3 3); Dip., S1

Institut Agama Islam Negeri Sunan Gunung Jati/IAIN Sunan Gunung Jati/Sunan Gunung Jati State Institute for Islamic Studies; Jl. Raya Timur Km. 14, No. 197, Ujung Berung, Bandung, Jawa Barat; YF 1968; EN 11,010; FT 219 (S2 3, S3 1); S1

Institut Agama Islam Negeri Sunan Kalijaga/IAIN Sunan Kalijaga/Sunan Kalijaga State Institute for Islamic Studies; Jl. Marsda Adisucipto, Demangan, DI Yogyakarta; YF 1960; EN 7505; FT 209 (S2 19, S3 3); S1, S2, S3

Institut Agama Islam Negeri Syarif Hidayatullah/IAIN Syarif Hidayatullah/Syarif Hidayatullah State Institute for Islamic Studies; Jl. Ir. H. Juanda, Ciputat, 15412, Tangerang, Jawa Barat; YF 1957; EN 6039; FT 179 (S2 34, S3 17); S1, S2, S3

Institut Agama Islam Negeri Walisongo/IAIN Walisongo/Walisongo State Institute for Islamic Studies; Jl. Walisongo No. 5, Semarang, Jawa Tengah; YF 1970; EN 6048; FT 150 (S2 5, S3 0); S1

Institut Keguruan dan Ilmu Pendidikan Bandung/IKIP Bandung/Bandung Institute of Teacher Training; Jl. Dr. Setiabudi No. 229, Bandung, Jawa Barat; YF 1954; EN 11,500; FT 986 (S2 124, S3 49); Dip., S1, S2, S3

Institut Keguruan dan Ilmu Pendidikan Jakarta/IKIP Jakarta/Jakarta Institute of Teacher Training; Jl. Rawamangun Muka, Jakarta Timur, DKI Jakarta; YF 1963; EN 9155; FT 797 (S2 64, S3 55); Dip., S1, S2, S3

Institut Keguruan dan Ilmu Pendidikan Malang/IKIP Malang/ Malang Institute of Teacher Training; Jl. Surabaya No. 6, Kotak Pos 65145, Malang, Jawa Timur; YF 1954; EN 8641; FT 788 (S2 107, S3 39); Dip., S1, S2, S3

Institut Keguruan dan Ilmu Pendidikan Manado/IKIP Manado/ Manado Institute of Teacher Training; Kampus IKIP Negeri Manado di Tondano, Sulawesi Utara; YF 1955; EN 5423; FT 854 (S2 72, S3 23); Dip., S1

Institut Keguruan dan Ilmu Pendidikan Medan/IKIP Medan/Medan Institute of Teacher Training; Jl. Merbau No. 38A, Kotak Pos 590, Medan, Sumatera Utara; YF 1950; EN 8366; FT 942 (S2 85, S3 13); Dip., S1

Institut Keguruan dan Ilmu Pendidikan Padang/IKIP Padang/ Padang Institute of Teacher Training; Kampus IKIP, Air Tawar, Padang, Sumatera Barat; YF 1954; EN 9160; FT 732 (S2 84, S3 31); Dip., S1, S2*

Institut Keguruan dan Ilmu Pendidikan Semarang/IKIP Semarang/Semarang Institute of Teacher Training; Jl. Kelud Utara No. III, Kotak Pos 50232, Semarang, Jawa Tengah; YF 1965; EN 13,279; FT 655 (S2 53, S3 19); Dip., S1

Institut Keguruan dan Ilmu Pendidikan Surabaya/IKIP Surabaya/Surabaya Institute of Teacher Training; Jl. Kayoon 72-74, Surabaya, Jawa Timur; YF 1964; EN 9246; FT 660 (S2 75, S3 19); Dip., S1

Institut Keguruan dan Ilmu Pendidikan Ujung Pandang/IKIP Ujung Pandang/Ujung Pandang Institute of Teacher Training; Kampus IKIP Gunung Sari Baru, Ujung Pandang; Sulawesi Selatan; YF 1965; EN 8554; FT 664 (S2 73, S3 33); Dip., S1, S2*

Institut Keguruan dan Ilmu Pendidikan Yogyakarta/IKIP Yogya/Yogyakarta Institute of Teacher Training; Kampus IKIP, Karang Malang, DI Yogyakarta; YF 1963; EN 12,264; FT 746 (S2 112, S3 46); Dip., S1, S2*

Institut Pertanian Bogor/IPB/Bogor Institute of Agriculture (or Bogor Agricultural University); Jl. Raya Padjajaran, Bogor, Jawa Barat; YF 1963; EN 11,689; FT 1187 (S2 293, S3 225); Dip., S1, S2, S3

Institut Seni Indonesia Yogyakarta/ISI Yogya/Indonesian Institute of Art, Yogyakarta; Jl. Parangtritis Km. 6.5, Kotak Pos 210, DI Yogyakarta; YF 1984; EN 2140; FT 226 (S2 13, S3 0); Dip., S1

Institut Teknologi Bandung/ITB/Bandung Institute of Technology; Jl. Taman Sari No. 64, Bandung, Jawa Barat; YF 1959; EN 13,112; FT 1057 (S2 196, S3 258); Dip., S1, S2, S3

Institut Teknologi Sepuluh Nopember/ITS/Sepuluh Nopember Institute of Technology; Kampus ITS Keputih Sukolilo, Surabaya, Jawa Timur; YF 1960; EN 9864; FT 683 (S2 182, S3 76); Dip., S1, S2*

Sekolah Tinggi Seni Indonesia Denpasar/STSI Denpasar/Indonesian Advanced School of Art, Denpasar; Jl. Nusa Indah, Denpasar, Bali; YF 1969; EN 403; FT 78 (S2 3, S3 1); S1

Sekolah Tinggi Seni Indonesia Surakarta/STSI Surakarta/Indonesian Advanced School of Art, Surakarta; Kentingan Jebres, Surakarta 57126, Jawa Tengah; YF 1964; EN 827; FT 189 (S2 7, S3 3); Dip., S1

Universitas Airlangga/UNAIR/Airlangga University; Jl. Airlangga No. 4-6, Surabaya, Jawa Timur; YF 1954; EN 12,466; FT 1340 (S2 626, S3 85); Dip., S1, S2, S3, Sp.I

Universitas Andalas/UNAND/Andalas University; Jl. Limau Manis, Padang 25163, Sumatera Barat; YF 1956; EN 12,221; FT 1018 (S2 213, S3 51); Dip., S1, S2*, S3*, Sp.I

Universitas Bengkulu/UNIB/Bengkulu University; Jl. Raya Kandang Limun, Bengkulu, Sumatera; YF 1982; EN 2692; FT 495 (S2 87, S3 7); Dip., S1

Universitas Brawijaya/UNIBRAW/Brawijaya University; Jl. Mayjen Haryono No. 169, Malang, Jawa Timur; YF 1963; EN 14,688; FT 1151 (S2 265, S3 45); Dip., S1, S2*, S3*, Sp.I

Universitas Cenderawasih/UNCEN/Cenderawasih University; Jl. Sentani Abe Pura, PO Box 422, Jayapura, Irian Jaya; YF 1962; EN 3909; FT 335 (S2 23, S3 2); Dip., S1

Universitas Diponegoro/UNDIP/Diponegoro University; Jl. Imam Bardjo SH. No. 1, Kotak Pos 270, Semarang, Jawa Tengah; YF 1960; EN 18,472; FT 1412 (S2 250, S3 44); Dip., S1, S2*, Sp.I

Universitas Gadjah Mada/UGM/Gadjah Mada University; Bulak Sumur, DI Yogyakarta; YF 1949; EN 32,035; FT 2062 (S2 631, S3 296); Dip., S1, S2, S3, Sp.I

Universitas Haluoleo/UNHALU/Haluoleo University; Jl. Mayjen S. Parman, Kendari, Sulawesi Tenggara; YF 1981; EN 5819; FT 289 (S2 20, S3 1); Dip., S1

Universitas Hasanuddin/UNHAS/Hasanuddin University; Kampus Tamalanrea, Jl. Perintis Kemerdekaan, Ujung Pandang, 90245, Sulawesi Selatan; YF 1956; EN 20,945; FT 1554 (S2 396, S3 139); Dip., S1, S2, S3*, Sp.I

Universitas Indonesia/UI/University of Indonesia; Kampus UI, Depok, Jawa Barat; YF 1950; EN 20,679; FT 2410 (S2 799, S3 250); Dip., S1, S2, S3, Sp.I

Universitas Jambi/UNJAM/Jambi University; Jl. Prof. Dr. Sri Soedewi Masjchun Sofwan SH., Jambi, Sumatera; YF 1963; EN 6165; FT 426 (S2 38, S3 0); Dip., S1

Universitas Jember/UNEJ/Jember University; Jl. Veteran No. 3, Kotak Pos 59, Jember, Jawa Timur; YF 1964; EN 11,325; FT 685 (S2 106, S3 6); Dip., S1

Universitas Jenderal Soedirman/UNSOED/Jenderal Soedirman University; Kampus UNSOED Grendeng, Purwokerto, Jawa Tengah; YF 1963; EN 7915; FT 668 (S2 86, S3 10); Dip., S1

Universitas Lambung Mangkurat/UNLAM/Lambung Mangkurat University; Jl. Brigjen. H. Hasan Basry, Kotak Pos 219, Banjarmasin, Kalimantan Selatan; YF 1960; EN 8885; FT 659 (S2 61, S3 10); Dip., S1

Universitas Lampung/UNILA/Lampung University; Jl. Prof. Dr. Sumantri Brojonegoro No. 1, Bandar Lampung, Lampung; YF 1965; EN 8099; FT 731 (S2 108, S3 9); Dip., S1

Universitas Mataram/UNRAM/Mataram University; Jl. Pendidikan, Mataram, Kotak Pos 20 Ampenan, Lombok, Nusa Tenggara Barat; YF 1962; EN 6764; FT 535 (S2 78, S3 3); Dip., S1

Universitas Mulawarman/UNMUL/Mulawarman University; Kampus Gn. Kelua No. 5, Kotak Pos 68, Samarinda, Kalimantan Timur; YF 1962; EN 5014; FT 426 (S2 62, S3 18); Dip., S1, S2*

Universitas Nusa Cendana/UNDANA/Nusa Cendana University; Jl. Adi Sucipto, Penfui, Kupang, Timor, Nusa Tenggara Timur; YF 1962; EN 6409; FT 668 (S2 75, S3 2); Dip., S1

Universitas Padjadjaran/UNPAD/Padjadjaran University; Jl. Dipati Ukur No. 35, Bandung, Jawa Barat; YF 1957; EN 15,438; FT 1611 (S2 332, S3 137); Dip., S1, S2, S3, Sp.I

Universitas Palangkaraya/UNPAR/Palangkaraya University; Kampus UNPAR, Tanjung Nyahu, Jl. Yos Sudarso, Palangkaraya, 73111A, Kalimantan Tengah; YF 1963; EN 3928; FT 407 (S2 22, S3 1) Dip., S1

Universitas Pattimura/UNPATTI/Pattimura University; Jl. Ahmad Yani, Kotak Pos 95, Ambon, Maluku; YF 1956; EN 7516; FT 497 (S2 65, S3 4); Dip., S1

Universitas Riau/UNRI/Riau University; Jl. Pattimura 9, Pekanbaru, Riau, Sumatera; YF 1962; EN 7925; FT 660 (S2 76, S3 10); Dip., S1

Universitas Sam Ratulangi/UNSRAT/Sam Ratulangi University; Kampus UNSRAT, Bahu, Manado, Sulawesi Utara; YF 1961; EN 13,644; FT 1319 (S2 160, S3 19); Dip., S1, S2*, S3*, Sp.I

Universitas Sebelas Maret/UNS/Sebelas Maret University; Jl. Ir. Sutami No. 36A, Kentingan, Surakarta, Jawa Tengah; YF 1976; EN 16,475; FT 1219 (S2 191, S3 17); Dip., S1, Sp.I

Universitas Sriwijaya/UNSRI/Sriwijaya University; Jl. Srijaya Negara, Palembang, Sumatera Selatan; YF 1960; EN 10,174; FT 1043 (S2 240, S3 29); Dip., S1, Sp.I

Universitas Sumatera Utara/USU/University of North Sumatra; Jl. Universitas No. 9, Kampus USU, Medan, Sumatera Utara; YF 1957; EN 15,939; FT 1622 (S2 203, S3 56); Dip., S1, S2*, Sp.I

Universitas Syiah Kuala/UNSYIAH/Syiah Kuala University; Komplek Darussalam, Banda Aceh, Daerah Istimewa Aceh, Sumatera; YF 1961; EN 15,684; FT 863 (S2 141, S3 28); Dip., S1

Universitas Tadulako/UNTAD/Tadulako University; Kampus Bumi Bahari Tadulako, Tondo, Palu, Sulawesi Tengah; YF 1981; EN 6562; FT 584 (S2 36, S3 2); Dip., S1

Universitas Tanjungpura/UNTAN/Tanjungpura University; Jl. Imam Bonjol, Pontianak, 78124, Kalimantan Barat; YF 1963; EN 8413; FT 625 (S2 121, S3 8); Dip., S1

Universitas Terbuka/UT/Open University; Jl. Cabe Raya, Pondok Cabe, Kotak Pos 6666, Ciputat, Tangerang, Jawa Barat; YF 1984; EN 12,2086; FT 336 (S2 43, S3 15); Dip., S1

Universitas Udayana/UNUD/Udayana University; Kampus Bukit Jimbaran, Denpasar, Bali; YF 1962; EN 14,152; FT 1498 (S2 256, S3 53); Dip., S1

Appendix B. Private Tertiary Institutions

The following lists all private tertiary institutions in Indonesia as of 1990, according to the *Direktori Perguruan Tinggi Swasta di Indonesia 1990* (Directory of Private Tertiary Institutions in Indonesia 1990) and includes additional self-reported information. Each entry supplies the institution's name, address, year founded (YF), total enrollment (EN), fulltime teachers (FT), part-time teachers (PT), the diploma and/or degree offered, and equalized study programs (if any). S2* indicates credit-earning programs. A hyphen (-) occurs where no information was available. "Indonesia" must be added to all addresses.

Akademi Administrasi Amuntai, Jl. Lambung Mangkurat No. 383, P.O. Box 4, Palampitan Amuntai, Kalimantan Selatan; YF 1984; EN 85; FT 6; PT 27; Dip.

Akademi Administrasi Kertanegara, Jl. Budi 21, Cawang, Jakarta Timur, DKI Jakarta; YF 1980; EN 151; FT 15; PT 13; Dip.

Akademi Administrasi Keuangan Bentara Indonesia, Jl. Letjen Sutoyo No. 43, Surakarta, Jawa Tengah; YF 1984; EN 487; FT 5; PT 18; Dip.

Akademi Administrasi Keuangan Indonesia, Jl. Pangkalan Jati IV, Jakarta Timur, DKI Jakarta; YF 1982; EN 1325; FT 5; PT 27; Dip.

Akademi Administrasi Keuangan Jakarta, Jl. Jembatan Selatan No. 6 Blok A, Jakarta Selatan, DKI Jakarta; YF 1968; EN. 178; FT 31; PT 40; Dip.

Akademi Administrasi Magetan, Jl. Tripendita No. 4, Magetan, Jawa Timur; YF 1985; EN 130; FT 11; PT 34; Dip.

Akademi Administrasi Niaga Surabaya, Jl. Dr. Sutomo No. 49, Surabaya, Jawa Timur; YF 1986; EN 74; FT 7; PT 3; Dip.

Akademi Administrasi Notokusumo, Jl. Blunyahrejo, Karangwaru, Yogyakarta, DI Yogyakarta; YF 1979; EN 232; FT 9; PT 22; Dip.

Akademi Administrasi Pembangunan Dharma Wacana, Jl. Kenanga No. 3-Melyojati 16-C, Metro, Lampung; YF 1983; EN 405; FT 12; PT 38; Dip.

Akademi Administrasi Pembangunan Indonesia, Jl. Palapa Raya 2, Jakarta Selatan, DKI Jakarta; YF 1970; EN 112; FT 22; PT 5; Dip.

Akademi Administrasi Pembangunan Muhammadiyah Saunan, Jl. Sutan Syahril No.1, Ketapang Kalimantan Barat; YF 1981; EN 178; FT 3; PT 17; Dip.

Akademi Administrasi Pembangunan Palu, Jl. Yos Sudarso 2, Palu, Sulawesi Tengah; YF 1982; EN 170; FT 6; PT 37; Dip.

Akademi Administrasi Pembangunan PGRI, Jl. Letnan Sunarto 45, Bangkalan, Jawa Timur; YF 1984; EN 180; FT 4; PT 40; Dip.

Akademi Administrasi Pembangunan Rantau, Jl. Brigjen. Hasan Basri No.9, Rantau, Kalimantan Selatan; YF 1984; EN 156; FT 3; PT 27; Dip.

Akademi Administrasi Pembangunan Satria Wyata Mandala, Jl. Pepera, Nabire, Irian Jaya; YF 1986; EN 160; FT 5; PT 28; Dip.

Akademi Administrasi Pembangunan St. Ursula, Jl. Wirajaya No. 3, Ende, Nusa Tenggara Timur; YF 1982; EN 272; FT 9; PT 24; Dip.

Akademi Administrasi Setih Setio Jambi, Jl. Perwira, Muara Bungo, Jambi; YF 1982; EN 66; FT 5; PT 15; Dip.

Akademi Administrasi Tabalong, Jl. P. Antasari No. 17, Tanjung, Kalimantan Selatan; YF 1984; EN 98; FT 4; PT 15; Dip.

Akademi Administrasi Widya Dharma, Jl. Arief Rahman Hakim No. 93, Pontianak, Kalimantan Barat; YF 1983; EN 164; FT 8; PT 15; Dip.

Akademi Administrasi YPISA, Jl. Jend. Sudirman No. 89, Sungai Penuh, Jambi; YF 1983; EN 126; FT 4; PT 14; Dip.

Akademi Akuntansi Artawiyata Indonesia LPI, Jl. Teuku Cik Ditiro No. 9, Jakarta Pusat, DKI Jakarta; YF 1966; EN 200; FT 17; PT 16; Dip.

Akademi Akuntansi Bandung, Jl. Merdeka No. 33, Bandung, Jawa Barat; YF 1970; EN 855; FT 26; PT 42; Dip.

Akademi Akuntansi Borobudur, Jl. Raya Kali Malang 1, Jakarta Timur, DKI Jakarta; YF 1972; EN 1,931; FT 81; PT 37; Dip.: Accounting.

Akademi Akuntansi dan Manajemen Lubuk Begalung, Jl. Ujung Tanah, Lubuk Begalung, Sumatera Barat; YF 1985; EN 86; FT 8; PT 18; Dip.

Akademi Akuntansi dan Manajemen Semarang, Jl. Pamularsih Raya No. 16, Semarang, Jawa Tengah; YF 1979; EN 1137; FT 14; PT 40; Dip.

Akademi Akuntansi Denpasar, Jl. Nangka, Gang Kalisuci 2, Singaraja, Bali; YF 1983; EN 345; FT 5; PT 24; Dip.

Akademi Akuntansi Dr. Much. Thalib, Jl. Melawai XII, Jakarta Selatan, DKI Jakarta; YF 1978; EN 99; FT 4; PT 1; Dip.

Akademi Akuntansi Gatot Soebroto, Jl. Matraman Raya 88, Jakarta Pusat; YF 1987; EN 187; FT 11; PT 40; Dip.

Akademi Akuntansi Indonesia LPI, Tamalanrea Km. 9, Ujung Pandang, Sulawesi Selatan; YF 1970; EN 219; FT 17; PT 38; Dip.

Akademi Akuntansi Indonesia Padang, Jl. Purus Dalam, Padang, Sumatera Barat; YF 1972; EN 1209; FT 12; PT 39; Dip.: Accounting.

Akademi Akuntansi Jakarta, Jl. Salemba Raya 284-C, Jakarta Pusat, DKI Jakarta; YF 1969; EN 274; FT 16; PT 42; Dip.

Akademi Akuntansi Jayabaya, Jl. A. Yani-By-Pass, Jakpus, DKI Jakarta, YF 1962; EN 381; FT 11; PT 25; Dip.: Accounting.

Akademi Akuntansi Lampung, Jl. Teuku Umar-Pelita 24-B, Bandar Lampung, Lampung; YF 1980; EN 235; FT 13; PT 16; Dip.

Akademi Akuntansi Manado, Jl. Jend Sudirman 45, Manado, Sulawesi Utara; YF 1976; EN 1364; FT 4; PT 18; Dip.

Akademi Akuntansi Muhammadiyah, Jl. Kramat Raya 49, Jakarta Pusat, DKI Jakarta; YF 1983; EN 111; FT 9; PT 19; Dip.

Akademi Akuntansi Nasional, Jl. Sawo Manila, Pejaten, Jakarta Selatan, DKI Jakarta; YF 1972; EN 286; FT 18; PT 37; Dip.

Akademi Akuntansi Palangkaraya, Jl. Haji Ikap No.17, Palangkaraya, Kalimantan Tengah; YF 1985; EN 450; FT 7; PT 20; Dip.

Akademi Akuntansi Sakhyakirti, Jl. Sultan M. Mansyur 32 Ilir, Palembang, Sumatera Selatan; YF 1980; EN 207; FT 6; PT 30; Dip.

Akademi Akuntansi St. Pignatelli, Kampus Karangasem Laweyan, PO Box. 27, Surakarta, Jawa Tengah; YF 1970; EN 154; FT 8; PT 14; Dip.

Akademi Akuntansi Surabaya, Jl. Babarsari 41, Surabaya, Jawa Timur; YF 1967; EN 572; FT 9; PT 11; Dip.

Akademi Akuntansi Syafa'at Indonesia, Jl. Joe 4, Pasar Minggu, Jakarta Selatan, DKI Jakarta; YF 1987; EN 127; FT 11; PT 13; Dip.

Akademi Akuntansi Trisakti, Jl. Kyai Tapa, Grogol, DKI Jakarta; YF 1966; EN 422; FT 33; PT 35; Dip.: Accounting.

Akademi Akuntansi Veteran, Jl. Pondok Labu, Jakarta Selatan, DKI Jakarta; YF 1981; EN 961; FT 40; PT 11; Dip.

Akademi Akuntansi "YAI", Jl. Biru Laut Timur, Jakarta Utara, DKI Jakarta; YF 1977; EN 2406; FT 131; PT 57; Dip.: Accounting.

Akademi Akuntansi YKP, Jl. Surokarsan No. 2, Yogyakarta, DI Yogyakarta; YF 1972; EN 459; FT 13; PT 20; Dip.

Akademi Akuntansi YKPN Yogyakarta, Jl. Gagak Rimang No. 3, DI Yogyakarta; YF 1970; EN 2042; FT 39; PT 34; Dip.

Akademi Akuntansi Yogyakarta, Jl. Glagah Sari No. 63, DI Yogyakarta; YF 1968; EN 777; FT 15; PT 20; Dip.

Akademi Akuntansi YPK Medan, Jl. Pandan No. 6, Medan, Sumatera Utara; YF 1969; EN 355; FT 14; PT 25; Dip.

Akademi Asuransi Trisakti, Jl. Kyai Tapa Gd. A, Grogol, Jakarta; YF 1984; EN 203; FT 6; PT 37; Dip.

Akademi Bahasa 17 Agustus 1945 Semarang, Jl. Seteran Dalam No. 9, Semarang, Jawa Tengah; YF 1969; EN 883; FT 26; PT 31; Dip.

Akademi Bahasa Asing Atmajaya, Jl. Serui 18, Ujung Pandang, Sulawesi Selatan; YF 1965; EN 197; FT 15; PT 11; Dip.

Akademi Bahasa Asing Bhakti Pertiwi, Jl. Sunan Muria 6, Jember, Jawa Timur; YF 1986; EN 90; FT 1; PT 15; Dip.

Akademi Bahasa Asing Bina Budaya, Jl. Yogyakarta No. 41, Malang, Jawa Timur; YF 1984; EN 280; FT 4; PT 40; Dip.

Akademi Bahasa Asing Borobudur, Jl. Raya Kalimalang 1, Jakarta Timur, DKI Jakarta; YF 1972; EN 849; FT 55; PT 30; Dip.: English Language.

Akademi Bahasa Asing Budi Dharma, Jl. Kesehatan, Bukittinggi, Sumatera Barat; YF 1973; EN 602; FT 5; PT 15; Dip.

Akademi Bahasa Asing Kertanegara, Jl. Budi 21, Cawang, Jaktim; DKI Jakarta; YF 1980; EN 100; FT 8; PT 15; Dip.

Akademi Bahasa Asing "LPI", Jl. Cikini Raya No. 64, Jakpus; DKI Jakarta; YF 1965; EN 1,762; FT 94; PT 18; Dip.: English Language.

Akademi Bahasa Asing Manado, Jl. 14 Februari 159, Manado, Sulawesi Utara; YF 1983; EN 140; FT 7; PT 27; Dip.

Akademi Bahasa Asing Methodist Palembang, Jl. Jend. Sudirman Km. 3.5, Palembang, Sumatera Selatan; YF 1969; EN 293; FT 9; PT 21; Dip.

Akademi Bahasa Asing Nasional, Jl. Sawo Manila, Pejaten, Jaksel; DKI Jakarta; YF 1970; EN 64; FT 1; PT 16; Dip.

Akademi Bahasa Asing Pertiwi Indonesia, Jl. Melawai XI/189, Jaksel, DKI Jakarta; YF 1968; EN 466; FT 8; PT 15; Dip.

Akademi Bahasa Asing Setiabudi "LPN," Jl. RS. Fatmawati 45, Jaksel, DKI Jakarta; YF 1972; EN 37; FT 12; PT 14; Dip.

Akademi Bahasa Asing St. Pignatelli, Kampus Karangasem Laweyan P.O. Box 27, Surakarta, Jawa Tengah; YF 1968; EN 306; FT 10; PT 8; Dip.

Akademi Bahasa Asing Surabaya, Jl. Rajawali No. 29, Surabaya, Jawa Timur; YF 1975; EN 75; FT 7; PT 14; Dip.

Akademi Bahasa Asing Swadaya Medan, Jl. Jose Rizal No. 3, Medan, Sumatera Utara; YF 1967; EN 2,475; FT 23; PT 38; Dip.: English Language.

Akademi Bahasa Asing Trinitas, Jl. Pemuda No. 116, Semarang, Jawa Tengah; YF 1970; EN 45; FT 5; PT 6; Dip.

Akademi Bahasa Asing "UMI", Jl. Kakatua 27, Ujung Pandang, Sulawesi Selatan; YF 1970; EN 400; FT 7; PT 27; Dip.

Akademi Bahasa Asing WEBB, Jl. Pemuda No. 19, Surabaya, Jawa Timur; YF 1975; EN 66; FT 2; PT 9; Dip.

Akademi Bahasa Asing YAB, Jl. RS. Fatmawati 45, Jaksel; DKI Jakarta; YF 1974; EN 1,450; FT 20; PT-; Dip.

Akademi Bahasa Asing YIPK Yogyakarta, Jl. Kumendaman MD-VI/125, Yogyakarta, DIY; YF 1968; EN 329; FT 21; PT 23; Dip.

Akademi Bahasa Asing Yogyakarta, Jl. Saharjo UH-II/673, Muja-Muju, Yogyakarta, DIY; YF 1969; EN 284; FT 19; PT 4; Dip.

Akademi Bahasa Asing "YPUP", Jl. Andi Tonro 17, Ujung Pandang, Sulawesi Selatan; YF 1974; EN 165; FT 7; PT 11; Dip.

Akademi Bahasa Asing Yunisla, Jl. Pagar Alam No. 31, Kedaton, Bandar Lampung, Lampung; YF 1974; EN 254; FT 9; PT 21; Dip.

Akademi Filsafat Gereja Kalimantan Evangelis, Jl. Jend. Sudirman No. 11, Banjarmasin, Kalimantan Selatan; YF 1963; EN 142; FT 9; PT 8; Dip.

Akademi Hubungan Internasional Borobudur, Jl. HOS. Cokroaminoto 66, Jakpus; DKI Jakarta; YF 1965; EN 68; FT 17; PT 17; Dip.

Akademi Hukum Nasional, Jl. Urip Sumoharjo KM-9, Ujung Pandang, Sulawesi Selatan; YF 1970; EN 173; FT 12; PT 32; Dip.

Akademi Ilmu Gizi Indonesia, Jl. Haji Mappanyukki 41, Ujung Pandang, Sulawesi Selatan; YF 1975; EN 732; FT 11; PT 18; Dip.

Akademi Ilmu Hukum dan Kepengacaraan, Jl. Gembong No. 48, Surabaya, Jawa Timur; YF 1981; EN 610; FT 51; PT 64; Dip.

Akademi Ilmu Komunikasi Medan, Jl. Gedung Arca No. 52, Medan, Sumatera Utara; YF 1976; EN 230; FT 22; PT 12; Dip.

Akademi Ilmu Komunikasi Padang, Jl. Andalas No. 5-B, Padang, Sumatera Barat; YF 1984; EN 160; FT 6; PT 17; Dip.

Akademi Informatika dan Komputer Yadika, Jl. Makmur-Arteri, Keb. Lama, Jaksel, DKI Jakarta; YF 1984; EN 79; FT 7; PT 11; Dip.

Akademi Kehutanan Pemda Tk. II Jawa Barat, Jl. Raya Tanjungsari-Kampus STIP, Sumedang, Jawa Barat.

Akademi Kehutanan Propinsi DATI I JABAR, Jl. Cirebon No. 4-A, Bandung, Jawa Barat; YF 1967; EN 489; FT 17; PT 86; Dip.

Akademi Kepariwisataan Semarang, Jl. Bendan Ngisor, Semarang, Jawa Tengah; YF 1970; EN 705; FT 27; PT 20; Dip.

Akademi Kesejahteraan Sosial "AKK", Jl. Nitikan No. 69, Yogyakarta, DIY; YF 1973; EN 497; FT 18; PT 51; Dip.

Akademi Kesejahteraan Sosial AKTA Tarakanita, Jl. Tantular, Priwulung P.O. Box 267, Yogyakarta, DIY; YF 1967; EN 613; FT 26; PT 21; Dip.: Social Welfare, Food Technology, Clothing Technology, Housing/Human Shelter Technology.

Akademi Kesejahteraan Sosial Bandung, Jl. Lembong No. 19, Bandung, Jawa Barat; YF 1971; EN 177; FT 9; PT 14; Dip.

Akademi Kesejahteraan Sosial Ibu Kartini, Jl. Sultan Agung No. 77, Semarang, Jawa Tengah; YF 1984; EN 248; FT 8; PT 73; Dip.

Akademi Ketatalaksanaan Pelayaran Niaga, Jl. Magelang Mesan Sinduadi P.O. Box 42; Yogyakarta; DI Yogyakarta; YF 1960; EN 106; FT 13; PT 14; Dip.

Akademi Ketatalaksanaan Pelayaran Niaga Bahtera, Jl. Tentara Rakyat Mataram No. 2; Yogyakarta; DI Yogyakarta; YF 1969; EN 81; FT 10; PT 12; Dip.

Akademi Keuangan dan Akuntansi Wika Jasa, Jl. Pawiyatan Luhur, Bendan Ngisor, Semarang, Jawa Tengah; YF 1975; EN 3105; FT 73; PT 79; Dip.

Akademi Keuangan dan Perbankan Borobudur, Jl. Raya Kalimalang 1, Jaktim; DKI Jakarta; YF 1971; EN 1902; FT 101; PT 83; Dip.: Finance and Banking.

Akademi Keuangan dan Perbankan Indonesia Bandung, Jl. Kampus I/37-39, Bandung, Jawa Barat; YF 1972; EN 902; FT 29; PT 41; Dip.

Akademi Keuangan dan Perbankan Indonesia LPI, Jl. Datumuseng 34, Ujung Pandang, Sulawesi Selatan; YF 1970; EN 261; FT 9; PT 23; Dip.

Akademi Keuangan dan Perbankan Manado, Jl. 14 Februari, LR 20 Mei, Manado, Sulawesi Utara; YF 1976; EN 2,336; FT 9; PT 38; Dip.

Akademi Keuangan dan Perbankan Merdeka, Jl. Saninten No. 1, Bandung, Jawa Barat; YF 1972; EN 145; FT 6; PT 25; Dip.

Akademi Keuangan dan Perbankan Pasundan, Jl. RE. Martadinata P.O. Box 61, Tasikmalaya, Jabar; YF 1972; EN 108; FT 5; PT 24; Dip.

Akademi Keuangan dan Perbankan Pembangunan, Jl. Chotib Sulaiman, Padang, Sumatera Barat; YF 1972; EN 1,802; FT 4; PT 40; Dip.: Finance and Banking.

Akademi Keuangan dan Perbankan Surakarta, Kampus AKP Cenklik, Nusukan, Surakarta, Jawa Tengah; YF 1969; EN 1,115; FT 27; PT 23; Dip.: Finance and Banking.

Akademi Keuangan dan Perbankan Swadaya, Jl. Jose Rizal No. 3-A, Medan, Sumatera Utara; YF 1958; EN 1,455; FT 26; PT 38; Dip.: Finance and Banking.

Akademi Keuangan dan Perbankan Tridinanti, Jl. Kapt. Marzuki 2446, Palembang, Sumatera Selatan; YF 1990; EN 1,185; FT 48; PT 79; Dip.: Banking.

Akademi Keuangan dan Perbankan YIPK, Jl. Sorosutan UH-17/18, Yogyakarta, DIY; YF 1967; EN 298; FT 16; PT 22; Dip.

Akademi Kimia Analis "YKPI," Jl. Padjadjaran-Bangbarung Ujung, Bogor, Jawa Barat; YF 1986; EN 149; FT 5; PT 30; Dip.

Akademi Kimia Industri St. Paulus Semarang, Jl. Serja Dalam I/10, Semarang, Jawa Tengah; YF 1983; EN 75; FT 13; PT 22; Dip.

Akademi Komunikasi Bandung, Jl. RAA. Wiranatakusumah No. 205, Bandung, Jawa Barat; YF 1973; EN 106; FT 11; PT 7; Dip.

Akademi Komunikasi Manado, Jl. Adinegoro, Malalayang I, Manado, Sulawesi Utara; YF 1974; EN 510; FT 6; PT 42; Dip.

Akademi Komunikasi Yogyakarta, Jl. Babarsari, Komp. PTS, DI Yogyakarta; YF 1979; EN 164; FT 14; PT 28; Dip.

Akademi Litigasi Indonesia, Jl. Perc. Negara VII/49, Jakpus, DKI Jakarta; YF 1987; EN 470; FT 11; PT 57; Dip.

Akademi Manajemen Banda Aceh, Jl. Merduwati No. 9-C, Banda Aceh, DI Aceh; YF 1974; EN 2,180; FT 11; PT 18; Dip.

Akademi Manajemen dan Informatika Komputer Bandung, Jl. Jakarta No. 28, Bandung, Jawa Barat; YF 1983; EN 647; FT 5; PT-.

Akademi Manajemen dan Informatika Komputer Bunda Mulia, Jl. AM. Sangaji No. 20, Jakpus, DKI Jakarta; YF 1986; EN 452; FT 10; PT 37; Dip.

Akademi Manajemen dan Informatika Komputer Dharma Karya, Jl. Melawai XIII No. 207A, Jaksel; DKI Jakarta; YF 1981; EN 310; FT 5; PT 23; Dip.

Akademi Manajemen dan Informatika Komputer Propatria, Jl. Jagakarsa Raya, Pasar Minggu, Jaksel; DKI Jakarta; YF 1981; EN 213; FT 7; PT 17; Dip.

Akademi Manajemen dan Informatika Veteran, Jl. Dr. Angka, Purwokerto, Jawa Tengah; YF 1988; EN 95; FT 3; PT 20; Dip.

Akademi Manajemen dan Komputer YP-IPPI, Jl. Petojo Barat III/2, Jakpus DKI Jakarta; YF 1983; EN 317; FT 5; PT 8; Dip.

Akademi Manajemen Indonesia Surakarta, Sumber Jetis Rt.27/Rk.III Banjarsari, Surakarta, Jawa Tengah; YF 1969; EN 162; FT 12; PT 7; Dip.

Akademi Manajemen Industri (AAPPI), Jl. S. Parman Kav. 68, Slipi, Jakbar, DKI Jakarta; YF 1957; EN 549; FT 5; PT 50; Dip.

Akademi Manajemen Industri Propinsi Dati I Jawa Barat, Jl. Pahlawan No. 61, Bandung, Jawa Barat; YF 1967; EN 2,518; FT 23; PT 62; Dip.

Akademi Manajemen Industri Surakarta, Jl. Yos Sudarso No. 38, Surakarta, Jawa Tengah; YF 1988; EN 55; FT 7; PT 23; Dip.

Akademi Manajemen Informatika dan Komputer Dian Nuswantoro , Jl. Veteran No. 45, Semarang, Jawa Tengah; YF 1990; EN-; FT 9 PT 0; Dip.

Akademi Manajemen Informatika dan Komputer Harapan Bangsa, Jl. Raya Solo Baru AC-09, Surakarta, Jawa Tengah; YF 1990; EN-; FT 7; PT 17; Dip.

Akademi Manajemen Informatika dan Komputer ICI, Jl. Merdeka No. 36, Bandung, Jawa Barat; YF 1986; EN 160; FT 5; PT 20; Dip.

Akademi Manajemen Informatika dan Komputer Kesatria, Jl. M. Joni No. 22, Medan, Sumatera Utara; YF 1986; EN 80; FT 6; PT 10; Dip.

Akademi Manajemen Informatika dan Komputer Remox, Jl. Mayjen Sutoyo No. 23, Bengkulu; YF 1989; EN 49; FT 13; PT 16; Dip.

Akademi Manajemen Informatika dan Komputer Sumatera Barat, Jl. A. Rahman Hakim No. 57, Padang, Sumatera Barat; YF 1985; EN 640; FT 6; PT 9; Dip.

Akademi Manajemen Informatika dan Komputer Yadika, Jl. Makmur, Pondok Indah, Jakarta Selatan, DKI Jakarta; YF 1984; EN 79; FT 7; PT 11; Dip.

Akademi Manajemen Informatika dan Komputer Yogyakarta, Jl. Raya Janti, Karang Jambe, DI Yogyakarta; YF 1979; EN 763; FT 14; PT 18; Dip.

Akademi Manajemen Informatika Komputer Practicia, Jl. Pucangadi 130, Surabaya, Jawa Timur; YF 1985; EN 105; FT 20; PT 8; Dip.

Akademi Manajemen Informatika Komputer Sigma, Jl. Jend. Sudirman Km. 3.5, Palembang, Sumatera Selatan; YF 1983; EN 277; FT 27; PT 31; Dip.

Akademi Manajemen Jakarta (YPPI), Jl. Bima 42, Cijantung, Jaktim; YF 1969; EN 42; FT 38; PT 33; Dip.

Akademi Manajemen Kesatuan Bogor, Jl. Ranggagading No. 1, Bogor, Jawa Barat; YF 1972; EN 116; FT 2; PT 14; Dip.

Akademi Manajemen Keuangan Banjarmasin, Jl. Mt. Haryono No.19, Banjarmasin, Kalimantan Selatan; YF 1982; EN 251; FT 5; PT 12; Dip.

Akademi Manajemen Keuangan Lampung, Jl. Jend. Sudirman No. 39, Rawa Laut, Tanjungkarang, Lampung; YF 1983; EN 121; FT 5; PT 21; Dip.

Akademi Manajemen Keuangan "Raya" Palangkaraya, Jl. Cilik Riwut Km.3, Palangkaraya, Kalimantan Tengah; YF 1981; EN 234; FT 4; PT 36; Dip.

Akademi Manajemen Koperasi, Jl. Borobudur Barat No. 26, Malang, Jawa Timur; YF 1983; EN 94; FT 6; PT 19; Dip.

Akademi Manajemen Koperasi, Jl. Jaksa Agung Suprato 140, Banyuwangi, Jawa Timur; YF 1986; EN 56; FT 6; PT 17; Dip.

Akademi Manajemen Koperasi, Kampus Palem Pare P.O. Box 20 Pare, Kediri, Jawa Timur; YF 1987; EN 161; FT 8; PT 31; Dip.

Akademi Manajemen Koperasi 17 Agustus 1945, Jl. Selomowaru, Surabaya, Jawa Timur; YF-; EN 220; FT 2; PT 13; Dip.

Akademi Manajemen Koperasi Barabai, Jl. Kembang Melur, PO Box 2, Barabai, Kalimantan Selatan; YF 1982; EN 186; FT 3; PT 32; Dip.

Akademi Manajemen Koperasi Bengkulu, Jl. Jend. A. Yani-Ibul Manna, Bengkulu, YF 1985; EN 109; FT 3; PT 14; Dip.

Akademi Manajemen Koperasi Graha Karya, Jl. Gajahmada, Muara Bulian, Jambi; YF 1987; EN 149; FT 8; PT 17; Dip.

Akademi Manajemen Koperasi Kosgoro, Jl. A. Yani, Pontianak, Kalimantan Barat; YF 1981; EN 291; FT 1; PT 36; Dip.

Akademi Manajemen Koperasi Padang, Jl. Abdullah Achmad No. 8, Padang, Sumatera Barat; YF 1981; EN 825; FT 25; PT 21; Dip.

Akademi Manajemen Koperasi Palembang, Jl. Letnan Murod Talang Ratu Km. 5, Palembang, Sumatera Selatan; YF 1984; EN 537; FT 25; PT 41; Dip.

Akademi Manajemen Koperasi Pekanbaru, Jl. Maniyar Sakti Km. 12, Pekanbaru, Riau; YF 1987; EN 430; FT 7; PT 17; Dip.

Akademi Manajemen Koperasi Semarang, Jl. Menoreh Utara Raya 11, Semarang, Jawa Tengah; YF 1986; EN 818; FT 15; PT 34; Dip.

Akademi Manajemen Koperasi Surya, Jl. Suturyo Tengah, Surabaya, Jawa Timur; YF 1984; EN 92; FT 4; PT 15; Dip.

Akademi Manajemen Koperasi Tantular Jl. Mayjen Panjaitan No. 12, Madiun, Jawa Timur; YF 1980; EN 218; FT 2; PT 27; Dip.

Akademi Manajemen Koperasi Ujung Pandang, Jl. Bajiminasa 18, Ujung Pandang, Sulawesi Selatan; YF 1962; EN 2,065; FT 22; PT 52; Dip.

Akademi Manajemen Kupang, Jl. Adisucipto, Penfui, Kupang, Nusa Tenggara Timur; YF 1981; EN 758; FT 9; PT 25; Dip.

Akademi Manajemen Mataram, Jl. Pendidikan No. 1, Mataram, Nusa Tenggara Barat; YF 1983; EN 905; FT 15; PT 31; Dip.

Akademi Manajemen Muhammadiyah, Jl. Suprapto No. 60, Banyuwangi, Jawa Timur; YF 1984; EN 57; FT 4; PT 22; Dip.

Akademi Manajemen "Orlab", Jl. Pulo Nangka Timur I, Jaktim; DKI Jakarta; YF 1986; EN 232; FT 11; PT 12; Dip.

Akademi Manajemen Pariwisata AKTRIPA Yapari, Jl. Ir. H. Juanda No. 92, Bandung, Jawa Barat; YF 1962; EN 1,468; FT 33; PT 54; Dip.: Tourism Development, Tourism, Hotel Administration.

Akademi Manajemen Perpajakan Ujung Pandang, Jl. Lembeh 63, Ujung Pandang, Sulawesi Selatan; YF 1971; EN 255; FT 12; PT 18; Dip.

Akademi Manajemen Perusahaan Eben Haezer, Jl. Diponegoro 4, P.O. Box 120, Manado, Sulawesi Utara; YF 1982; EN 179; FT 2; PT 25; Dip.

Akademi Manajemen Perusahaan Indonesia, Jl. Arjuna No. 61, Surabaya, Jawa Timur; YF 1975; EN 80; FT 3; PT 8; Dip.

Akademi Manajemen Perusahaan Jayabaya, Jl. A. Yani By-Pass, Jakpus, DKI Jakarta; YF 1958; EN 161; FT 9; PT 23; Dip.: Business Management.

Akademi Manajemen Perusahaan Kuala Kapuas, Jl. Tambun Bungai, Kuala Kapuas, Kalimantan Tengah; YF 1971; EN 302; FT 7; PT 25; Dip.

Akademi Manajemen Perusahaan Panca Bhakti, Jl. Yos Sudarso, Pontianak, Kalimantan Barat; YF 1979; EN 263; FT 4; PT 22; Dip.

Akademi Manajemen Perusahaan Tanjung Selor, Jl. Kamp. Baru Dalam, Tarakan, Kalimantan Timur; YF 1980; EN 157; FT 6; PT 6; Dip.

Akademi Manajemen Perusahaan YKPN, Jl. Langensari No. 45, DI Yogyakarta; YF 1976; EN 1,860; FT 15; PT 39; Dip.

Akademi Manajemen Putra Jaya, Jl. Tentara Rakyat Mataram 11-B, DI Yogyakarta; YF 1983; EN 150; FT 16; PT 26; Dip.

Akademi Manajemen Sabang-Merauke, Jl. Mawar, Sabang, DI Aceh.

Akademi Manajemen Salatiga, Jl. Diponegoro No. 39, Salatiga, Jawa Tengah; YF 1984; EN 420; FT 5; PT 28; Dip.

Akademi Manajemen YAPK, Jl. Menteng Raya 11, Jakarta Pusat, DKI Jakarta; YF 1973; EN 78; FT 36; PT 36; Dip.

Akademi Maritim Djadajat, Jl. Gorontalo 2, Tj, Priok, Jakarta Utara, DKI Jakarta; YF 1963; EN 95; FT 8; PT 10; Dip.

Akademi Maritim Indonesia, Jl. Landak 15A, Ujung Pandang, Sulawesi Selatan; YF 1971; EN 486; FT 12; PT 29; Dip.

Akademi Maritim Indonesia, Jl. Pacuan Kuda 1-5 Pulo Mas, Jakarta Pusat, DKI Jakarta; YF 1960; EN 141; FT 17; PT 39; Dip.

Akademi Maritim Indonesia, Jl. Pierre Tendean, Bitung, Sulawesi Utara; YF 1989; EN 225; FT 6; PT 41; Dip.

Akademi Maritim Indonesia-Medan, Jl. Pertempuran No. 125 Pl. Brayan, Medan, Sumatera Utara; YF 1960; EN 420; FT 13; PT 33; Dip.

Akademi Maritim Nasional Indonesia, Jl. Tlogosari No. 180, Semarang, Jawa Tengah; YF 1964; EN 108; FT 13; PT 26; Dip.

Akademi Maritim Nasional Jaya, Jl. Perintis Kemerdekaan Barat, Jakut, DKI Jakarta; YF 1966; EN 97; FT 24; PT 13; Dip.

Akademi Maritim Suaka Bahari Cirebon, Jl. Widarasari III/3 Komp. Fatahillah, Cirebon, Jawa Barat; YF 1987; EN 234; FT 8; PT 18; Dip.

Akademi Maritim Veteran Republik Indonesia, Jl. Bunung Latimojong 15, Ujung Pandang, Sulawesi Selatan; YF 1963; EN 281; FT 7; PT 37; Dip.

Akademi Matematika dan Ilmu Pengetahuan Alam Al-Wasliyah, Jl. Sisingamangaraja No. 20, Medan, Sumatera Utara; YF 1989; EN 328; FT 7; PT 27; Dip.

Akademi Pariwisata Ambarukmo Place, Komp. Ambarukmo Place, DI Yogyakarta; YF 1987; EN 449; FT 14; PT 30; Dip.

Akademi Pariwisata Buana Wisata, Jl. Kementrian Lor 3-A, DI Yogyakarta; YF 1974; EN 153; FT 12; PT 21; Dip.

Akademi Pariwisata Bunda, Jl. A. Rahman Hakim No. 5, Padang, Sumatera Barat; YF 1983; EN 355; FT 7; PT 23; Dip.

Akademi Pariwisata dan Perhotelan Buana Wisata, Jl. Letjen Suprapto 104, Jakpus, DKI Jakarta; YF 1970; EN 84; FT 16; PT 46; Dip.

Akademi Pariwisata dan Perhotelan Dharma Agung, Jl. Bantam No. 1, Medan, Sumatera Utara; YF 1979; EN 569; FT 4; PT 12; Dip.: Hotel Administration, Tourism.

Akademi Pariwisata Denpasar, Jl. Tukad Balian 15, Renon, Denpasar, Bali; YF 1987; EN 286; FT 8; PT 40; Dip.

Akademi Pariwisata Engku Putri Hamidah, Jl. Diponegoro, Pekanbaru, Riau; YF 1989; EN 74; FT 4; PT 68; Dip.

Akademi Pariwisata Indonesia, Jl. Pahlawan Revolusi, Gg. H. Achmad, Pondok Bambu, Jaktim, DKI Jakarta; YF 1968; EN 639; FT 16; PT 67; Dip.

Akademi Pariwisata Indonesia Yogyakarta, Jl. Wisata, Babarsari TB-XV/15, DI Yogyakarta; YF 1971; EN 1,091; FT 13; PT 21; Dip.

Akademi Pariwisata Manado, Jl. Sam Ratulangi, Manado, Sulawesi Utara; YF 1985; EN 157; FT 7; PT 18; Dip.

Akademi Pariwisata Nasional, Jl. Sawo Manila, Pejaten, Jaksel, DKI Jakarta; YF 1985; EN 259; FT 4; PT 45; Dip.

Akademi Pariwisata Prapanca, Jl. Medokan Semampir Aws No. 5, Surabaya, Jawa Timur; YF 1987; EN 187; FT 10; PT 15; Dip.

Akademi Pariwisata Satya Widya, Jl. Bendul Merisi IX/48, Surabaya, Jawa Timur; YF 1986; EN 573; FT 4; PT 23; Dip.

Akademi Pariwisata Tadika Puri, Jl. Soekarno-Hatta Km. 6, Bandung, Jawa Barat; YF 1983; EN 132; FT 9; PT 27; Dip.

Akademi Pariwisata Tridaya, Jl. Pangkalan Jati II, Jaktim, DKI Jakarta; YF 1990; EN-; FT-; PT-; Dip.

Akademi Pariwisata Trisakti, Jl. IKPN, Tanah Kusir, Jaksel, DKI Jakarta; YF 1969; EN 957; FT 23; PT 48; Dip.: Hotel Administration, Tourism.

Akademi Pariwisata "YPAG," Jl. Haji Mappanyukki 41, Ujung Pandang, Sulawesi Selatan; YF 1975; EN 224; FT 9; PT 36; Dip.

Akademi Pelayanan Niaga Indonesia, Jl. Mgr. A. Sugiyopranoto SY. No. 37, Semarang, Jawa Tengah; YF 1964; EN 412; FT 9; PT 60; Dip.

Akademi Pembangunan Pertanian Sumatera Barat, Jl. Pasar Raya No. 22, Padang, Sumatera Barat; YF 1981; EN 71; FT 11; PT 26; Dip.

Akademi Perawatan Karya Husada, Jl. Kyai Saleh No. 3, Semarang, Jawa Tengah; YF 1982; EN 275; FT 14; PT 33; Dip.

Akademi Perawatan RS. DGI Cikini, Jl. Raden Saleh No. 40, Jakarta Pusat, DKI Jakarta; YF 1969; EN 147; FT 31; PT 31; Dip.

Akademi Perawatan RS. St. Carolus, Jl. Salemba Raya No. 41, Jakpus, DKI Jakarta; YF 1962; EN 248; FT 29; PT 35; Dip.: Nursing.

Akademi Perbankan Internasional, Jl. Pintu Besi I/2 Pasar Baru, Jakpus, DKI Jakarta; YF 1970; EN 135; FT 7; PT 17; Dip.

Akademi Perbankan LPI Jakarta, Jl. Cikini Raya No. 88, Jakpus, DKI Jakarta; YF 1965; EN 2,541; FT 97; PT 11; Dip.: Finance and Banking.

Akademi Perbankan Muhammadiyah, Jl. Kramat Raya No. 49, Jakpus, DKI Jakarta; YF 1968; EN 620; FT 45; PT 10; Dip.: Finance and Banking.

Akademi Perbankan Patrisia, Jl. Kebon Sirih No. 46, Jakpus, DKI Jakarta; YF 1967; EN 372; FT 17; PT 41; Dip.

Akademi Perbankan Setiabudi, Jl. Petojo Melintang No. 26-A, Jakpus, DKI Jakarta; YF 1964; EN 288; FT 6; PT 32; Dip.

Akademi Perbankan Yapenanta, Jl. Gunung Sahari, Kalilio 3, Jakpus, DKI Jakarta; YF 1963; EN 66; FT 9; PT 16; Dip.

Akademi Perbankan YPK, Jl. Wijaya II/62 Keb. Baru, Jaksel, DKI Jakarta; YF 1969; EN 205; FT 5; PT 20; Dip.

Akademi Perdagangan Triguna, Jl. Hang Lekir III/7, Jaksel, DKI Jakarta; YF 1986; EN 93; FT 7; PT 13; Dip.

Akademi Perdagangan YAPIM, Jl. Dr. Sam Ratulangi 46, Maros, Sulawesi Selatan; YF 1989; EN 30; FT 9; PT 7; Dip.

Akademi Perikanan Kalinyamat Jepara, Jl. HMS. No. 1 Krian, Jepara, Jawa Tengah; YF 1987; EN 198; FT 8; PT 9; Dip.

Akademi Perikanan Karya Husada, Jl. Kyai Saleh No. 3, Semarang, Jawa Tengah; YF 1990; EN 120; FT 15; PT 47; Dip.

Akademi Perikanan Yogyakarta, Jl. Kenari No. 65 Muja-muju, Yogyakarta, DIY; YF 1987; EN 111; FT 7; PT 15; Dip.

Akademi Perniagaan Perusahaan Medan, Jl. Jambi No. 23-D, Medan, Sumatera Utara; YF 1956; EN 3,893; FT 6; PT 18; Dip.: Business Management, Commercial Management.

Akademi Pertamanan Jakarta, Jl. Jagakarsa Raya, Lenteng Agung, Jaksel, DKI Jakarta; YF 1981; EN 133; FT 7; PT 14; Dip.

Akademi Pertanian Dharma Wacana Metro, Jl. Kenangan No. 3-Melyojati 16-C, Metro, Lampung; YF 1983; EN 174; FT 17; PT 27; Dip.

Akademi Pertanian Gajah Mungkur, Kampus Buluksumur, Wonogiri, Jawa Tengah; YF 1983; EN 153; FT 12; PT 25; Dip.

Akademi Pertanian HKTI Purwokerto, Jl. Letjen Pol. Sumarto Gg.VI/63, Purwokerto, Jawa Tengah; YF 1981; EN 152; FT 5; PT 17; Dip.

Akademi Pertanian Meulaboh, Jl. Yos Sudarso, Ujung Kereung, Meulaboh, DI Aceh; YF 1984; EN 167; FT 4; PT 22; Dip.

Akademi Pertanian Muhammadiyah Pemalang, Jl. Jend. Sudirman Tengah No. 226, Pemalang, Jawa Tengah; YF 1989; EN 160; FT 10; PT 10; Dip.

Akademi Pertanian Pandanaran Boyolali, Jl. Pandanaran No. 405, Boyolali, Jawa Tengah; YF 1989; EN 234; FT 7; PT 33; Dip.

Akademi Pertanian Perg. Taman Siswa, Jl. Teuku Umar No. 1, Padang, Sumatera Barat; YF 1983; EN 185; FT 13; PT 3; Dip.

Akademi Pertanian Ragam Tunas, Jl. Kapt. Dulhag No. 7 Kotabumi, Lampung Utara, Lampung; YF 1987; EN 47; FT 12; PT 37; Dip.

Akademi Pertanian Sragen, Jl. Raya Sukowati, Sragen, Jawa Tengah; YF 1988; EN 46; FT 7; PT 13; Dip.

Akademi Pertanian Surabaya, Jl. Pemuda No. 17-A, Surabaya, Jawa Timur; YF 1974; EN 225; FT 5; PT 4; Dip.

Akademi Pertanian Surya Dharma, Jl. Ki Maja Gang Pertama, Way Halim, Kedaton, Bandar Lampung, Lampung; YF 1984; EN 161; FT 9; PT 53; Dip.

Akademi Pertanian Yogyakarta, Jl. Sangaji Km. 6, DI Yogyakarta; YF 1984; EN 293; FT 7; PT 23; Dip.

Akademi Peternakan Brahma Putra, Jl. Bakalsari UH-VI/237, DI Yogyakarta; YF 1973; EN 535; FT 13; PT 32; Dip.

Akademi Peternakan Karanganyar, Jl. Lawu No. 115, Karanganyar, Jawa Tengah; YF 1985; EN 399; FT 14; PT 10; Dip.

Akademi Politeknik Jawa Dwipa Ungaran, Jl. Diponegoro No. 206, Ungaran, Jawa Tengah; YF-; EN-; FT-; PT-; Dip.

Akademi Sekretaris dan Manajemen Arjuna, Jl. Bengawan Solo 37, Malang, Jawa Timur; YF 1984; EN 240; FT 2; PT 7; Dip.

Akademi Sekretaris dan Manajemen Atmajaya, Jl. Lamadukelleng 7, Ujung Pandang, Sulawesi Selatan; YF 1982; EN 462; FT 25; PT 21; Dip.

Akademi Sekretaris dan Manajemen Bandung, Jl. Lodaya No. 38, Bandung, Jawa Barat; YF 1971; EN 352; FT 15; PT 17; Dip.

Akademi Sekretaris dan Manajemen Budi Murni, Jl. Timor No. 34, Medan, Sumatera Utara; YF 1980; EN 80; FT 11; PT 16; Dip.

Akademi Sekretaris dan Manajemen El-Fatah, Jl. Sam Ratulangi 55, Manado, Sulawesi Utara; YF 1977; EN 366; FT 6; PT 28; Dip.

Akademi Sekretaris dan Manajemen Indonesia, Jl. Kapt. Pierre Tendean No. 28, Balikpapan, Kalimantan Timur; YF 1983; EN 361; FT 3; PT 18; Dip.

Akademi Sekretaris dan Manajemen Indonesia, Jl. RTA. Milono Km. 1, Palangkaraya, Kalimantan Tengah; YF 1984; EN 255; FT 3; PT 30; Dip.

Akademi Sekretaris dan Manajemen Indonesia Jakarta, Jl. Pacuan Kuda No. 1-5 Pulo Mas, Jaktim, DKI Jakarta; YF 1962; EN 3982; FT 78; PT 117; Dip.: Management, Secretarial Science.

Akademi Sekretaris dan Manajemen Indonesia Padang, Jl. Padang Pasir No. 30, Padang, Sumatera Barat; YF 1979; EN 46; FT 5; PT 18; Dip.

Akademi Sekretaris dan Manajemen Indonesia Surabaya, Jl. Puncak Permai Ut. 45-47, Surabaya, Jawa Timur; YF 1970; EN 377; FT 6; PT 19; Dip.

Akademi Sekretaris dan Manajemen Indonesia Surakarta, Jl. Yosodipuro No. 38, Surakarta, Jawa Tengah; YF 1978; EN 1,324; FT 21; PT 18; Dip.

Akademi Sekretaris dan Manajemen Isthikayana, Jl. MT. Haryono No. 29, DI Yogyakarta; YF 1975; EN 360; FT 17; PT 17; Dip.

Akademi Sekretaris dan Manajemen Jambi, Jl. HOS. Cokroaminoto, Jambi; YF 1969; EN 601; FT 11; PT 29; Dip.

Akademi Sekretaris dan Manajemen Khalsa, Jl. Teuku Umar No. 14-16, Medan, Sumatera Utara; YF 1984; EN 169; FT 4; PT 20; Dip.

Akademi Sekretaris dan Manajemen Maria Gorreti, Jl. Bahagia No. 1, Pematang Siantar, Sumatera Utara; YF 1986; EN 98; FT 8; PT 37; Dip.

Akademi Sekretaris dan Manajemen Marsudirini, Jl. Bener No. 14 Tegalrejo, DI Yogyakarta; YF 1975; EN 421; FT 13; PT 14; Dip.

Akademi Sekretaris dan Manajemen Masyarakat Pase, Jl. Teuku Umar No. 36, Langsa, DI Aceh; YF 1989; EN 210; FT 6; PT 20; Dip.

Akademi Sekretaris dan Manajemen Pagar Alam, Jl. Teuku Umar No. 67, Bandar Lampung; YF 1987; EN 89; FT 10; PT 27; Dip.

Akademi Sekretaris dan Manajemen Pagar Alam Bandar Lampung, Jl. Raya Teuku Umar No. 26 Labuhan Ratu, Bandar Lampung, Lampung; YF 1972; EN 934; FT 46; PT 26; Dip.: Management, Secretarial Science.

Akademi Sekretaris dan Manajemen Palu, Jl. Dr. Suharso 36A, Palu, Sulteng; YF 1971; EN 1,420; FT 23; PT 36; Dip.

Akademi Sekretaris dan Manajemen Publik, Jl. Macini Tengah 50-54, Ujung Pandang, Sulawesi Selatan; YF 1979; EN 745; FT 22; PT 45; Dip.

Akademi Sekretaris dan Manajemen Purnama, Jl. Tirtayasa V, Jaksel, DKI Jakarta; YF 1975; EN 193; FT 6; PT 13; Dip.

Akademi Sekretaris dan Manajemen Saint Mary, Jl. Ir. H. Juanda No. 29, Jakpus, DKI Jakarta; YF 1985; EN 1,752; FT 8; PT 85; Dip.

Akademi Sekretaris dan Manajemen Sriwijaya, Jl. Merdeka No. 25, Palembang, Sumatera Selatan; YF 1980; EN 281; FT 11; PT 38; Dip.

Akademi Sekretaris dan Manajemen Tanah Rencong, Jl. Samudra Lancang Garam, Lhokseumawe, DI Aceh; YF 1989; EN 94; FT 3; PT 18; Dip.

Akademi Sekretaris dan Manajemen Taruna Bhakti, Jl. RE. Martadinata No. 52, Bandung, Jawa Barat; YF 1971; EN 621; FT 7; PT 25; Dip.

Akademi Sekretaris dan Manajemen Tugama, Jl. Cemara No. 32, Medan, Sumatera Utara; YF 1969; EN 115; FT 13; PT 14; Dip.

Akademi Sekretaris dan Manajemen Widya Dharma, Jl. Arief Rahman Hakim No. 93, Pontianak, Kalimantan Barat; YF 1983; EN 316; FT 3; PT 34; Dip.

Akademi Sekretaris LPK Tarakanita, Komp. Billy Moon, Pondok Kelapa, Jaktim, DKI Jakarta; YF 1968; EN 1,182; FT 21; PT 30; Dip.

Akademi Sekretaris Marsudirini Santa Maria, Jl. Ronggowarsito No. 8, Surakarta, Jawa Tengah; YF 1972; EN 487; FT 10; PT 15; Dip.

Akademi Sekretaris Regina Confessorum, Jl. Gunung Sahari II/7, Jakpus, DKI Jakarta; YF 1986; EN 53; FT 4; PT 11; Dip.

Akademi Seni dan Desain ISWI, Jl. Kebon Kacang Raya No. 5, Jakpus, DKI Jakarta; YF 1981; EN 142; FT 19; PT 13; Dip.

Akademi Teknik Bakti Teknologi, Jl. Buntaran I/45, Malang, Jawa Timur; YF 1984; EN 243; FT 16; PT 50; Dip.

Akademi Teknik dan Manajemen Industri YLPI, Jl. Bukit Datuk, Dumai, Riau; YF 1972; EN 225; FT 21; Dip.

Akademi Teknik Desain Interior, Jl. Jagakarsa Raya, Pasar Minggu, Jaksel, DKI Jakarta; YF 1981; EN 269; FT-; PT 15; Dip.

Akademi Teknik Glugur Medan, Jl. Glugur No. 140, Medan, Sumatera Utara; YF-; EN-; FT-; PT-; Dip.

Akademi Teknik Grafika Indonesia, Jl. Pasar Jum'at, Lebak Bulus, Jakarta Selatan, DKI Jakarta; YF 1965; EN 173; FT 9; PT 32; Dip.

Akademi Teknik Harapan "Yaspendar," Jl. Imam Bonjol No. 35, Medan, Sumatera Utara; YF-; EN-; FT-; PT-; Dip.

Akademi Teknik Indonesia, Jl. Sungai Sambas II/Blok B, Jaksel, DKI Jakarta; YF 1969; EN 128; FT 16; PT 8; Dip.

Akademi Teknik Kendari, Jl. RE. Martadinata 1, Kendari, Sulawesi Tenggara; YF 1985; EN 803; FT 16; PT 20; Dip.

Akademi Teknik Kimia Surakarta, Jl. Letjen Sutoyo, Surakarta, Jawa Tengah; YF 1989; EN 87; FT 7; PT 14; Dip.

Akademi Teknik Kupang, Jl. Jend. Suharto 71, Kupang, Nusa Tenggara Timur; YF 1972; EN 594; FT 3; PT 32; Dip.

Akademi Teknik Mesin Industri Surakarta, Jl. Adisucipto P.O. Box 15, Surakarta, Jawa Tengah; YF 1967; EN 171; FT 50; PT 7; Dip.: Industrial Mechanical Engineering.

Akademi Teknik Mpu Barada R., Jl. Rajikwasi No. 21, Bondowoso, Jawa Timur; YF 1982; EN 28; FT 2; PT 2; Dip.

Akademi Teknik Nasional Surabaya, Jl. Ngagel Madya I/35, Surabaya, Jawa Timur; YF 1977; EN 61; FT 5; PT 2; Dip.

Akademi Teknik Padang, Jl. Kandis Nanggalo, Padang, Sumatera Barat; YF 1972; EN 342; FT 26; PT 68; Dip.

Akademi Teknik Pembangunan Bandung, Jl. Tamansari No. 24, Bandung, Jawa Barat; YF 1982; EN 105; FT 5; PT 31; Dip.

Akademi Teknik Pembangunan Nasional Banjar Baru, Jl. Ir. Pangeran M. Noor 10, Banjar Baru, Kalimantan Selatan; YF 1986; EN 152; FT 10; PT 94; Dip.

Akademi Teknik Veteran, Jl. RS. Fatmawati, Pondok Labu, Jaksel, DKI Jakarta; YF 1982; EN 356; FT 6; PT 24; Dip.

Akademi Teknik Warga Surakarta, Jl. Kol. Sutarto No. 92, Surakara, Jawa Tengah; YF 1974; EN 401; FT 25; PT 18; Dip.

Akademi Teknik Wiworotomo Purwokerto, Jl. Laksda Yos Sudarso No. 3, Purwokerto, Jawa Tengah; YF 1984; EN 136; FT 5; PT 36; Dip.

Akademi Teknik YKPN Yogyakarta, Jl. Gagak Rimang 1, Balapan, Yogyakarta, DI Yogyakarta; YF 1972; EN 428; FT 28; PT 14; Dip.

Akademi Teknologi Grafika Trisakti, Jl. Kyai Tapa, Grogol, Jakarta Barat, DKI Jakarta; YF 1985; EN 176; FT 14; PT 18; Dip.

Akademi Teknologi Industri, Jl. Pancarkeling No. 7, Surabaya, Jawa Timur; YF 1970; EN 377; FT 11; PT 10; Dip.

Akademi Teknologi Industri, Jl. Teuku Cik Ditiro No. 7, Banda Aceh, DI Aceh; YF 1989; EN 56; FT 4; PT 29; Dip.

Akademi Teknologi Industri Palembang, Jl. Baladewa-Padang Selasa, Palembang, Sumatera Selatan; YF 1982; EN 376; FT 79; PT 38; Dip.

Akademi Teknologi Industri Tekstil, Jl. Perak Timur No. 358, Surabaya, Jawa Timur; YF 1967; EN 320; FT 5; PT 31; Dip.

Akademi Teknologi Industri Veteran, Jl. Gajahmada No. 123, Semarang, Jawa Tengah; YF 1987; EN 125; FT 8; PT 20; Dip.

Akademi Teknologi Pekerjaan Umum, Jl. Garut No. 11, Bandung, Jawa Barat, 78453; YF 1965; EN 3,035; FT 82; PT 195; Dip.

Akademi Teknologi Ronggolawe Cepu, Jl. Kampus Ronggolawe Blok B-1 Mentul, Cepu, Jawa Tengah; YF 1985; EN 532; FT 22; PT 72; Dip.

Akademi Teknologi Sapta Taruna, Jl. Pemuda Kav. 52 Rawamangun, Jaktim, DKI Jakarta; YF 1984; EN 478; FT 10; PT 68; Dip.

Akademi Teknologi Semarak, Jl. Jend. Sudirman No. 5, Bengkulu; YF 1983; EN 184; FT 9; PT 31; Dip.

Akademi Teknologi Semarang, Jl. Cinde Raya No. 27, Semarang, Jawa Tengah; YF 1979; EN 396; FT 12; PT 88; Dip.

Institut Hindu Dharma, Jl. Sangalangit, Tembau, Denpasar, Bali; YF 1963; EN 1,674; FT 45; PT 9; S1.

Institut Ilmu Sosial dan Ilmu Politik, Jl. Raya Lenteng Agung No. 32, Jaksel, DKI; YF 1953; EN 3,253; FT 153; PT 57; S1: Journalism, Public Relations, Communications.

Institut Keguruan dan Ilmu Pendidikan Al-Wasliyah, Jl. Sisingamangaraja Km. 5, Medan, Sumatera Utara; YF 1963; EN 1,176; FT 58; PT 55; Dip; S1.

Institut Keguruan dan Ilmu Pendidikan Budi Utomo, Jl. Arjuna No. 19-A, Malang, Jawa Timur; YF 1984; EN 3,434; FT 256; PT 50; S1.

Institut Keguruan dan Ilmu Pendidikan Gunung Sitoli, Jl. Yos Sudarso 118, Gunung Sitoli, Sumatera Utara; YF 1965; EN 2,154; FT 43; PT 124; Dip.; S1.

Institut Keguruan dan Ilmu Pendidikan Mataram, Jl. Pemuda, Mataram, Nusa Tenggara Barat; YF 1968; EN 3,740; FT 38; PT 141; Dip.; S1.

Institut Keguruan dan Ilmu Pendidikan Muhammadiyah, Jl. Limau II Keb. Baru, Jaksel, DKI Jakarta; YF 1957; EN 6,848; FT 56; PT 3; Dip.: History of Education, Business Administration Education, Philosophy and Sociology of Education; English Language; Education; Indonesian Language; Indonesian Literature Education; S1: Philosophy and Sociology of Education.

Institut Keguruan dan Ilmu Pendidikan Muhammadiyah Purwokerto, Kampus Institut Keguruan dan Ilmu Pendidikan Dukuhlawuh, Purwokerto, Jawa Tengah; YF 1965; EN 2,037; FT 41; PT 60; S1.

Institut Keguruan dan Ilmu Pendidikan Muhammadiyah Purworejo, Jl. KHA. Dachlan No. 3, Purworejo, Jawa Tengah; YF 1964; EN 1,353; FT 32; PT 70; S1.

Institut Keguruan dan Ilmu Pendidikan Muhammadiyah Yogyakarta, Jl. Kapas No. 9 Semaki, Yogyakarta, DI Yogyakarta; YF 1962; EN 2,817; FT 40; PT 65; Dip.; S1.

Institut Keguruan dan Ilmu Pendidikan PGRI Bali, Jl. Patih Jelantik 5-A, Denpasar, Bali; YF 1965; EN 2,189; FT 81; PT 295; S1.

Institut Keguruan dan Ilmu Pendidikan PGRI Banyuwangi, Jl. A. Yani 82B, Banyuwangi, Jawa Timur; YF 1978; EN 1,963; FT 35; PT 87; S1.

Institut Keguruan dan Ilmu Pendidikan PGRI Bojonegoro, Jl. Jagung Suprapto 73, Bojonegoro, Jawa Timur; YF 1976; EN 1,810; FT 44; PT 56; Dip.; S1.

Institut Keguruan dan Ilmu Pendidikan PGRI Jember, Jl. Jawa No. 10, Jember, Jawa Timur; YF 1979; EN 2,047; FT 35; PT 90; Dip.; S1.

Institut Keguruan dan Ilmu Pendidikan PGRI Kalimantan Timur, Jl. Pahlawan, Samarinda, Kalimantan Timur; YF 1979; EN 390; FT 5; PT 72; Dip.; S1.

Institut Keguruan dan Ilmu Pendidikan PGRI Kediri, Jl. K.H.A. Dachlan 76, Kediri, Jawa Timur; YF 1977; EN 3,197; FT 209; PT 252; Dip.; S1.

Institut Keguruan dan Ilmu Pendidikan PGRI Madiun, Jl. Setiabudi No. 85, Madiun, Jawa Timur; YF 1975; EN 2,924; FT 67; PT 205; Dip.; S1.

Institut Keguruan dan Ilmu Pendidikan PGRI Malang, Jl. Sudanco Supriadi 48, Malang, Jawa Timur; YF 1975; EN 5,364; FT 298; PT 6; Dip.; S1.

Institut Keguruan dan Ilmu Pendidikan PGRI Semarang, Jl. Lontar No. 1, Semarang, Jawa Tengah; YF 1981; EN 2,025; FT 53; PT 50; S1.

Institut Keguruan dan Ilmu Pendidikan PGRI Surabaya, Jl. Ngagel Dadi III-B/37, Surabaya, Jawa Timur; YF 1971; EN 7,441; FT 167; PT 311; Dip.; S1.

Institut Keguruan dan Ilmu Pendidikan PGRI Tuban, Jl. Manunggal No. 61, Tuban, Jawa Timur; YF 1978; EN 1,232; FT 42; PT 74; Dip.; S1.

Institut Keguruan dan Ilmu Pendidikan PGRI Wates, Jl. Kembang No. 65 Margosari, Wates, DI Yogyakarta; YF 1968; EN 1,008; FT 36; PT 23; S1.

Institut Keguruan dan Ilmu Pendidikan PGRI Yogyakarta, Jl. PGRI No. 1 Sonosewu Km. 3, DI Yogyakarta; YF 1961; EN 2,817; FT 40; PT 65; Dip.; S1.

Institut Keguruan dan Ilmu Pendidikan Sanata Dharma, Jl. Mrican P.O. Box 29, DI Yogyakarta; YF 1955; EN 3,546; FT 124; PT 111; Dip.: English Language Education, Mathematics Education, Physics Education; S1: Curriculum and Education Technology, Theology, History Education, Cooperative Education, Accounting Education; Indonesian Language and Literature Education, English Language Education, Mathematics Education, Physics Education.

Institut Keguruan dan Ilmu Pendidikan Saraswati Tabanan, Jl. Pahlawan No. 2, Tabanan, Bali; YF 1965; EN 877; FT 54; PT 43; Dip.; S1.

Institut Keguruan dan Ilmu Pendidikan Veteran Semarang, Jl. Pawiyatan Luhur IV Bendan Duwur, Semarang, Jawa Tengah; YF 1967; EN 1,900; FT 74; PT 85; Dip.; S1.

Institut Keguruan dan Ilmu Pendidikan Veteran Sukoharjo, Kampus Jombor, Sukoharjo, Jawa Tengah; YF 1968; EN 2,744; FT 79; PT 101; Dip.; S1.

Institut Keguruan dan Ilmu Pendidikan Veteran Yogyakarta, Jl. Glondongan TB XV, Babarsari, DI Yogyakarta; YF 1967; EN 825; FT 32; PT 33; S1.

Institut Keguruan dan Ilmu Pendidikan Widya Darma Surabaya, Jl. Ketintang No. 147, Surabaya, Jawa Timur; YF 1981; EN 1,301; FT 37; PT 58; Dip.; S1.

Institut Keguruan dan Ilmu Pendidikan Yayasan Pendidikan Klaten, Jl. Cungkrungan, Karanganom, Klaten, Jawa Tengah; YF 1965; EN 2,133; FT 43; PT 55; S1.

Institut Kesenian Jakarta, Jl. Cikini Raya 73, Jakpus, DKI Jakarta; YF 1970; EN 497; FT 49; PT 23; Dip.; S1.

Institut Manajemen Koperasi Indonesia, Jl. Raya Bdg-Sdg Km. 20.5, Jatinangor, Sumedang, Jawa Barat; YF 1982; EN 5,164; FT 41; PT 92; S1.

Institut Pertanian (Intan) Yogyakarta, Jl. Magelang Km. 5.6, P.O. Box 59, Yogyakarta, DI Yogyakarta; YF 1983; EN 416; FT 14; PT 42; S1.

Institut Pertanian Malang, Desa Mojolangu, Lowokwaru, Malang, Jawa Timur; YF 1985; EN 412; FT 25; PT 72; S1.

Institut Pertanian Sitiper, Jl. Betung No. 2 Papringan, DI Yogyakarta; YF 1958; EN 416; FT 14; PT 42; S1: Socioeconomics of Agriculture; Agriculture.

Institut Sains dan Teknologi "AKPRIND", Jl. Kalisalak 28 Komp. Balapan, DI Yogyakarta,; YF 1986; EN 1,648; FT 69; PT 158; Dip.; S1.

Institut Sains dan Teknologi Al-Kamal, Jl. Kedoya, Keb. Jeruk, Jakbar DKI Jakarta; YF 1987; EN 74; FT 4; PT 21; S1.

Institut Sains dan Teknologi Nasional Jakarta, Jl. Moh. Kahfi II Srengseng, Jaksel, DKI Jakarta; YF 1950; EN 6,307; FT 151; PT 605; Dip.: Civil Engineering; Mechanical Engineering; Electrical Engineering; S1: Civil Engineering; Mechanical Engineering; Electrical Engineering.

Institut Sains dan Teknologi Palapa, Jl. Kecubung No. 2 Tlogo Mas, Malang, Jawa Timur; YF 1985; EN 859; FT 36; PT 62; Dip.; S1.

Institut Sains dan Teknologi Pembangunan Indonesia, Jl. Jend. Sudirman No. 42, Ujung Pandang, Sulawesi Selatan; YF 1987; EN 91; FT 15; PT 24; S1.

Institut Sains dan Teknologi Pembangunan Nusantara, Jl. Gajahmada, Gunung Pangilun, Padang, Sumatera Barat; YF 1987; EN 196; FT 25; PT 81; Dip.; S1.

Institut Sains dan Teknologi TD Pardede Medan, Jl. Binjai Km. 10, Medan, Sumatera Utara; YF 1987; EN 1,350; FT 25; PT 42; Dip.: Textile Technology; Textile Industrial Management.; S1: Textile Technology.

Institut Teknologi Adhitama, Jl. A. Rahman Hakim, Surabaya, Jawa Timur; YF 1963; EN 3,325; FT 104; PT 145; Dip.; S1.

Institut Teknologi Adityawarman, Jl. Rancabentang No. 11, Bandung, Jawa Barat; YF 1985; EN 176; FT 6; PT 33; Dip.; S1.

Institut Teknologi Budi Utomo, Jl. Raya Mawar Merah 23, Jaktim; DKI Jakarta; YF 1984; EN 1,102; FT 85; PT 105; Dip.; S1.

Institut Teknologi Indonesia, Jl. Puspitek ITI, Serpong, Tangerang, Jawa Barat; YF 1984; EN 3,618; FT 68; PT 172; S1.

Institut Teknologi Medan, Jl. Gedung Arca 52, Medan, Sumatera Utara; YF 1960; EN 2,154; FT 43; PT 124; S1.

Institut Teknologi Minaesa, Jl. Pinabetengan No. 2, Tompaso, Minahasa, Sulawesi Utara; YF 1987; EN 366; FT 29; PT 35; S1.

Institut Teknologi Nasional Bandung, Jl. Penghulu H. Mustafa 17, Bandung, Jawa Barat; YF 1972; EN 3,725; FT 30; PT 163; Dip.; S1.

Institut Teknologi Nasional Malang, Jl. Bend. Sigura-gura 2, Malang, Jawa Timur; YF 1969; EN 7,099; FT 181; PT 127; Dip.: Mechanical Engineering; S1: Civil Engineering; Mechanical Engineering; Dip.; S1.

Institut Teknologi Pembangunan, Jl. Balongsari Praja V/1, Surabaya, Jawa Timur; YF 1981; EN 2,239; FT 49; PT 170; S1.

Politeknik Semarang, Jl. Singasari VI/8, Semarang, Jawa Tengah; Dip.

Sekolah Tinggi Agama Hindu Amlapura, Jl. Ngurah Rai 132, Amlapura, Bali; YF 1984; EN 63; FT 7; PT 17; Dip.; S1.

Sekolah Tinggi Agama Hindu Singaraja, Jl. Pulau Timor 24, PO Box 15, Singaraja, Bali; YF 1970; EN 974; FT 18; PT 11; Dip.; S1.

Sekolah Tinggi Bahasa Asing Harapan, Jl. Imam Bonjol No. 35, Medan, Sumatera Utara; YF 1970; EN 1,335; FT 12; PT 23; Dip.: English Language.

Sekolah Tinggi Bahasa Asing Prayoga, Jl. Chairil Anwar No. 14, Padang, Sumatera Barat; YF 1976; EN 5,908; FT 10; PT 23; Dip.: English Language.

Sekolah Tinggi Bahasa Asing Putera Kusuma, Jl. Raya Narogong Km. 3.6, Bekasi, Jawa Barat; YF 1985; EN 31; FT 4; PT 6; S1.

Sekolah Tinggi Bahasa Asing Swadaya, Jl. Jose Rizal No. 3-4, Medan, Sumatera Utara; YF 1967; EN 2,475; FT 23; PT 38; Dip.: English Language.

Sekolah Tinggi Bahasa Asing Widya Mandala, Jl. Manggis No.15-17, Madiun, Jawa Timur; YF 1985; EN 46; FT 5; PT 4; Dip.

Sekolah Tinggi Bahasa Asing Yapari, Jl. Purnawarman No. 24, Bandung, Jawa Barat; YF 1963; EN 1,935; FT 27; PT 36; Dip.; S1.

Sekolah Tinggi Bahasa dan Sastra Malang, Jl. Semeru No. 80, Malang, Jawa Timur; YF 1971; EN 911; FT 8; PT 31; Dip.

Sekolah Tinggi Farming Semarang, Jl. Pawiyatan Luhur IV/15, Semarang, Jawa Tengah; YF 1960; EN 1,188; FT 31; PT 22; Dip.: Agriculture; Animal Science; Estate Crops; Fisheries; Horticulture; Forestry; S1.

Sekolah Tinggi Filsafat Driyakara, Jl. Percetakan Negara, Jakpus, DKI Jakarta; YF 1969; EN 199; FT 16; PT 19; S1: Sociocultural Philosophy; Philosophy and Theology.

Sekolah Tinggi Filsafat Jakarta, Jl. Proklamasi 27, Jakpus, DKI Jakarta; YF 1934; EN 176; FT 14; PT 16; S1.

Sekolah Tinggi Filsafat Kateketik Pranadnya Widya, Jl. Abubakar Ali No. 1, DI Yogyakarta; YF 1962; EN 394; FT 21; PT 23; S1.

Sekolah Tinggi Filsafat Katolik Ledalero, Jl. Katedral No. 5 Flores, Ende, Nusa Tenggara Timur; YF 1971; EN 764; FT 36; PT 10; S1: Catholic Philosophy.

Sekolah Tinggi Filsafat Seminari Pineleng, Jl. Raya Tomohon, Pineleng, Sulawesi Utara; YF 1935; EN 322; FT 15; PT 10; S1.

Sekolah Tinggi Filsafat Theologi Fajar Timur, Jl. Takonde No. 9-12, Abepura, Irian Jaya; YF 1967; EN 116; FT 15; PT 3; S1.

Sekolah Tinggi Filsafat Theologi Gereja Kristen Injili, Jl. Argapura No. 21, Jayapura, Irian Jaya; YF 1971; EN 314; FT 12; PT 15; Dip.; S1.

Sekolah Tinggi Filsafat Theologi Indonesia Timur, Jl. Baji Dakka No. 7, Ujung Pandang, Sulawesi Selatan; YF 1948; Enroll 274; FT 12; PT 13; S1.

Sekolah Tinggi Filsafat Theologi Jaffray, Jl. Gunung Merapi 103, Ujung Pandang, Sulawesi Selatan; YF 1932; EN 131; FT 21; PT 9; S1.

Sekolah Tinggi Filsafat Theologi Widya Sasana, Jl. Terusan Rajabasa No. 2, Malang, Jawa Timur; YF 1971; EN 264; FT 13; PT 11; Dip.

Sekolah Tinggi Administrasi Adabiah, Jl. Perintis Kemerdekaan, Padang, Sumatera Barat; YF 1984; EN 392; FT 20; PT 14; S1.

Sekolah Tinggi Ilmu Administrasi Al-Amin Sorong, Jl. Merpati 17, Remu, Sorong, Irian Jaya; YF 1982; EN 375; FT 5; PT 23; S1.

Sekolah Tinggi Ilmu Administrasi Al-Gazali Barru, Jl. Achmad Yani 8, Barru, Sulawesi Selatan; YF 1968; EN 440; FT 6; PT 29; S1.

Sekolah Tinggi Ilmu Administrasi Al-Gazali Soppeng, Jl. Samudra No. 16, Watansoppeng, Sulawesi Selatan; YF 1968; EN 135; FT 6; PT 61; S1.

Sekolah Tinggi Ilmu Administrasi Al-Wasliyah, Jl. Sisingamangaraja Km. 5.5, Medan, Sumatera Utara.

Sekolah Tinggi Ilmu Administrasi Angkasa Bandung, Jl. Lanud. Sulaiman, Margahayu, Bandung, Jawa Barat; YF 1967; EN 288; FT 20; PT 48; S1.

Sekolah Tinggi Ilmu Administrasi Bagasasi, Jl. Kimangunsarkoro No. 40, Bekasi, Jawa Barat; YF 1983; EN 195; FT 8; PT 24; S1.

Sekolah Tinggi Ilmu Administrasi Bayu Angga, Jl. TGP, Probolinggo, Jawa Timur; YF 1981; EN 362; FT 19; PT 26; Dip.

Sekolah Tinggi Ilmu Administrasi Bengkulu, Jl. Cimanuk Km. 6.5, Padang Harapan, Bengkulu; YF 1987; EN 251; FT 28; PT 25; Dip.; S1.

Sekolah Tinggi Ilmu Administrasi Bina Banua, Jl. Hikmah Banua Km. 6, Banjarmasin, Kalimantan Selatan; YF 1982; EN 811; FT 40; PT 17; S1.

Sekolah Tinggi Ilmu Administrasi Denpasar, Jl. Tukad Balian 15, Renon, Denpasar, Bali; YF 1983; EN 231; FT 25; PT 29; S1.

Sekolah Tinggi Ilmu Administrasi Iskandar Thani, Jl. Iskandar Muda, Banda Aceh, DI Aceh; YF 1987; EN 640; FT 7; PT 67; S1.

Sekolah Tinggi Ilmu Administrasi Karya Dharma Merauke, Jl. Kinaan, Merauke, Irian Jaya; YF 1984; EN 180; FT 4; PT 44; S1.

Sekolah Tinggi Ilmu Administrasi Kawula Indonesia, Jl. Cipinang Muara I/11, Jakarta Timur, DKI Jakarta; YF 1983; S1.

Sekolah Tinggi Ilmu Administrasi Kutawaringin Subang, Jl. S. Parman No. 1, Subang, Jawa Barat; YF 1982; EN 325; FT 4; PT 47; S1.

Sekolah Tinggi Ilmu Administrasi LLPN Padang, Jl. Jhoni Anwar No. 17-A, Padang, Sumatera Barat; YF 1984; EN 89; FT 8; PT 8; Dip.; S1.

Sekolah Tinggi Ilmu Administrasi Malang, Jl. Raya Tlogomas 35 P.O. Box 94, Malang, Jawa Timur; YF 1981; EN 497; FT 12; PT 105; S1.

Sekolah Tinggi Ilmu Administrasi Mandala Ilomata, Jl. Salemba Tengah 46, Jakarta Pusat, DKI Jakarta; YF 1983; EN 510; FT 10; PT 56; S1.

Sekolah Tinggi Ilmu Administrasi Masyarakat Indonesia, Jl. Teladan No. 15, Medan, Sumatera Utara; YF 1979; EN 1,107; FT 11; PT 21; Dip.; S1.

Sekolah Tinggi Ilmu Administrasi Mataram, Jl. Bung Karno Pesongsoran, Mataram, Nusa Tenggara Barat; YF 1986; EN 610; FT 23; PT 27; S1.

Sekolah Tinggi Ilmu Administrasi Maulana Yusuf Banten, Jl. Trip K. Jamaksari No. 44, Serang, Jawa Barat; YF 1962; EN 729; FT 26; PT 31; S1.

Sekolah Tinggi Ilmu Administrasi Muhammadiyah Samarinda, Jl. P. Hidayatullah No. 46, Samarinda, Kalimantan Timur; YF-; EN-; FT-; PT-; Dip.

Sekolah Tinggi Ilmu Administrasi Muhammadiyah Selong, Jl. Pahlawan 67, Selong, Nusa Tenggara Barat; YF 1983; EN 196; FT 9; PT 30; S1.

Sekolah Tinggi Ilmu Administrasi Panca Marga, Jl. Hasanuddin No. 64, Palu, Sulteng; YF 1985; EN 658; FT-; PT-; S1.

Sekolah Tinggi Ilmu Administrasi Pembangunan, Jl. Lumba-lumba No. 9, Jember, Jawa Timur; YF 1981; EN 90; FT 11; PT 25; S1.

Sekolah Tinggi Ilmu Administrasi Puangrimaggalatung, Jl. Puangrimaggalatung, Sengkang, Sulawesi Selatan; YF 1982; EN 385; FT 35; PT-; Dip.; S1.

Sekolah Tinggi Ilmu Administrasi Tasikmalaya, Jl. Nagrak Karala P.O. Box 67, Tasikmalaya, Jawa Barat; YF 1974; EN 545; FT 12; PT 33; S1.

Sekolah Tinggi Ilmu Administrasi Trinitas Ambon, Jl. Pattimura 1, Ambon, Maluku; YF 1982; EN 1,840; FT 24; PT 41; S1.

Sekolah Tinggi Ilmu Administrasi Yapis Biak, Jl. Condronegoro, Samofa, Biak, Irian Jaya; YF 1981; EN 300; FT 8; PT 29; S1.

Sekolah Tinggi Ilmu Administrasi Yappan, Jl. Lenteng Agung, Pasar Minggu, Jakarta Selatan, DKI Jakarta; YF 1973; EN 2,500; FT 64; PT 41; S1.

Sekolah Tinggi Ilmu Administrasi Yappi, Jl. Andi Mappanyuki 11, Ujung Pandang, Sulawesi Selatan; YF 1973; EN 769; FT 13; PT 41; S1.

Sekolah Tinggi Ilmu Administrasi YPI-AMI, Jl. Ancol Selatan, Jakarta Utara, DKI Jakarta; YF 1982; EN 180; FT 11; PT 29; S1.

Sekolah Tinggi Ilmu Administrasi YPPM Majalengka, Jl. Raya Barat Km. 2, Majalengka, Jawa Barat; YF 1984; EN 156; FT 8; PT 34; S1.

Sekolah Tinggi Ilmu Bahasa dan Sastra Satya Widya, Jl. Bendul Merisi IX/4-B, Surabaya, Jawa Timur; YF 1968; EN 595; FT 9; PT 28; S1.

Sekolah Tinggi Ilmu Ekonomi Agus Salim, Jl. Merapi No. 15, Padang, Sumatera Barat; YF 1987; EN 133; FT 8; PT 12; S1.

Sekolah Tinggi Ilmu Ekonomi Amsir, Jl. Bau Messepe 52A, Pare-Pare, Sulawesi Selatan; YF 1985; EN 185; FT 42; PT 27; S1.

Sekolah Tinggi Ilmu Ekonomi Artha Budi Iswara, Jl. Pumpungan III/29, Surabaya, Jawa Timur; YF 1969; EN 431; FT 29; PT 34; Dip.; S1.

Sekolah Tinggi Ilmu Ekonomi Baitul Rachman, Jl. Damar I No. 16, Padang, Sumatera Barat; YF 1985; EN 208; FT 6; PT 26; Dip.; S1.

Sekolah Tinggi Ilmu Ekonomi Bajiminasa, Jl. Bajiminasa, Ujung Pandang, Sulawesi Selatan; YF 1989; EN 243; FT 18; PT 66; S1.

Sekolah Tinggi Ilmu Ekonomi Balikpapan, Jl. Gunung Pasir No. 261, Balikpapan, Kalimantan Timur; YF 1983; EN 189; FT 5; PT 36; S1.

Sekolah Tinggi Ilmu Ekonomi Bandung, Jl. Penghulu H. Mustafa Gg. Pelita II, Bandung, Jawa Barat; YF 1973; EN 1,881; FT 17; PT 70; S1.

Sekolah Tinggi Ilmu Ekonomi Benteng Huraba, Jl. Ujung Gurap, Padang Sidempuan, Sumatera Utara; YF 1986; EN 87; FT 6; PT 18; S1.

Sekolah Tinggi Ilmu Ekonomi Bhakti Api '50, Jl. Sabar, Keb. Lama, Jakarta Selatan, DKI Jakarta; YF 1979; EN 316; FT 8; PT 44; Dip.: Business Management; S1.

Sekolah Tinggi Ilmu Ekonomi Dua Lima Pohalaa, Jl. Jend. Sudirman 16, Gorontalo, Sulawesi Utara; YF 1983; EN 448; FT 12; PT 59; S1.

Sekolah Tinggi Ilmu Ekonomi Duta Nusantara, Jl. Karya Ujung Medan, Sumatera Utara; YF 1990; EN 100; FT 12; PT 13; Dip.

Sekolah Tinggi Ilmu Ekonomi Dwi Putra, Jl. Serua Raya, Ciputat, Jakarta Selatan, DKI Jakarta; YF 1986; EN 80; FT 10; PT 7; Dip.

Sekolah Tinggi Ilmu Ekonomi GAMA, Jl. Gejayan Mrican No. 5, DI Yogyakarta; YF 1983; EN 136; FT 15; PT 28; S1.

Sekolah Tinggi Ilmu Ekonomi Gunadarma, Jl. Salemba Raya No. 53, Jakarta Pusat, DKI Jakarta; YF 1990; EN 589; FT 42; PT 16; Dip.; S1.

Sekolah Tinggi Ilmu Ekonomi Gunung Sewu, Jl. Hayam Wuruk 108, Jakarta Barat, DKI Jakarta; YF 1986; EN 260; FT 9; PT 20; S1.

Sekolah Tinggi Ilmu Ekonomi Harapan, Jl. Imam Bonjol No. 35, Medan, Sumatera Utara; YF 1974; EN 1,565; FT 19; PT 40; Dip.: Office Management; S1.

Sekolah Tinggi Ilmu Ekonomi Harapan Kasih, Jl. Di Panjaitan 61, Manado, Sulawesi Utara; YF 1984; EN 383; FT 5; PT 69; S1.

Sekolah Tinggi Ilmu Ekonomi IBEK, Jl. Mandala Utara 33-A, Jakarta Barat, DKI Jakarta; YF 1987; EN 315; FT 30; PT 56; Dip.; S1.

Sekolah Tinggi Ilmu Ekonomi Indonesia, Jl. Kayu Jati Raya No. 11A, Jakarta Timur, DKI Jakarta; YF 1969; EN 2,583; FT 131; PT 48; Dip.: Accounting; S1: Accounting; Management.

Sekolah Tinggi Ilmu Ekonomi "Indonesia," Jl. Menur Pumpungan 30, Surabaya, Jawa Timur; YF 1971; EN 2,917; FT 79; PT 48; Dip.; S1.

Sekolah Tinggi Ilmu Ekonomi Indonesia, Jl. Mega Mendung No. 9, Malang, Jawa Timur; YF 1983; EN 549; FT 25; PT 35; Dip.; S1.

Sekolah Tinggi Ilmu Ekonomi Indonesia, Jl. Seulawah, Lampuneurut, Banda Aceh, DI Aceh; YF 1975; EN 2,555; FT 18; PT 72; S1.

Sekolah Tinggi Ilmu Ekonomi Indonesia, Jl. Timor 82, Ujung Pandang, Sulawesi Selatan; YF 1974; EN 527; FT 11; PT 38; S1.

Sekolah Tinggi Ilmu Ekonomi Indonesia Banjarmasin, Jl. Hasan Basri No. 11, Banjarmasin, Kalimantan Selatan; YF 1974; EN 164; FT 17; PT 37; Dip.; S1.

Sekolah Tinggi Ilmu Ekonomi Indonesia Jaya Negara, Jl. Jagung Suprapto 87, Malang, Jawa Timur; YF 1973; EN 1,279; FT 12; PT 32; S1: Financial Management.

Sekolah Tinggi Ilmu Ekonomi Indonesia Membangun, Jl. Soekarno-Hatta 25/206 A, Bandung, Jawa Barat; YF 1985; EN 1,448; FT 65; Dip.; S1.

Sekolah Tinggi Ilmu Ekonomi Jagakarsa, Jl. Raya Tanjung Barat 152, Jakarta Selatan, DKI Jakarta; YF 1989; EN 441; FT 1; PT 45; S1.

Sekolah Tinggi Ilmu Ekonomi Jakarta Raya, Jl. Matraman Raya 119, Jakarta Timur, DKI Jakarta; YF 1985; EN 167; FT 8; PT 22; S1.

Sekolah Tinggi Ilmu Ekonomi Jember, Jl. Pahlawan No. 64, Jember, Jawa Timur; YF 1980; EN 365; FT 8; PT 32; S1.

Sekolah Tinggi Ilmu Ekonomi Kerjasama, Jl. Purwangan No. 39, Yogyakarta, DI Yogyakarta; YF 1988; EN 283; FT 23; PT 33; Dip.: Business Management, Finance and Banking; S1.

Sekolah Tinggi Ilmu Ekonomi Keuangan dan Perbankan Indonesia, Jl. TMP, Kalibata, Jakarta Selatan, DKI Jakarta; YF 1982; EN 687; FT 42; PT 51; S1.

Sekolah Tinggi Ilmu Ekonomi Keuangan dan Perbankan Padang, Jl. Chatib Sulaiman, Padang, Sumatera Barat; YF 1985; EN 427; FT 11; PT 43; S1.

Sekolah Tinggi Ilmu Ekonomi Kosgoro, Jl. Chairil Anwar II/13-A, Jember, Jawa Timur; YF 1983; EN 85; FT 8; PT 11; S1.

Sekolah Tinggi Ilmu Ekonomi Kusuma Negara, Jl. Pendidikan Cijantung, Jakarta Timur, DKI Jakarta; YF 1976; EN 77; FT 9; PT 22; S1.

Sekolah Tinggi Ilmu Ekonomi Kusumanegara, Jl. Mastrip No. 51, Blitar, Jawa Timur; YF 1985; EN 280; FT 5; PT 18; Dip.; S1.

Sekolah Tinggi Ilmu Ekonomi Lampung, Jl. Teuku Umar No. 67 Kedaton, Bandar Lampung, Lampung; YF 1987; EN 237; FT 11; PT 24; S1.

Sekolah Tinggi Ilmu Ekonomi Mahardika, Jl. Barata Jaya XXII/1, Surabaya, Jawa Timur; YF 1981; EN 255; FT 45; PT 49; S1.

Sekolah Tinggi Ilmu Ekonomi Malangkucecwara, Jl. Terusan Kalasan, Blimbing, Malang, Jawa Timur; YF 1971; EN 3,275; FT 58; PT 62; S1: Financial Management, Accounting.

Sekolah Tinggi Ilmu Ekonomi Mandala, Jl. Sumatera 118-120, Jember, Jawa Timur; YF 1978; EN 1194; FT 16; PT 27; Dip.; S1.

Sekolah Tinggi Ilmu Ekonomi "45" Mataram, Jl. Bung Karno Pasongsoran, Mataram, Nusa Tenggara Barat; YF 1984; EN 610; FT 13; PT 27; Dip.; S1.

Sekolah Tinggi Ilmu Ekonomi Muhammadiyah, Jl. KHA. Dachlan 7, Banda Aceh, DI Aceh; YF 1989; EN 208; FT 7; PT 22; S1.

Sekolah Tinggi Ilmu Ekonomi Muhammadiyah Metro, Jl. Kampus Lembayung No. 15-A, Metro, Lampung; YF 1987; EN 237; FT 12; PT 15; S1.

Sekolah Tinggi Ilmu Ekonomi Muhammadiyah Palopo, Jl. Rambutan, Palopo, Sulawesi Selatan; YF 1986; EN 412; FT 12; PT 26; S1.

Sekolah Tinggi Ilmu Ekonomi Nasional Banjarmasin, Jl. Kuin Selatan No. 1, Banjarmasin Kalimantan Selatan; YF 1984; EN 286; FT 8; PT 24; S1.

Sekolah Tinggi Ilmu Ekonomi Nusa Bangsa, Jl. Abdullah Lubis 4B, Medan, Sumatera Utara; YF 1978; EN 319; FT 12; PT 45; S1.

Sekolah Tinggi Ilmu Ekonomi Ottow Van Geisler, Jl. Kotaraja Dalam, Jayapura, Irian Jaya; YF 1981; EN 736; FT 17; PT 6; S1.

Sekolah Tinggi Ilmu Ekonomi Palangkaraya, Jl. Yos Sudarso No.1, Palangkaraya, Kalimantan Tengah; YF 1978; EN 885; FT 87; PT 110; S1.

Sekolah Tinggi Ilmu Ekonomi Panca Bhakti, Jl. Dr. Suharso 36-A, Palu, Sulteng; YF 1971; Dip.; S1.

Sekolah Tinggi Ilmu Ekonomi Pasaman, Jl. Moh. Yamin No. 1, Pasaman, Sumatera Barat; YF 1984; EN 164; FT 15; PT 11; S1.

Sekolah Tinggi Ilmu Ekonomi Pasundan, Jl. Turangga No. 37-39, Bandung, Jawa Barat; YF 1971; EN 567; FT 12; PT 26; Dip.; S1.

Sekolah Tinggi Ilmu Ekonomi Pelita Bangsa, Jl. Kebun Lada No. 24, Binjai, Sumatera Utara; YF 1985; EN 64; FT 4; PT 9; S1.

Sekolah Tinggi Ilmu Ekonomi Pembangunan Indonesia, Jl. Jend. Sudirman 42, Ujung Pandang, Sulawesi Selatan; FT 1987; EN 500; FT 10; PT 43; S1.

Sekolah Tinggi Ilmu Ekonomi Perbanas, Jl. Perbanas, Karet-Kuningan, Setiabudi, Jakarta Selatan, DKI Jakarta; YF 1969; EN 6,298; FT 93; PT 379; Dip.: Bank Management; Accounting; S1: Accounting, Financial Management and Banking.

Sekolah Tinggi Ilmu Ekonomi Perbanas Medan, Jl. Gaperta Ujung No. 56, Medan, Sumatera Utara; YF 1989; EN 394; FT 7; PT 42; S1.

Sekolah Tinggi Ilmu Ekonomi Perbanas Surabaya, Jl. Nginden Semolo 36, Surabaya, Jawa Timur; YF 1970; EN 937; FT 28; PT 51; S1.

Sekolah Tinggi Ilmu Ekonomi Perdagangan Padang, Jl. Bandar Purus No. 71, Padang, Sumatera Barat; YF 1987; EN 71; FT 10; PT 19; S1.

Sekolah Tinggi Ilmu Ekonomi Pertiba, Jl. Kacang Pedang No. 9, Pangkal Pinang, Sumatera Selatan; YF 1982; EN 226; FT 9; PT 24; S1.

Sekolah Tinggi Ilmu Ekonomi Pontianak, Jl. Perintis Kemerdekaan, Pontianak, Kalimantan Barat; YF 1983; EN 499; FT 3; PT 20; S1.

Sekolah Tinggi Ilmu Ekonomi Sabang, Jl. Mawar, Sabang, Banda Aceh, DI Aceh; YF 1986; EN 1,099; FT 27; PT 74; S1.

Sekolah Tinggi Ilmu Ekonomi Sampit, Jl. Padat Karya Baamang, Sampit, Kalimantan Tengah; YF 1986; EN 130; FT 8; PT 24; S1.

Sekolah Tinggi Ilmu Ekonomi Sari Bakti, Jl. Kebon Kacang Raya 142, Jakarta Pusat, DKI Jakarta; YF 1986; EN 95; FT 9; PT 69; S1.

Sekolah Tinggi Ilmu Ekonomi Satya Widya, Jl. Menur No. 2-A, Surabaya, Jawa Timur; YF 1968; EN 193; FT 9; PT 32; S1.

Sekolah Tinggi Ilmu Ekonomi Sumatera Barat, Jl. Dr. M. Jamil No. 29, Padang Pariaman, Sumatera Barat; YF 1984; EN 194; FT 8; PT 42; S1.

Sekolah Tinggi Ilmu Ekonomi Swadaya, Jl. Jose Rizal 3-A, Medan, Sumatera Utara; YF 1985; EN 242; FT 8; PT 24; S1.

Sekolah Tinggi Ilmu Ekonomi Tjut Nyak Dhien, Jl. Jambi No. 23-D, Medan, Sumatera Utara; YF 1968; EN 200; FT 16; PT 10; S1.

Sekolah Tinggi Ilmu Ekonomi Tri Dharma, Jl. Cikutra Baru Raya No. 28, Bandung, Jawa Barat; YF 1974; EN 842; FT 23; PT 40; S1.

Sekolah Tinggi Ilmu Ekonomi Tri Dharma Widya, Jl. Cikini Raya 64, Jakarta Pusat, DKI Jakarta; YF 1984; EN 265; FT 19; PT 17; Dip.; S1.

Sekolah Tinggi Ilmu Ekonomi "Unisda," Jl. Raya Sukodadi 4, Lamongan, Jawa Timur; YF 1978; EN 320; FT 4; PT 23; S1.

Sekolah Tinggi Ilmu Ekonomi Urip Sumohardjo, Jl. Urip Sumohardjo 5-7, Surabaya, Jawa Timur; YF 1961; EN 424; FT 13; PT 9; Dip.

Sekolah Tinggi Ilmu Ekonomi Widya Artha, Jl. Barata Jaya XIX/16, Surabaya, Jawa Timur; YF 1981; EN 180; FT 6; PT 21; S1.

Sekolah Tinggi Ilmu Ekonomi Widya Gama, Jl. Pelita II/4, Lumajang, Jawa Timur; YF 1985; EN 183; FT 21; PT 42; S1.

Sekolah Tinggi Ilmu Ekonomi Widya Wiwaha, Jl. Lawanu, Sorosutan UH-17/XX, DI Yogyakarta; YF 1982; EN 628; FT 20; PT 34; S1.

Sekolah Tinggi Ilmu Ekonomi Wilwatikta, Jl. Bali, Surabaya, Jawa Timur; YF 1980; EN 280; FT 4; PT 21; S1.

Sekolah Tinggi Ilmu Ekonomi "YAI," Jl. Salemba Raya No. 10, Jakarta Pusat, DKI Jakarta; YF 1985; EN 2,466; FT 138; PT 39; S1: Accounting.

Sekolah Tinggi Ilmu Ekonomi Yapis Jayapura, Jl. Sam Ratulangi No. 11, Jayapura, Irian Jaya; YF 1974; EN 1,096; FT 7; PT 25; S1.

Sekolah Tinggi Ilmu Ekonomi Yayasan Pendidikan Bongaya Makasar, Jl. Bongaya 28, Ujung Pandang, Sulawesi Selatan; YF 1968; EN 1,862; FT 13; PT 30; Dip.; S1.

Sekolah Tinggi Ilmu Ekonomi Yayasan Sulawesi Utara, Jl. Arie Lasut-Wowonasa, Manado, Sulawesi Utara; YF 1983; EN 448; FT 12; PT 59; S1.

Sekolah Tinggi Ilmu Ekonomi Yayasan Swadaya, Jl. Cidurian No. 2, Jakarta Pusat, DKI Jakarta; YF 1969; EN 1,094; FT 42; PT 77; Dip.: Financial Management and Banking, Accounting; S1.

Sekolah Tinggi Ilmu Ekonomi "YBUP" Makasar, Jl. Letjen Pol Mappaundang 28, Ujung Pandang, Sulawesi Selatan; YF 1987; EN 920; FT 27; PT 36; Dip.; S1.

Sekolah Tinggi Ilmu Ekonomi YKPN, Jl. Gagak Rimang No. 2, DI Yogyakarta; YF 1980; EN 2,558; FT 98; PT 94; S1.

Sekolah Tinggi Ilmu Ekonomi YPKP Bandung, Jl. Surapati No. 225, Bandung, Jawa Barat; YF 1968; EN 3,277; FT 108; PT 99; Dip.: Finance and Banking; S1.

Sekolah Tinggi Ilmu Ekonomi YPUP, Jl. Andi Tonro 17, Ujung Pandang, Sulawesi Selatan; YF 1981; EN 1,200; FT 10; PT 50; Dip.; S1.

Sekolah Tinggi Ilmu Hukum Al-Gazali Soppeng, Jl. Samudra 16, Watansoppeng, Sulawesi Selatan; YF 1986; EN 129; FT 4; PT 19; Dip.

Sekolah Tinggi Ilmu Hukum Bandung, Jl. Cihampelas No. 8, Bandung, Jawa Barat; YF 1958; EN 1,123; FT 52; PT 46; S1: Civil Law, Criminal Law.

Sekolah Tinggi Ilmu Hukum Benteng Huraba, Jl. Ujung Gurap, Padang Sidempuan, Sumatera Utara; YF 1986; EN 136; FT 6; PT 12; S1.

Sekolah Tinggi Ilmu Hukum Galuh Ciamis, Kampus Pulo Maju, Kawali, Ciamis, Jawa Barat; YF 1984; EN 462; FT 17; PT 43; S1.

Sekolah Tinggi Ilmu Hukum Galunggung, Jl. Dr. Sukarjo No. 47, Tasikmalaya, Jawa Barat; YF 1974; EN 200; FT 17; PT 41; S1.

Sekolah Tinggi Ilmu Hukum Garut, Jl. Nusa Indah No. 24, Garut, Jawa Barat; YF 1983; EN 312; FT 2; PT 17; S1.

Sekolah Tinggi Ilmu Hukum Habaring Hurung, Jl. Padat Karya Baamang, Sampit, Kalimantan Tengah; YF 1985; EN 266; FT 7; PT 2; S1.

Sekolah Tinggi Ilmu Hukum Jend. Sudirman, Jl. Swandak Timur 3, Lumajang, Jawa Timur; YF 1981; EN 127; FT 4; PT 21; S1.

Sekolah Tinggi Ilmu Hukum Lubuk Sikaping, Jl. Moh. Yamin, Lubuk Sikaping, Pasaman, Sumatera Barat; YF 1985; EN 67; FT 7; PT 9; S1.

Sekolah Tinggi Ilmu Hukum Manokwari, Jl. Karya ABRI Sanggeng, Manokwari, Irian Jaya; YF 1975; EN 566; FT 13; PT 49; S1.

Sekolah Tinggi Ilmu Hukum Muhammadiyah, Jl. KHA. Dachlan No. 7, Banda Aceh, DI Aceh; YF 1969; EN 245; FT 8; PT 17; S1.

Sekolah Tinggi Ilmu Hukum Muhammadiyah Bima, Jl. Anggrek 1 Ranggo, Bima, Nusa Tenggara Barat; YF 1987; EN 151; FT 20; PT 10; S1.

Sekolah Tinggi Ilmu Hukum Muhammadiyah Kotabumi, Jl. Raya Prokimal, PO Box. 57, Kotabumi, Lampung; YF 1987; EN 111; FT 16; PT 7; S1.

Sekolah Tinggi Ilmu Hukum Painan, Jl. Siswa SMEA PGRI, Painan, Sumatera Barat; YF 1986; EN 121; FT 7; PT 9; S1.

Sekolah Tinggi Ilmu Hukum Pasundan, Jl. Pasundan No. 85, Sukabumi, Jawa Barat; YF 1964; EN 602; FT 14; PT 31; S1.

Sekolah Tinggi Ilmu Hukum Pertiba, Jl. Kacang Pedang No. 9, Pangkal Pinang, Sumatera Selatan; YF 1982; EN 365; FT 8; PT 35; S1.

Sekolah Tinggi Ilmu Hukum Purnawarman, Jl. A. Yani No. 172, Purwakarta, Jawa Barat; YF 1973; EN 226; FT 20; PT 32; S1.

Sekolah Tinggi Ilmu Hukum Sultan Adam, Jl. S. Parman, Simp. Purnama 22-A, Banjarmasin, Kalimantan Selatan; YF 1983; EN 493; FT 6; PT 40; S1.

Sekolah Tinggi Ilmu Hukum Sultan M. Tsyafiuddin, Jl. Sultan M. Tsyafiuddin No. 83, Singkawang, Kalimantan Barat; YF 1978; EN 203; FT 4; PT 24; Dip.; S1.

Sekolah Tinggi Ilmu Hukum Sunan Giri, Jl. Joyo Merjosari 240-A, Malang, Jawa Timur; YF 1979; EN 218; FT 8; PT 17; S1.

Sekolah Tinggi Ilmu Hukum Suryakencana, Jl. Pasir Gede Raya, Cianjur, Jawa Barat; YF 1973; EN 1,058; FT 22; PT 33; S1.

Sekolah Tinggi Ilmu Hukum Tambun Bungai, Jl. Yos Sudarso No. 35, Palangkaraya, Kalimantan Tengah; YF 1975; EN 577; FT 16; PT 36; S1.

Sekolah Tinggi Ilmu Hukum Tjoet Nyak Dhien Medan, Jl. Jambi No. 23-D, Medan, Sumatera Utara; YF 1986; EN 52; FT 19; PT 27; S1.

Sekolah Tinggi Ilmu Hukum "Unisda," Jl. Raya Sukodadi 4, Lamongan, Jawa Timur; YF 1987; EN 180; FT 7; PT 24; S1.

Sekolah Tinggi Ilmu Hukum Yayasan Nasional, Jl. Medan Km. 4, P. Siantar, Sumatera Utara; YF 1957; EN 65; FT 18; PT 19; S1.

Sekolah Tinggi Ilmu Hukum Zainul Hasan, Jl. Raya Semampur 360, Probolinggo, Jawa Timur; YF 1981; EN 218; FT 8; PT 17; S1.

Sekolah Tinggi Ilmu Kehutanan Pantu Kulu, Jl. T. Nyak Arief Darussalam, Banda Aceh, DI Aceh; YF 1986; EN 264; FT 7; PT 18; S1.

Sekolah Tinggi Ilmu Kesejahteraan Sosial Manado, Jl. Santo Yoseph, Kleak, Manado, Sulawesi Utara; YF 1984; EN 144; FT 18; PT 22; S1.

Sekolah Tinggi Ilmu Kesejahteraan Sosial Tamalanrea, Jl. Amanagappa 12, Ujung Pandang, Sulawesi Selatan; YF 1969; EN 405; FT 24; PT 25; Dip.

Sekolah Tinggi Ilmu Kesejahteraan Sosial Ujung Pandang, Jl. Cenderawasih 398, Ujung Pandang, Sulawesi Selatan; YF 1974; EN 459; FT 20; PT 34; S1.

Sekolah Tinggi Ilmu Komunikasi Diponegoro, Jl. Gajahmada No. 119-A, Semarang, Jawa Tengah; YF 1969; EN 934; FT 22; PT 55; S1.

Sekolah Tinggi Ilmu Komunikasi Mahakam, Jl. Dahlia No. 71, Samarinda, Kalimantan Timur; YF 1984; EN 99; FT 8; PT 15; S1.

Sekolah Tinggi Ilmu Manajemen Banjarmasin, Jl. Jend. Sudirman No. 14, Banjarmasin, Kalimantan Selatan; YF-; EN-; FT-; PT-.

Sekolah Tinggi Ilmu Manajemen Handayani, Jl. Tukad Banyusari 17B, Denpasar, Bali; YF 1979; EN 845; FT 17; PT 53; Dip.; S1.

Sekolah Tinggi Ilmu Manajemen Indonesia Banjarmasin, Jl. Kuripan No. 26, Banjarmasin, Kalimantan Selatan; YF 1983; EN 737; FT 10; PT 47; Dip.; S1.

Sekolah Tinggi Ilmu Manajemen Informatika dan Komputer Indonesia, Jl. Kiyai Tapa 216-A, Jakarta Barat, DKI Jakarta; YF 1985; EN 440; FT 10; PT 21; S1.

Sekolah Tinggi Ilmu Manajemen Informatika dan Komputer Jakarta, Jl. Radio Dalam, Jakarta Selatan, DKI Jakarta; YF 1978; EN 925; FT 12; PT 63; Dip.; S1.

Sekolah Tinggi Ilmu Manajemen Informatika dan Komputer Kuwera, Jl. Madrasah 14, Cilandak, Jakarta Selatan, DKI Jakarta; YF 1981; EN 251; FT 6; PT 19; S1.

Sekolah Tinggi Ilmu Manajemen Jakarta, Jl. Halimun 2, Guntur, Jaksel, DKI Jakarta; YF 1986; EN 164; FT 40; PT 25; Dip.; S1.

Sekolah Tinggi Ilmu Manajemen Komputer Bina Nusantara, Jl. KH. Syahdan 9 Kemanggisan, Jakarta Barat, DKI Jakarta; YF 1981; EN 5,705; FT 45; PT 155; Dip.: Management Information Systems, Information Science, Computer Engineering; S1.

Sekolah Tinggi Ilmu Manajemen Kosgoro, Jl. Taman Margasatwa 19, Jaksel, DKI Jakarta; YF 1986; EN 228; FT 42; PT 7; S1.

Sekolah Tinggi Ilmu Manajemen Sumatera Barat, Jl. Abdul Ahmad No. 8, Padang, Sumatera Barat; YF 1984; EN 232; FT 20; PT 7; S1.

Sekolah Tinggi Ilmu Manajemen "YLPG", Jl. Pacuan Kuda 1-5, Jaktim, DKI Jakarta; YF 1985; EN 736; FT 14; PT 28; S1.

Sekolah Tinggi Ilmu Pertanian Al-Gazali, Jl. Perintis Kemerdekaan 29, Ujung Pandang, Sulawesi Selatan; YF 1984; EN 444; FT 8; PT 48; S1.

Sekolah Tinggi Ilmu Pertanian "YAPI", Jl. Kapasa, Tol KM-8, Ujung Pandang, Sulawesi Selatan; YF 1981; EN 215; FT 14; PT 35; S1.

Sekolah Tinggi Ilmu Pengetahuan Sosial Wiraswasta, Jl. Abepura 31 P.O. Box 391, Jayapura, Irian Jaya; YF 1985; EN 225; FT 8; PT 28; S1.

Sekolah Tinggi Ilmu Pengetahuan Sosial Yappi, Jl. Lanto D-9, Pasewang, Jeneponto, Sulawesi Selatan; YF 1986; EN 103; FT 8; PT 20; S1.

Sekolah Tinggi Ilmu Sosial dan Ilmu Politik 17 Agustus 1945, Jl. Bontotangga 2, Ujung Pandang, Sulawesi Selatan; YF 1952; EN 794; FT 7; PT 50; S1.

Sekolah Tinggi Ilmu Sosial dan Ilmu Politik Candradimuka, Jl. Swadaya Sekip Ujung 20 Ilir, Palembang, Sumatera Selatan; YF 1979; EN 1,276; FT 39; PT 49; S1.

Sekolah Tinggi Ilmu Sosial dan Ilmu Politik Dharma Wacana, Jl. Kenanga No. 3, Melyojati 16-C, Metro, Lampung; YF 1987; EN 90; FT 4; PT 37; S1.

Sekolah Tinggi Ilmu Sosial dan Ilmu Politik Dharmawangsa, Jl. Misbah No. 18-A, Medan, Sumatera Utara; YF-; EN-; FT-; PT-; Dip.; S1.

Sekolah Tinggi Ilmu Sosial dan Ilmu Politik Garut, Jl. Tarogong No. 265-A, Garut, Jawa Barat; YF 1974; EN 3,277; FT 108; PT 99; S1.

Sekolah Tinggi Ilmu Sosial dan Ilmu Politik Imam Bonjol, Jl. Koto Tinggi No. 5, Padang, Sumatera Barat; YF 1985; EN 111; FT 3; PT 12; S1.

Sekolah Tinggi Ilmu Sosial dan Ilmu Politik Kartika Bangsa, Jl. Gedok Kuning No. 140, DI Yogyakarta; YF 1981; EN 533; FT 12; PT 30; S1.

Sekolah Tinggi Ilmu Sosial dan Ilmu Politik Lampung, Jl. Gajahmada No. 34, Bandar Lampung, Lampung; YF 1977; EN 1,983; FT 15; PT 72; S1.

Sekolah Tinggi Ilmu Sosial dan Ilmu Politik Margarana, Jl. Mataram Malkangin, Tabanan, Bali; YF 1980; EN 160; FT 10; PT 32; S1.

Sekolah Tinggi Ilmu Sosial dan Ilmu Politik Mbojo, Jl. Sukarno-Hatta, Mpunda Raba, Bima, Nusa Tenggara Barat; YF 1985; EN 202; FT 13; PT 27; S1.

Sekolah Tinggi Ilmu Sosial dan Ilmu Politik Merdeka, Jl. Tumining, P.O. Box 184, Manado, Sulawesi Utara; YF 1969; EN 937; FT 24; PT 49; S1.

Sekolah Tinggi Ilmu Sosial dan Ilmu Politik Muhammadiyah, Jl. Mastrip No. 18, Madiun, Jawa Timur; YF 1977; EN 240; FT 4; PT 16; S1.

Sekolah Tinggi Ilmu Sosial dan Ilmu Politik Padang, Jl. A. Rahman Hakim No. 6, Padang, Sumatera Barat; YF 1985; EN 111; FT 3; PT 12; S1.

Sekolah Tinggi Ilmu Sosial dan Ilmu Politik Panca Bhakti, Jl. Dr. Suharso 36A, Palu, Sulteng; YF 1988; EN 726; FT 24; PT 27; S1.

Sekolah Tinggi Ilmu Sosial dan Ilmu Politik Panca Sakti, Jl. Tengah Sawah No. 44, Bukittinggi, Sumatera Barat; YF 1987; EN 174; FT 12; PT 38; S1.

Sekolah Tinggi Ilmu Sosial dan Ilmu Politik Pusaka Nusantara, Jl. Pahlawan Revolusi, Jakarta Timur, DKI Jakarta; YF 1986; EN 446; FT 12; PT 42; S1.

Sekolah Tinggi Ilmu Sosial dan Ilmu Politik Silas Papare, Jl. Guarabesi 10 P.O. Box 1990, Jayapura, Irian Jaya; YF 1984; EN 475; FT 3; PT 33; S1.

Sekolah Tinggi Ilmu Sosial dan Ilmu Politik Veteran RI., Jl. Diponegoro 33, Palopo, Sulawesi Selatan; YF 1963; EN 942; FT 10; PT 39; S1.

Sekolah Tinggi Ilmu Sosial dan Ilmu Politik Waskita Dharma, Jl. Sawojajar V/28, Malang, Jawa Timur; YF 1984; EN 1,250; FT 15; PT 20; S1.

Sekolah Tinggi Ilmu Sosial dan Ilmu Politik Widuri, Jl. Palmerah Barat 353, Jakarta Pusat, DKI Jakarta; YF 1960; EN 198; FT 20; PT 48; S1: Social Welfare.

Sekolah Tinggi Ilmu Sosial dan Ilmu Politik Wirabhakti, Jl. Cempaka No. 1, Denpasar, Bali; YF 1985; EN 278; FT 13; PT 18; Dip.; S1.

Sekolah Tinggi Informatika dan Komputer Indonesia, Jl. Tidar No. 110, Malang, Jawa Timur; YF 1978; EN 240; FT 4; PT 18; Dip.; S1.

Sekolah Tinggi Kedokteran Gigi, Jl. Slamet Riyadi 2, Jember, Jawa Timur; YF 1986; EN 264; FT 12; PT 4; S1.

Sekolah Tinggi Kedokteran Gigi Padang, Jl. Damar I/16, Padang, Sumatera Barat; YF 1985; EN 142; FT 12; PT 71; S1.

Sekolah Tinggi Keguruan dan Ilmu Pendidikan Abdi Pendidikan, Jl. Bengkawas Km. 3, Bukittinggi, Sumatera Barat; YF 1984; EN 702; FT 6; PT 52; Dip.; S1.

Sekolah Tinggi Keguruan dan Ilmu Pendidikan Ahlusunnah, Jl. Diponegoro No. 8, Bukittinggi, Sumatera Barat; YF 1984; EN 601; FT 13; PT 65; Dip.; S1.

Sekolah Tinggi Keguruan dan Ilmu Pendidikan 11 April, Jl. P. Geusan Ulun No. 104, Sumedang, Jawa Barat; YF 1982; EN 664; FT 11; PT 33; Dip.; S1.

Sekolah Tinggi Keguruan dan Ilmu Pendidikan Bangko, Jl. Jend. Sudirman Km. 2, Komp. Merantau, Bangko, Jambi; YF 1980; EN 353; FT 73; PT 27; S1.

Sekolah Tinggi Keguruan dan Ilmu Pendidikan Bima, Jl. Gatot Subroto-Mande, Sadia, Bima, Nusa Tenggara Barat; YF 1976; EN 456; FT 23; PT 17; Dip.; S1.

Sekolah Tinggi Keguruan dan Ilmu Pendidikan Budi Daya Binjai, Jl. KHA. Karim No. 11, Binjai, Sumatera Utara; YF 1984; EN 166; FT 14; PT 43; Dip.; S1.

Sekolah Tinggi Keguruan dan Ilmu Pendidikan Catur Sakti, Jl. Dr. Wahidin, Bantul, DI Yogyakarta; YF 1966; EN 204; FT 20; PT 9; S1.

Sekolah Tinggi Keguruan dan Ilmu Pendidikan Cikroaminoto Palopo, Jl. Anggrek, Palopo, Sulawesi Selatan; YF 1967; EN 1,039; FT 11; PT 32; Dip.; S1.

Sekolah Tinggi Keguruan dan Ilmu Pendidikan Cokroaminoto Pinrang, Jl. Lasinrang, Pinrang, Sulawesi Selatan; YF 1974; EN 503; FT 17; PT 44; Dip.; S1.

Sekolah Tinggi Keguruan dan Ilmu Pendidikan Darul Dakwah WI., Jl. Stadion Manding, Polewali, Sulawesi Selatan; YF 1975; EN 596; FT 12; PT 30; Dip.; S1.

Sekolah Tinggi Keguruan dan Ilmu Pendidikan Dharma Bhakti, Jl. Pasar Mudik No. 91-A, Padang, Sumatera Barat; YF 1986; EN 657; FT 12; PT 55; S1.

Sekolah Tinggi Keguruan dan Ilmu Pendidikan Hamzanwadi, Jl. Pahlawan Pancor, Selong, Nusa Tenggara Barat; YF 1978; EN 518; FT 28; PT 34; Dip.; S1.

Sekolah Tinggi Keguruan dan Ilmu Pendidikan Katekis Ruteng, Jl. A. Yani No. 10, Ruteng, Nusa Tenggara Timur; YF 1960; EN 199; FT 11; PT 20; Dip.: Catechetical Education.

Sekolah Tinggi Keguruan dan Ilmu Pendidikan Kristen Makale, Jl. Tikoalu 2, Makale, Sulawesi Selatan; YF 1967; EN 515; FT 10; PT 18; Dip.; S1.

Sekolah Tinggi Keguruan dan Ilmu Pendidikan Kuningan, Jl. Pramuka No. 67, Kuningan, Jawa Barat; YF 1979; EN 573; FT 13; PT 31; Dip.; S1.

Sekolah Tinggi Keguruan dan Ilmu Pendidikan Kusumanegara, Jl. Raya Bogor Km. 24, Jakarta Timur, DKI Jakarta; YF 1976; EN 99; FT 6; PT 12; S1.

Sekolah Tinggi Keguruan dan Ilmu Pendidikan Lubuk Linggau, Jl. Majapahit, Taba Pingin, Lubuk Linggau, Sumatera Selatan; YF 1987; EN 176; FT 13; PT 16; S1.

Sekolah Tinggi Keguruan dan Ilmu Pendidikan Lumajang, Jl. A. Yani No. 10, Lumajang, Jawa Timur; YF-; EN-; FT-; PT-; Dip.; S1.

Sekolah Tinggi Keguruan dan Ilmu Pendidikan Muhammadiyah, Jl. Tritura No. 7, Lumajang, Jawa Timur; YF 1982; EN 189; FT 7; PT 17; S1.

Sekolah Tinggi Keguruan dan Ilmu Pendidikan Muhammadiyah Barru, Jl. Padaelo Tanete, Barru, Sulawesi Selatan; YF 1974; EN 205; FT 12; PT 25; Dip.

Sekolah Tinggi Keguruan dan Ilmu Pendidikan Muhammadiyah Bengkulu, Jl. Bali No. 31, Bengkulu, Bengkulu; YF 1970; EN 1,140; FT 69; PT 98; S1.

Sekolah Tinggi Keguruan dan Ilmu Pendidikan Muhammadiyah Bone, Jl. Biru 139, Watampone, Sulawesi Selatan; YF 1973; EN 904; FT 12; PT 54; Dip.; S1.

Sekolah Tinggi Keguruan dan Ilmu Pendidikan Muhammadiyah Bulukumba, Jl. R. Suprapto 9, Bulukumba, Sulawesi Selatan; YF 1966; EN 331; FT 8; PT 34; Dip.; S1.

Sekolah Tinggi Keguruan dan Ilmu Pendidikan Muhammadiyah Enrekang, Jl. Jend. Sudirman 1, Enrekang, Sulawesi Selatan; YF 1973; EN 422; FT 14; PT 36; Dip.; S1.

Sekolah Tinggi Keguruan dan Ilmu Pendidikan Muhammadiyah Kotabumi, Jl. Raya Sindangsari, P.O. Box 57, Kotabumi, Lampung; YF 1975; EN 547; FT 15; PT 11; Dip.; S1.

Sekolah Tinggi Keguruan dan Ilmu Pendidikan Muhammadiyah Metro, Jl. Kampus Lembanyung No. 15-A, Metro, Lampung; YF 1969; EN 2,224; FT 70; PT 41; Dip.; S1.

Sekolah Tinggi Keguruan dan Ilmu Pendidikan Muhammadiyah Pare-Pare, Jl. Muhammadiyah 8, Pare-Pare, Sulawesi Selatan; YF 1983; EN 428; FT 14; PT 41; Dip.

Sekolah Tinggi Keguruan dan Ilmu Pendidikan Muhammadiyah Ring Sewu, Jl. Makam KH. Cholib No. 95, Pringsewu, Lampung; YF 1975; EN 1,593; FT 51; PT 45; S1.

Sekolah Tinggi Keguruan dan Ilmu Pendidikan Muhammadiyah Sampit, Jl. Pinang No. 14, Sampit, Kalimantan Tengah; YF 1986; EN 130; FT 8; PT 24; S1.

Sekolah Tinggi Keguruan dan Ilmu Pendidikan Pasundan, Jl. Terusan No. 32, Cimahi, Jawa Barat; YF 1986; EN 504; FT 15; PT-; Dip.; S1.

Sekolah Tinggi Keguruan dan Ilmu Pendidikan Pelita Bangsa, Jl. Kebun Lada No. 24, Binjai, Sumatera Utara; YF 1985; EN 44; FT 4; PT 9; S1.

Sekolah Tinggi Keguruan dan Ilmu Pendidikan Pembangunan Indonesia, Jl. Jend. Sudirman 42, Ujung Pandang, Sulawesi Selatan; YF 1987; EN 40; FT 10; PT 54; S1.

Sekolah Tinggi Keguruan dan Ilmu Pendidikan PGRI Bangkalan, Jl. Soekarno-Hatta No. 52, Bangkalan, Madura, Jawa Timur; YF 1976; EN 223; FT 12; PT 32; Dip.; S1.

Sekolah Tinggi Keguruan dan Ilmu Pendidikan PGRI Banjarmasin, Jl. Batu Tiban No. 32, Banjarmasin, Kalimantan Selatan; YF 1989; S1.

Sekolah Tinggi Keguruan dan Ilmu Pendidikan PGRI Blitar, Jl. Kalimantan, Blitar, Jawa Timur; YF 1971; EN 217; FT 11; PT 76; Dip.; S1.

Sekolah Tinggi Keguruan dan Ilmu Pendidikan PGRI Jakarta, Jl. Ragunan, Pasar Minggu, Jakarta Selatan, DKI Jakarta; YF 1974; EN 148; FT 6; PT 72; Dip.; S1.

Sekolah Tinggi Keguruan dan Ilmu Pendidikan PGRI Jombang, Jl. Pattimura II/85, Jombang, Jawa Timur; YF 1986; EN 1,741; FT 2; PT 73; Dip.; S1.

Sekolah Tinggi Keguruan dan Ilmu Pendidikan PGRI Kotabumi, Jl. Raden Intan Km. 4, Kotabumi, Lampung; YF 1987; EN 312; FT 16; PT 21; S1.

Sekolah Tinggi Keguruan dan Ilmu Pendidikan PGRI Lamongan, Jl. Sunan Giri, Lamongan, Jawa Timur; YF 1976; EN 192; FT 8; PT 27; Dip.

Sekolah Tinggi Keguruan dan Ilmu Pendidikan PGRI Lampung, Jl. Chairil Anwar No. 79, Bandar Lampung, Lampung; YF 1982; EN 1,416; FT 52; PT 59; Dip; S1.

Sekolah Tinggi Keguruan dan Ilmu Pendidikan PGRI Magetan, Jl. Kemasan 1, Magetan, Jawa Timur; YF 1975; EN 380; FT 4; PT 18; Dip.

Sekolah Tinggi Keguruan dan Ilmu Pendidikan PGRI Metro, Jl. Kampus Baru 38 Batanghari, Batanghari, Metro, Lampung; YF 1983; EN 624; FT 15; PT 27; S1.

Sekolah Tinggi Keguruan dan Ilmu Pendidikan PGRI Mojokerto, Jl. Veteran No. 9, Mojokerto, Jawa Timur; YF 1986; EN 281; FT 16; PT 21; Dip.

Sekolah Tinggi Keguruan dan Ilmu Pendidikan PGRI Nganjuk, Jl. Abd. Rahman Saleh 21, Nganjuk, Jawa Timur; YF 1978; EN 831; FT 9; PT 62; Dip.

Sekolah Tinggi Keguruan dan Ilmu Pendidikan PGRI Ngawi, Jl. Raya Klitik, Ngawi, Jawa Timur; YF 1974; EN 902; FT 30; PT 12; Dip.; S1.

Sekolah Tinggi Keguruan dan Ilmu Pendidikan PGRI Padang, Jl. Sudirman No. 1-A, Padang, Sumatera Barat; YF 1984; EN 1,469; FT 25; PT 121; Dip.; S1.

Sekolah Tinggi Keguruan dan Ilmu Pendidikan PGRI Palembang, Jl. A. Yani Lorong Gotongroyong 9/10, Palembang, Sumatera Selatan; YF 1984; EN 864; FT 41; PT 93; S1.

Sekolah Tinggi Keguruan dan Ilmu Pendidikan PGRI Pasuruan, Jl. Indragiri 10 Tambakrejo, Pasuruan, Jawa Timur; YF 1975; EN 412; FT 12; PT 22; Dip.; S1.

Sekolah Tinggi Keguruan dan Ilmu Pendidikan PGRI Ponorogo, Jl. Kabupaten No. 3, Ponorogo, Jawa Timur; YF 1976; EN 901; FT 19; PT 36; Dip.

Sekolah Tinggi Keguruan dan Ilmu Pendidikan PGRI Pontianak, Jl. Kalimantan No. 17, Pontianak, Kalimantan Barat; YF 1981; EN 662; FT 19; PT 66; Dip.; S1.

Sekolah Tinggi Keguruan dan Ilmu Pendidikan PGRI Probolinggo, Jl. Mawar No. 10, Probolinggo, Jawa Timur; YF 1976; EN 657; FT 20; PT 62; Dip.

Sekolah Tinggi Keguruan dan Ilmu Pendidikan PGRI Sampang, Jl. Raya Tarjon Indah, Sampang, Jawa Timur; YF 1975; EN 320; FT 12; PT 14; Dip.

Sekolah Tinggi Keguruan dan Ilmu Pendidikan PGRI Sidoarjo, Jl. Kampus Kemiri, Sidoarjo, Jawa Timur; YF 1985; EN 223; FT 4; PT 28; S1.

Sekolah Tinggi Keguruan dan Ilmu Pendidikan PGRI Situbondo, Jl. Argopuro Gg. VII, Situbondo, Jawa Timur; YF 1980; EN 586; FT 18; PT 38; Dip.

Sekolah Tinggi Keguruan dan Ilmu Pendidikan PGRI Sukabumi, Jl. Bhayangkara No. 146, Sukabumi, Jawa Barat; YF 1987; EN 333; FT 7; PT 43; S1.

Sekolah Tinggi Keguruan dan Ilmu Pendidikan PGRI Sumenep, Jl. Trunojoyo 21 Moncol, Sumenep, Jawa Timur; YF 1975; EN 298; FT 9; PT 32; Dip.

Sekolah Tinggi Keguruan dan Ilmu Pendidikan PGRI Trenggalek, Jl. Supriadi No. 22, Trenggalek, Jawa Timur; YF 1982; EN 350; FT 4; Dip.; S1.

Sekolah Tinggi Keguruan dan Ilmu Pendidikan PGRI Tulungagung, Jl. Mayor Suyadi Timur 7, Tulungagung, Jawa Timur; YF 1972; EN 612; FT 14; PT 44; Dip.

Sekolah Tinggi Keguruan dan Ilmu Pendidikan Purnama, Jl. Tirtayasa V, Jakarta Selatan, DKI Jakarta; YF 1975; EN 770; FT 45; PT 10; S1.

Sekolah Tinggi Keguruan dan Ilmu Pendidikan Riama, Jl. Gereja No. 6, Simpang Marindal, Medan, Sumatera Utara; YF 1976; EN 709; FT 30; PT 27; Dip.; S1.

Sekolah Tinggi Keguruan dan Ilmu Pendidikan Serambi Mekah, Jl. T. Cik Ditiro 19, Banda Aceh, DI Aceh; YF 1985; EN 770; FT 12; PT 94; Dip.; S1.

Sekolah Tinggi Keguruan dan Ilmu Pendidikan Siliwangi, Jl. Seram No. 5, Bandung, Jawa Barat; YF 1986; EN 570; FT 15; PT 42; Dip.; S1.

Sekolah Tinggi Keguruan dan Ilmu Pendidikan Sumbawa Besar, Jl. Yos Sudarso No. 9, Sumbawa Besar, Nusa Tenggara Barat; YF 1975; EN 225; FT 21; PT 36; Dip.; S1.

Sekolah Tinggi Keguruan dan Ilmu Pendidikan Suryakencana, Jl. Pasir Gede Raya (Blk RSU), Cianjur, Jawa Barat; YF 1981; EN 708; FT 26; PT 32; S1.

Sekolah Tinggi Keguruan dan Ilmu Pendidikan Tapanuli Selatan, Jl. Ujung Gurap, Padang Sidempuan, Sumatera Utara; YF 1981; EN 820; FT 24; PT 54; S1.

Sekolah Tinggi Keguruan dan Ilmu Pendidikan Teladan, Jl. Gedung Arca No. 49, Medan, Sumatera Utara; YF 1987; EN 127; FT 10; PT 11; S1.

Sekolah Tinggi Keguruan dan Ilmu Pendidikan Tompotika, Jl. Taman Siswa 65, Luwuk Banggai, Sulteng; YF 1977; EN 390; FT 6; PT 31; Dip.

Sekolah Tinggi Keguruan dan Ilmu Pendidikan Tri Buana, Jl. Bratang Wetan I/16, Surabaya, Jawa Timur; YF 1981; EN 302; FT 7; PT 35; S1.

Sekolah Tinggi Keguruan dan Ilmu Pendidikan "Unisda," Jl. Raya Sukodadi No. 4, Lamongan, Jawa Timur; YF 1987; EN 221; FT 4; PT 32; S1.

Sekolah Tinggi Keguruan dan Ilmu Pendidikan Veteran Sidenreng, Jl. Anggrek, Rappang, Sulawesi Selatan; YF 1977; EN 203; FT 9; PT 33; Dip.; S1.

Sekolah Tinggi Keguruan dan Ilmu Pendidikan Widya Mandala, Jl. Manggis No. 15-17, Madiun, Jawa Timur; YF 1960; EN 1,358; FT 24; PT 19; Dip.: Curriculum and Educational Technology; S1.

Sekolah Tinggi Keguruan dan Ilmu Pendidikan Widya Yuana, Jl. Mayjen. Panjaitan, Madiun, Jawa Timur; YF 1959; EN 172; FT 8; PT 9; Dip.

Sekolah Tinggi Keguruan dan Ilmu Pendidikan Wijaya Bhakti, Komp. Kehakiman, Utan Kayu, Jakarta Timur, DKI Jakarta; YF 1975; EN 265; FT 6; PT 24; S1.

Sekolah Tinggi Keguruan dan Ilmu Pendidikan YBPK-GKJW Surabaya, Jl. Luntas No. 32, Surabaya, Jawa Timur; YF 1983; EN 320; FT 8; PT 21; Dip.

Sekolah Tinggi Keguruan dan Ilmu Pendidikan YP. Bale, Jl. Wiranatakusumah, Bale Endah, Bandung, Jawa Barat; YF 1984; EN 531; FT 25; PT 32; Dip.; S1.

Sekolah Tinggi Kelautan Hatawana, Jl. IPN Kebon Nanas, Jakarta Timur, DKI Jakarta; YF 1987; EN 124; FT 8; PT 9; S1.

Sekolah Tinggi Kesenian Wilwatikta, Jl. Klampis Anom II, Surabaya, Jawa Timur; YF 1980; EN 2,886; FT 13; PT 42; Dip.; S1.

Sekolah Tinggi Keuangan dan Perbankan Semarang, Jl. Kendeng V, Bedan Nginsor, Semarang, Jawa Tengah; YF 1968; EN 3,132; FT 70; PT 40; Dip.

Sekolah Tinggi Keuangan Niaga dan Negara Pembangunan, Jl. Letjen Sutoyo, Cawang, Jaktim, DKI Jakarta; YF 1984; EN 316; FT 31; PT 40; Dip.; S1.

Sekolah Tinggi Komunikasi Almamater Wartawan, Jl. Kedokan Semamper, Surabaya, Jawa Timur; YF 1964; EN 280; FT 8; PT 21; S1.

Sekolah Tinggi Komunikasi Manado, Jl. Adi Negara Melayang 1, P.O. Box 204, Manado, Sulawesi Utara; YF 1985; EN 535; FT 6; PT 44; S1.

Sekolah Tinggi Komunikasi Pembangunan Medan, Jl. Sisingamangaraja No. 84, Medan, Sumatera Utara; YF 1987; EN 43; FT 10; PT 23; Dip.; S1.

Sekolah Tinggi Manajemen dan Informatika Putra Bhakti, Jl. Kutisari No. 66, Surabaya, Jawa Timur; YF 1983; EN 224; FT 13; PT 42; Dip.; S1.

Sekolah Tinggi Manajemen Informatika dan Komputer Budi Luhur, Jl. Raya Ciledug, Keb. Lama, Jakarta Selatan, DKI Jakarta; YF 1979; EN 3,822; FT 26; PT 60; Dip.: Information Technology, Management Systems; S1.

Sekolah Tinggi Manajemen Informatika dan Komputer Gunadarma, Jl. Salemba Raya 53, Jakarta Pusat, DKI Jakarta; YF 1984; EN 417; FT 10; PT 45; Dip.: Computer Engineering; Management Information Systems; S1: Computer Engineering, Management Information Systems, Information Technology.

Sekolah Tinggi Manajemen Informatika dan Komputer Muhammadiyah Sidoarjo, Kampus ST Manajemen Informatika dan Komputer Muhammadiyah, Sidoarjo, Jawa Timur; YF-; EN-; FT-; PT-; Dip.; S1.

Sekolah Tinggi Manajemen Informatika dan Komputer Samarinda, Jl. Pemandian, Samarinda, Kalimantan Timur; YF-; EN-; FT-; PT-.

Sekolah Tinggi Manajemen Transportasi Trisakti, Jl. Kyai Tapa, Grogol, Jakbar, DKI Jakarta; YF 1970; EN 434; FT 24; PT 55; Dip.: Air Transportation Management.

Sekolah Tinggi Muhammadiyah Sidenreng Rappang, Jl. Ressang 4, Rappang, Sulawesi Selatan; YF 1974; EN 171; FT 11; PT 17; Dip.; S1.

Sekolah Tinggi Olahraga dan Kesehatan Bina Guna, Jl. Aluminium 77, Tj. Mulia, Medan, Sumatera Utara; YF 1986; EN 167; FT 10; PT 20; S1.

Sekolah Tinggi Pembangunan Masyarakat Desa, Jl. Timoho No. 316, DI Yogyakarta; YF 1988; EN 3,400; FT 52; PT 47; Dip.; S1.

Sekolah Tinggi Perikanan Dharma Wangsa, Kampus Dharma Wangsa, Medan, Sumatera Utara; S1.

Sekolah Tinggi Perkebunan Yunisla, Jl. Pagar Alam No. 31, Bandar Lampung, Lampung; YF 1987; EN 71; FT 8; PT 9; S1.

Sekolah Tinggi Pertanian Al-Azhar, Jl. Pintu Air IV, Medan, Sumatera Utara; YF 1987; EN 100; FT 13; PT 38; S1.

Sekolah Tinggi Pertanian Al-Muslim, Jl. T. Abdulrahman 137 Madang, Biroeun, DI Aceh; YF 1990; EN 154; FT 9; PT 35; S1.

Sekolah Tinggi Pertanian Bandung, Jl. Raya Wiranata Kusuma, Bandung, Jawa Barat; YF 1984; EN 166; FT 16; PT 34; S1.

Sekolah Tinggi Pertanian Benteng Huraba, Jl. Ujung Gurap, Padang Sidempuan, Sumatera Utara; YF 1986; EN 134; FT 6; PT 18; S1.

Sekolah Tinggi Pertanian Dharma Wacana, Jl. Kenanga No. 3-Mulyojati 16-C, Metro, Lampung; YF 1983; EN 77; FT 10; PT 48; S1.

Sekolah Tinggi Pertanian Jawa Barat, Jl. Raya Cipadung No. 46, Bandung, Jawa Barat; YF 1988; EN 148; FT 11; PT 18; S1.

Sekolah Tinggi Pertanian Jember, Jl. Slamet Riyadi No. 64, Jember, Jawa Timur; YF 1979; EN 280; FT 5; PT 27; Dip.; S1.

Sekolah Tinggi Pertanian Lamongan, Kampus ST Pertanian "Unisda," Lamongan, Jawa Timur; YF 1978; EN 280; FT 7; PT 20; S1.

Sekolah Tinggi Pertanian Pembinaan Masyarakat Indonesia, Jl. Teladan No. 15, Medan, Sumatera Utara; YF 1979; EN 107; FT 11; PT 21; S1.

Sekolah Tinggi Pertanian Serambi Mekah, Jl. Gabus No. 33, Banda Aceh, DI Aceh; YF 1989; EN 76; FT 7; PT 21; S1.

Sekolah Tinggi Pertanian Serentak Bak-Ragam, Jl. Gajahmada, Muara Bulian, Jambi; YF 1987; EN 89; FT 12; PT 11; S1.

Sekolah Tinggi Pertanian Surya Dharma, Jl. Kyai Maja Gg. I Way Halim, Bandar Lampung, Lampung; YF 1987; EN 181; FT 9; PT 10; S1.

Sekolah Tinggi Pertanian Surya Nusantara, Jl. Moh. Yamin No. 1, Tebingtinggi, Sumatera Utara; YF 1985; EN 125; FT 9; PT 11; S1.

Sekolah Tinggi Pertanian Tanjungsari, Jl. Raya Tanjungsari, Sumedang, Jawa Barat; YF 1989; EN 154; FT 8; PT 15; Dip.; S1.

Sekolah Tinggi Pertanian Tjoet Nya Dhien, Jl. Jambi No. 230, Medan, Sumatera Utara; YF 1986; EN 157; FT 11; PT 21; S1.

Sekolah Tinggi Pertanian Yayasan Gajah Putih, Jl. Yos Sudarso No. 10, Takengon, DI Aceh; YF 1986; EN 154; FT 12; PT 18; S1.

Sekolah Tinggi Sains dan Teknologi Bandung, Jl. Ir. H. Juanda No. 130-C, Bandung, Jawa Barat; YF 1984; EN 909; FT 34; PT 78; S1.

Sekolah Tinggi Sains dan Teknologi Muhammadiyah, Jl. KHA. Dachlan No. 7, Banda Aceh, DI Aceh; YF 1989; S1.

Sekolah Tinggi Seni Indonesia Surakarta, Kentingan Jebres, Surakarta 57126, Jawa Tengah.

Sekolah Tinggi Seni Tari Indonesia, Jl. Nusa Indah, Denpasar, Bali.

Sekolah Tinggi Teknik Al-Azhar, Jl. Pintu Air IV, Medan, Sumatera Utara; YF 1987; EN 78; FT 7; PT 24; S1.

Sekolah Tinggi Teknik Harapan, Jl. Imam Bonjol No. 35, Medan, Sumatera Utara; YF 1989; EN 600; FT 3; PT 28; Dip.

Sekolah Tinggi Teknik Iskandar Thani, Jl. Iskandar Muda, Banda Aceh, DI Aceh; YF 1987; EN 422; FT 17; PT 37; S1.

Sekolah Tinggi Teknik Jakarta, Jl. Jatiwaringin Raya 39-41, Jakarta Timur, DKI Jakarta; YF 1971; EN 249; FT 56; PT 89; S1.

Sekolah Tinggi Teknik Mahakam, Kampus Sekolah Tinggi Teknik Mahakam, Samarinda, Kalimantan Timur; YF 1990; EN-; FT 6; PT 6; Dip.

Sekolah Tinggi Teknik Mataram, Jl. Pemuda, Mataram, Nusa Tenggara Barat; YF 1985; EN 260; FT 13; PT 22; S1.

Sekolah Tinggi Teknik Muhammadiyah, Jl. KHA. Dachlan No. 7, Banda Aceh, DI Aceh; YF 1989; S1.

Sekolah Tinggi Teknik Muhammadiyah Metro, Jl. Kampus Lembanyung No. 15-A, Metro, Lampung; YF 1986; EN 275; FT 8; PT 11; S1.

Sekolah Tinggi Teknik Pembinaan Masyarakat Indonesia, Jl. Teladan No. 15, Medan, Sumatera Utara; YF 1979; EN 107; FT 11; PT 21; Dip.; S1.

Sekolah Tinggi Teknik Rejasa, Jl. Gentengkali No. 27, Surabaya, Jawa Timur; YF 1982; EN 237; FT 7; PT 46; S1.

Sekolah Tinggi Teknik Surabaya, Jl. Ngagel Jaya Tengah 73-77, Surabaya, Jawa Timur; YF 1978; EN 280; FT 4; PT 16; Dip; S1.

Sekolah Tinggi Teknologi A. Yani Bandung, Jl. Cibeber,, Cimahi, Jawa Barat; YF 1974; EN 420; FT 21; PT-; Dip.; S1.

Sekolah Tinggi Teknologi Bina Tunggal, Jl. KH. Wahab Affan, Pondok Ungu, Bekasi, Jawa Barat; YF 1986; EN 136; FT 8; PT 26; S1.

Sekolah Tinggi Teknologi dan Kejuruan Surabaya, Jl. Mawar No. 31, Surabaya, Jawa Timur; YF 1985; EN 137; FT 7; PT 11; Dip.

Sekolah Tinggi Teknologi Dharmayadi, Jl. Sukarta 22, Panakukang, Ujung Pandang, Sulawesi Selatan; YF 1984; EN 590; FT 26; PT 52; S1.

Sekolah Tinggi Teknologi Dirgantara, Bandara Halim PK., Jaktim, DKI Jakarta; YF 1987; EN 278; FT 40; PT 44; Dip; S1.

Sekolah Tinggi Teknologi Indonesia, Jl. Raden Saleh No. 53, Jakpus, DKI Jakarta; YF 1987; EN 322; FT 14; PT 107; Dip.; S1.

Sekolah Tinggi Teknologi Indonesia Bandung, Jl. Dipati Ukur No. 26, Bandung, Jawa Barat.

Sekolah Tinggi Teknologi Industri, Jl. Kiputih, Sukolilo, Surabaya, Jawa Timur; YF 1969; EN 280; FT 6; PT 28; Dip.; S1.

Sekolah Tinggi Teknologi Industri Bandung, Jl. Gatot Sobroto, Pindad, Bandung, Jawa Barat; YF 1985; EN 1,501; FT 39; PT 47; S1.

Sekolah Tinggi Teknologi Industri Glugur, Jl. Glugur No. 140 By-Pass, Medan, Sumatera Utara; YF 1987; EN 200; FT 14; PT 23; Dip.; S1.

Sekolah Tinggi Teknologi Industri Padang, Jl. Imam Bonjol, P.O. Box 54, Padang, Sumatera Barat; YF 1982; EN 343; FT 9; PT 58; Dip.; S1.

Sekolah Tinggi Teknologi Industri Turen, Jl. Sudirman No. 209, Malang, Jawa Timur; YF 1986; EN 207; FT 10; PT 39; S1.

Sekolah Tinggi Teknologi Lingkungan Bantul, Jl. Janti, Gedung Kuning, Bantul, DI Yogyakarta; YF 1985; EN 598; FT 16; PT 40; S1.

Sekolah Tinggi Teknologi Mandala Bandung, Jl. Soekarno-Hatta (dekat Kantor Besar), Bandung, Jawa Barat; YF 1972; EN 1,441; FT 24; PT 87; Dip.; S1.

Sekolah Tinggi Teknologi Mineral Indonesia, Jl. Belitung No. 12, Bandung, Jawa Barat; YF-; EN-; FT-; PT.

Sekolah Tinggi Teknologi Nasional Yogyakarta, Jl. Yos Sudarso No. 27-A, Yogyakarta, DIY; YF 1973; EN 1,139; Dip.; S1.

Sekolah Tinggi Teknologi Raden Wijaya, Jl. Mayjen Sungkono No. 784, Mojokerto, Jawa Timur; YF 1979; EN 286; FT 6; PT 18; S1.

Sekolah Tinggi Theologia HKBP, Jl. Asahan No. 6, P. Siantar, Sumatera Utara; YF 1988; EN 297; FT 11; PT 5; S1.

Universitas 17 Agustus 1945 Banyuwangi, Jl. Adisucipto No. 26, Banyuwangi, Jawa Timur; YF 1980; EN 1,080; FT 85; PT 38; Dip.; S1.

Universitas 17 Agustus 1945 Cirebon, Jl. Perjuangan By-Pass, Cirebon, Jawa Barat; YF 1962; EN 1,691; FT 53; PT 259; S1.

Universitas 17 Agustus 1945 Jakarta, Jl. Sunter Permai, Podomoro, Jakut, DKI Jakarta; YF 1952; EN 2,717; FT 202; PT 306; S1: Public Administration, Business Administration, Criminal Law, Civil Law, Constitutional Law, International Law, Government, International Relations, Political Science, Communications.

Universitas 17 Agustus 1945 Samarinda, Jl. Air Putih, Samarinda, Kalimantan Timur; YF 1965; EN 2,167; FT 29; PT 220; S1.

Universitas 17 Agustus 1945 Semarang, Jl. Seteran Dalam No. 9, Semarang, Jawa Tengah; YF 1963; EN 10,908; FT 276; PT 266; S1.

Universitas 17 Agustus 1945 Surabaya, Jl. Semolowaru No. 45, Surabaya, Jawa Timur; YF 1958; EN 13,809; FT 213; PT 297; Dip.; S1: Management, Economics and Development Studies, Criminal Law, Civil Law, Constitutional Law, Public Administration, Business Administration.

Universitas "45" Mataram, Jl. Anak Agung Gede Ngurah, Cakranegara, Mataram, Nusa Tenggara Barat; YF 1983; EN 2,715; FT 61; PT 167; S1.

Universitas "45" Surabaya, Jl. Mayjen Sungkono, Surabaya, Jawa Timur; YF 1985; EN 337; FT 5; PT 48; S1.

Universitas "45" Ujung Pandang, Jl. Urip Sumoharjo KM-4, Ujung Pandang, Sulawesi Selatan; YF 1986; EN 4,463; FT 105; PT 305; S1.

Universitas Abdurrachman Saleh, Jl. Sudirman No. 7, Situbondo, Jawa Timur; YF 1981; EN 621; FT 39; PT 40; S1.

Universitas Abulyatama, Jl. Blang Bintang Km. 8.5, Banda Aceh, DI Aceh; YF 1982; EN 1,064; FT 64; PT 61; Dip.; S1: Economics and Development Studies, Civil Law, Constitutional Law, Agriculture, Agricultural Socioeconomics.

Universitas Achmad Yani, Jl. Achmad Yani Km. 5.5, Banjarmasin, Kalimantan Selatan; YF 1983; EN 1,818; FT 43; PT 164; S1.

Universitas Advent Indonesia, Jl. Kantor Pos, Cipaganti, Bandung, Jawa Barat; YF 1973; EN 564; FT 42; PT 61; Dip.; S1.

Universitas Al-Chairat, Jl. Sis. Aldjufrie No. 44, Palu, Sulteng; YF 1989; EN 496, FT 30; PT 51; S1.

Universitas Al-Falah, Jl. Taman Mayangkara 2-4, Surabaya, Jawa Timur; YF 1987; EN 96; FT 15; PT 60; S1.

Universitas Al-Wasliyah, Jl. Sisingamangaraja Km. 5.5, Medan, Sumatera Utara; YF 1986; EN 250; FT 15; PT 23; S1.

Universitas Amir Hamzah, Jl. HM. Joni No. 22, Medan, Sumatera Utara; YF 1981; EN 369; FT 18; PT 76; S1.

Universitas Asahan, Jl. A. Yani, Kisaran, Sumatera Utara; YF 1986; EN 920; FT 16; PT 38; S1.

Universitas Atma Jaya Ujung Pandang, Jl. Tanjung Alang 23, Ujung Pandang, Sulawesi Selatan; YF 1980; EN 1,121; FT 32; PT 92; S1.

Universitas Bali, Jl. Kartini 83, Denpasar, Bali; YF 1982; EN 135; FT 15; PT 40; S1.

Universitas Balikpapan, Jl. Pupuk P.O. Box 335, Balikpapan, Kalimantan Timur; YF 1981; EN 450; FT 36; PT 98; S1.

Universitas Bandar Lampung, Jl. Raya Teuku Umar No. 26, Tanjungkarang, Lampung; YF 1984; EN 3,802; FT 120; PT 94; S1.

Universitas Bandung Raya, Jl. Merdeka 39-41, Bandung, Jawa Barat; YF 1986; EN 1,648; FT 84; PT 216; Dip.; S1.

Universitas Bangkalan, Ds. Telang Kamal P.O. Box 2, Bangkalan, Jawa Timur; YF 1981; EN 1,015; FT 68; PT 94; Dip.; S1.

Universitas Baptis Surabaya, Jl. Ngagel Madya I/35, Surabaya, Jawa Timur; YF 1986; EN 305; FT 27; PT 2; S1.

Universitas Bhayangkara, Jl. A. Yani, Wonocolo, Surabaya, Jawa Timur; YF 1982; EN 2,997; FT 54; PT 188; S1.

Universitas Bojonegoro, Jl. Suyitno 11, Kalirejo, Bojonegoro, Jawa Timur; YF 1981; EN 574; FT 41; PT 56; S1.

Universitas Bondowoso, Jl. Diponegoro No. 247, Bondowoso, Jawa Timur; YF 1981; EN 938; FT 42; PT 89; S1.

Universitas Borobudur Jakarta, Jl. Raya Kali Malang 1, Jaktim, DKI Jakarta; YF 1982; EN 2,282; FT 161; PT 21; S1.

Universitas Bung Hatta, Jl. Sumatera, Ulak Karang, Padang, Sumatera Barat; YF 1981; EN 9,190; FT 87; PT 283; Dip.; S1.

Universitas Cokroaminoto, Jl. Perintis Kemerdekaan, DI Yogyakarta; YF 1979; EN 473; FT 22; PT 128; S1.

Universitas Darma Persada, Jl. Jend. Sudirman Kav. 57, Jakpus, DKI Jakarta; YF 1986; EN 829; FT 50; PT 106; Dip.; S1.

Universitas Darul U.I.C. Sudirman, Jl. Diponegoro 768 Ungaran, Semarang, Jawa Tengah; YF 1982; EN 479; FT 14; PT 64; S1.

Universitas Darul'Ulum, Jl. Merdeka 29-A, Jombang, Jawa Timur; YF 1965; EN 3378; FT 243; PT 137; Dip.; S1: Criminal Law, Civil Law, Constitutional Law.

Universitas Darussalam, Jl. Raya Tulehu, Ambon, Maluku; YF 1986; EN 455; FT 13; PT 51; S1.

Universitas Dayanu Ikhsanuddin, Jl. Yos Sudarso, Baubau, Sulawesi Tenggara; YF 1982; EN 1,567; FT 43; PT 128; S1.
Universitas Dharma Agung, Jl. Bantam No. 21, Medan, Sumatera Utara; YF 1957; EN 15,810; FT 115; PT 270; Dip.: Textile Technology, Textile Machinery, Textile Industry Management, Accounting, Nursing; S1: Economics and Development Studies, Management, Accounting, Criminal Law, Civil Law, Constitutional Law, Administrative Law, Government, Journalism, Public Relations, International Relations.
Universitas Dharmawangsa, Jl. Yos Sudarso 224, Medan, Sumatera Utara; YF 1985; EN 520; FT 14; PT 43; S1.
Universitas Dr. Soetomo, Jl. Selomowaru, Surabaya, Jawa Timur; YF 1981; EN 5,806; FT 79; PT 161; S1.
Universitas Dumoga Bone, Jl. A. Yani No. 184, Bolaang Mongondow, Sulawesi Utara; YF 1984; EN 267; FT 19; PT 58; S1.
Universitas Dwijendra, Jl. Kamboja, Denpasar, Bali; YF 1982; EN 885; FT 40; PT 127; Dip.; S1.
Universitas Eka Sakti, Jl. Veteran Dalam No. 26-B, Padang, Sumatera Barat; YF 1983; EN 680; FT 40; PT 38; S1.
Universitas Flores, Jl. Sukarno No. 6-8, Ende, Nusa Tenggara Timur; YF 1980; EN 600; FT 21; PT 44; Dip.; S1.
Universitas Gajayana, Jl. Merjosari-Lowokwaru, Malang, Jawa Timur; YF 1986; EN 2,145; FT 83; PT 93; Accounting; Dip.; S1.
Universitas Graha Nusantara, Jl. Merdeka No. 2, Padang Sidempuan, Sumatera Utara; YF 1986; EN 628; FT 18; PT 69; S1.
Universitas Gresik, Jl. Arief Rahman Hakim 2-B, Gresik, Jawa Timur; YF 1981; EN 645; FT 7; PT 102; S1.
Universitas Hang Tuah, Jl. Arief Rahman Hakim 150, Surabaya, Jawa Timur; YF 1987; EN 1,021; FT 62; PT 179; Dip.; S1.
Universitas HKBP Nommensen, Jl. Dr. Sutomo No. 4-A, Medan, Sumatera Utara; YF 1954; EN 12,071; FT 102; PT 291; Dip.: Pancasila/Civics, Christian Religious Education, Curriculum and Educational Technology, Indonesian Language and Literature Education, English Language, German Language; S1: Business Management, Economics and Development Studies.
Universitas IBA-Palembang, Jl. Mayor Ruslan, Palembang, Sumatera Selatan; YF 1987; EN 699; FT 55; PT 81; S1.
Universitas Ibnu Khaldun, Jl. Pemuda Kav 97, Jakarta Timur, DKI Jakarta; YF 1956; EN 509; FT 63; PT 65; S1: Public Administration, Journalism, Public Relations.
Universitas Ibnu Khaldun, Jl. RE Martadinata 2, Bogor, Jawa Barat; YF 1961; EN 1,285; FT 60; PT 117; S1.
Universitas Iskandar Muda, Jl. S. Alaidin Machmudsyah 15, Banda Aceh, DI. Aceh; YF 1990; S1.
Universitas Islam "45," Jl. Cut Mutiah 83, Bekasi, Jawa Barat; YF 1987; EN 1,435; FT 27; PT 78; S1.
Universitas Islam Al-Azhar, Jl. Bung Hatta No. 21, Mataram, Nusa Tenggara Barat; YF 1981; EN 1,706; FT 58; PT 123; S1.
Universitas Islam As-Syafiyah Uia, Jl. Raya Jatiwaringin, Jakarta Timur, DKI Jakarta; YF 1965; EN 415; FT 41; PT 112; S1.
Universitas Islam Atthairiyah, Jl. Melayu Besar 68 Tebet, Jaksel, DKI Jakarta; YF 1984; EN 154; FT 31; PT 68; S1.
Universitas Islam Bandung, Jl. Tamansari 1, Bandung, Jawa Barat; YF 1959; EN 3,053; FT 104; PT 304; S1.
Universitas Islam Batik, Jl. KH Agus Salim 10, Surakarta, Jawa Tengah; YF 1984; EN 712; FT 27; PT 84; S1.
Universitas Islam Indonesia, Jl. Cik Ditiro No. 1, DI Yogyakarta; YF 1945; EN 9,973; FT 180; PT 348; S1: Civil Law, Commercial Law, Traditional Law, Islamic Law, Criminal Law, Constitutional Law, Business Management, Islamic Education, Islamic Judicature.
Universitas Islam Jakarta (UID), Jl. Balai Rakyat Utan Kayu, Jaktim, DKI Jakarta; YF 1951; EN 2,028; FT 62; PT 61; S1: Management, Criminal Law, Civil Law, Constitutional Law.
Universitas Islam Jember, Jl. Kyai Mojo No. 39, P.O. Box 70, Jember, Jawa Timur; YF 1984; EN 630; FT 102; PT 98; S1.

Universitas Islam Kediri, Jl. Sersan Suharmaji 10-B, Kediri, Jawa Timur; YF 1983; EN 1,189; FT 64; PT 13; S1.

Universitas Islam M. Arsyad Al-Banjari, Komplek RS. Islam, Banjarmasin, Kalimantan Selatan; YF 1982; EN 1,350; FT 26; PT 152; S1.

Universitas Islam Malang, Jl. Mayjen Haryono No. 193, Malang, Jawa Timur; YF 1980; EN 4,127; FT 111; PT 614; S1.

Universitas Islam Nusantara, Jl. Sukarno-Hatta 10, Bandung, Jawa Barat; YF 1959; EN 9,889; FT 188; PT 540; Dip.; S1.

Universitas Islam Riau, Jl. Moh. Yamin No. 29, Penkanbaru, Riau; YF 1962; EN 7188; FT 108; PT 109; Dip.; S1: Criminal Law, Civil Law, Traditional Law, Islamic Law, Constitutional Law.

Universitas Islam Sultan Agung, Jl. Raya Kaligawe Km. 4, P.O. Box 236, Semarang, Jawa Tengah; YF 1982; EN 4,344; FT 75; PT 207; S1.

Universitas Islam Sumatera Utara, Jl. Sisingamangaraja-Teladan, Medan, Sumatera Utara; YF 1952; EN 6,716; FT 131; PT 213; Dip.: Curriculum and Educational Technology; S1: Criminal Law, Civil Law, Constitutional Law, Business Management, Economics and Development Studies, Curriculum and Educational Technology.

Universitas Islam-Syekh Yusuf, Jl. Harapan II Babakan, Tangerang, Jawa Barat; YF 1966; EN 1,231; FT 36; PT 111; Dip.; S1.

Universitas Islam Syek Yusuf, Jl. Kuningan Raya 10, Mampang Pr., Jaksel, DKI Jakarta; YF 1964; EN 589; FT 10; PT 40; S1.

Universitas Jafar Ghafur, Jl. Teuku Umar, Sigli, DI Aceh; YF 1982; EN 1,675; FT 49; PT 61; Dip.; S1.

Universitas Jakarta, Jl. Pulomas Barat, Jaktim, DKI Jakarta; YF 1965; EN 991; FT 97; PT 103; S1.

Universitas Janbadra, Jl. Tentara Rakyat Mataram 57, Yogyakarta, DI Yogya; YF 1958; EN 4,329; FT 69; PT 144; S1.

Universitas Jayabaya, Jl. Jend. Achmad Yani By Pass, Jakpus, DKI Jakarta; YF 1958; EN 4,919; FT 136; PT 201; Dip.: Civil Engineering, Mechanical Engineering; S1: Criminal Law, Civil Law, Constitutional Law, Business Management, Public Administration, Accounting, International Relations, Civil Engineering, Mechanical Engineering.

Universitas Jenggala, Jl. Sekardangan, Sidoarjo, Jawa Timur; YF 1983; EN 757; FT 18; PT 78; S1.

Universitas Juanda, Kampus UNIDA, Pintu Tol Ciawi, Bogor, Jawa Barat; YF 1986; EN 638; FT 27; PT 6; S1.

Universitas Karo, Jl. Pahlawan, Kabanjahe, Sumatera Utara; YF 1986; EN 170; FT 76; PT 96; S1.

Universitas Kartini, Jl. Kalidami No. 16, Surabaya, Jawa Timur; YF 1984; EN 368; FT 19; PT 43; S1.

Universitas Katolik Dharma Cendika, Jl. Deles I/29, Surabaya, Jawa Timur; YF 1986; EN 209; FT 17; PT 33; S1.

Universitas Katolik Indonesia Atmajaya, Jl. Babarsari No. 44, DI Yogyakarta; YF 1965; EN 5,852; FT 165; PT 124; S1: Business Management, Business Administration, English Language, Educational Psychology and Counselling, Civil Engineering and Hydrology, Civil Engineering and Construction, Civil Engineering and Transportation, Architecture, Civil Law, Criminal Law, Constitutional Law; S2*.

Universitas Katolik Indonesia Atmajaya, Jl. Jend. Sudirman No. 51, Jaksel, DKI Jakarta; YF 1960; EN 6,843; FT 180; PT 409; S1: Mechanical Engineering, Business Management, Educational Psychology and Counselling, English Language, Criminal Law, Civil Law, Constitutional Law, Business Administration.

Universitas Katolik Parahyangan, Jl. Ciumbuleuit 94, Bandung, Jawa Barat; YF 1955; EN 6,394; FT 329; PT 292; S1: Accounting, Management, Economics and Development Studies, Civil Law, Criminal Law, Constitutional Law, International Law, International Relations, Administration, Public Administration, Civil Engineering, Architecture; S2*.

Universitas Katolik St. Thomas, Jl. S. Parman No. 107, Medan, Sumatera Utara; YF 1984; EN 1,972; FT 59; PT 149; S1.

Universitas Katolik Sugiyapranata, Jl. Pawiyatan Luhur IV/I, Semarang, Jawa Tengah; YF 1982; EN 3,062; FT 109; PT 223; S1.

Universitas Katolik Widya Karya, Jl. Bondowoso No. 2, Malang, Jawa Timur; YF 1982; EN 1,209; FT 28; PT 181; Dip.; S1.

Universitas Katolik Widya Mandala, Jl. Dinoyo No. 42-44, Surabaya, Jawa Timur; YF 1960; EN 3,269; FT 110; PT 72; Dip.: English Language; S1.

Universitas Katolik Widya Mandira, Jl. A. Yani No. 50-52, Kupang, Nusa Tenggara Timur; YF 1982; EN 3,731; FT 201; PT 62; Dip.; S1.
Universitas Kediri, Jl. Mastrip No. 32, Kediri, Jawa Timur; YF 1981; EN 1,552; FT 151; PT 94; S1.
Universitas Kertanegara, Jl. Budi No. 21, Cawang, Jakarta Timur, DKI Jakarta; YF 1986; EN 510; FT 26; PT 51; S1.
Universitas Khaerun, Jl. Bandara Babullah, Ternate, Maluku; YF 1964; EN 1758; FT 79; PT 33; Dip.; S1.
Universitas Klabat, Jl. Waolanda Maramis, Manado, Sulawesi Utara; YF 1965; EN 475; FT 33; PT 122; Dip.; S1.
Universitas Krisnadwipayana, Kampus Unkris Jatiwaringin P.O. Box 7774/Jat. CM, Jaktim, DKI Jakarta; YF 1952; EN 6,640; FT 215; PT 388; S1: Criminal Law, Civil Law, Constitutional Law, Business Management, Business Administration, Public Administration.
Universitas Kristen Artha Wacana, Jl. Adisucipto, Oesapa, P.O. Box 147, Kupang, Nusa Tenggara Timur; YF 1985; EN 2,047; FT 41; PT 44; Dip.; S1.
Universitas Kristen Duta Wacana, Jl. Dr. Wahidin 5-19, DI Yogyakarta; YF 1962; EN 1,946; FT 41; PT 74; S1.
Universitas Kristen Imanuel, Jl. Solo Km. 11, P.O. Box 4/YPKP, DI Yogyakarta; YF 1982; EN 620; FT 42; PT 37; S1.
Universitas Kristen Indonesia, Jl. Mayjen Sutoyo, Cawang, Jaktim, DKI Jakarta; YF 1953; EN 9,662; FT 277; PT 563; Dip.; S1: English Literature, Business Management, Criminal Law, Civil Law, International Law, Constitutional Law, Public Administrative Law.
Universitas Kristen Indonesia Maluku, Jl. Letjen DI Panjaitan, Ambon, Maluku; YF 1985; EN 516; FT 73; PT 97; S1.
Universitas Kristen Indonesia Paulus, Jl. Cendrawasih 65, Ujung Pandang, Sulawesi Selatan; YF 1963; EN 3,165; FT 105; PT 142; S1.
Universitas Kristen Indonesia Tomohon, Jl. Kakas Kasen III, Tomohon, Sulawesi Utara; YF 1965; EN 1,231; FT 26; PT 102; S1.
Universitas Kristen Jawa Timur, Jl. Semeru No. 42, Malang, Jawa Timur; YF 1980; EN 477; FT 6; PT 110; Dip.; S1.
Universitas Kristen Krida Wacana; Tanjung Duren 4, Jakbar, DKI Jakarta; YF 1967; EN 2,110; FT 76; PT 3; S1: Telecommunications Engineering, Electronic Technology for Industry, Business Management.
Universitas Kristen Maranatha, Jl. Prof. Drg. Suria Sumantri, MPH No. 65, Bandung, Jawa Barat; YF 1965; EN 2,710; FT 143; PT 298; S1: Civil Engineering, Electrical Engineering.
Universitas Kristen Petra, Jl. Siwalankerto No. 121-131, Surabaya, Jawa Timur; YF 1961; EN 3,166; FT 131; PT 173; Dip.; S1: Building Construction; S1: Architecture, English Literature, Linguistics, Construction, Transportation, Irrigation Technology.
Universitas Kristen Satya Wacana, Jl. Diponegoro 52-60, Salatiga, Jawa Tengah; YF 1956; EN 7,875; FT 329; PT 0; Dip.: History Education, English Language; S1: History Education, Pancasila/Civics, Cooperatives Education, Office Management Education, Curriculum and Educational Technology, Educational Psychology and Counselling, English Language, Criminal Law, Civil Law, Constitutional Law, Administrative Law, Law and Development, Management, Human Resource Management, Budget Management, Production Management, Planning, Banking, Labor and Manpower Studies, Institutional Development Studies, Ecology, Plant Breeding, Plant Physiology, Agricultural Communication, Agribusiness, Terrestrial Ecology, Acquatic Ecology; Environmental Microbiology, Industrial Microbiology; S2*.
Universitas Kutai Kertanegara, Jl. Turangga No. 22, Tenggarong, Kalimantan Timur; YF 1981; EN 719; FT 10; PT 126; S1.
Universitas Lancang Kuning, Jl. Yos Sudarso Km. 6 Rumbai, Pekanbaru, Riau; YF 1982; EN 2,889; FT 41; PT 87; S1.
Universitas Langlangbuana, Jl. Karapitan 116, Bandung, Jawa Barat; YF 1982; EN 2,298; FT 82; PT 155; S1.
Universitas Lumajang, Jl. Sumberejo No. 12, Lumajang, Jawa Timur; YF 1985; EN 328; FT 24; PT 44; S1.
Universitas Madura Pemekasan, Jl. Jokotole No. 43, P.O. Box 62, Pamekasan, Jawa Timur; YF 1978; EN 1,210; FT 49; PT 135; S1.

Universitas Mahaputra Mohammad Yamin, Jl. Jend. Sudirman No. 5, Solok, Sumatera Barat; YF 1986; EN 2,545; FT 41; PT 157; Dip.; S1.

Universitas Mahasaraswati Denpasar, Jl. Kamboja, Denpasar, Bali; YF 1961; EN 4,114; FT 140; PT 222; Dip.; S1.

Universitas Mahasaraswati Mataram, Jl. Kali Barantas, KRG Sukun, Mataram, Nusa Tenggara Barat; YF 1981; EN 1,614; FT 50; PT 150; S1.

Universitas Mahendradatta, Jl. Ken Arok 5, Dakdakan, Denpasar, Bali; YF 1963; EN 588; FT 53; PT 93; S1.

Universitas Malikussaleh, Jl. Teuku Cik Ditiro 9, Lhokseumawe, DI Aceh; S1.

Universitas Mayjen Sungkono, Jl. Irian Jaya No. 42, Mojokerto, Jawa Timur; YF 1981; EN 915; FT 24; PT 83; S1.

Universitas Medan Area, Jl. Kolam No. 1 Sampali, Medan, Sumatera Utara; YF 1983; EN 7,283; FT 143; PT 294; S1: Criminal Law.

Universitas Mercu Buana, Jl. Raya Meruya Selatan, Kb. Jeruk, Jakbar, DKI Jakarta; YF 1985; EN 1,058; FT 28; PT 235; Dip.; S1: Management, Accounting, Agriculture, Socioeconomics of Agriculture, Civil Engineering, Architecture, Mechanical Engineering.

Universitas Merdeka Madiun, Jl. Serayu Taman, Madiun, Jawa Timur; YF 1979; EN 1,786; FT 48; PT 78; S1.

Universitas Merdeka Malang, Jl. Terusan Raya Dieng No. 62-64, Malang, Jawa Timur; YF 1964; EN 10,478; FT 222; PT 188; Dip.; S1: Accounting, Management, Civil Engineering, Civil Law, Criminal Law, Constitutional Law, Administrative Law.

Universitas Merdeka Pasuruan, Jl. Veteran No. 68, Pasuruan, Jawa Timur; YF 1984; EN 620; FT 13; PT 95; S1.

Universitas Merdeka Ponorogo, Jl. Pacar No. 1, Ponorogo, Jawa Timur; YF 1983; EN 625; FT 49; PT 33; S1.

Universitas Merdeka Surabaya, Jl. Kalimantan No. 11, Surabaya, Jawa Timur; YF 1972; EN 917; FT 43; PT 99; S1.

Universitas Methodis Indonesia, Jl. Hang Tuah No. 8, Medan, Sumatera Utara; YF 1965; EN 1,409; FT 50; PT 88; S1.

Universitas Moh. Sroedji, Jl. Sriwijaya No. 32, Jember, Jawa Timur; YF 1981; EN 1,756; FT 33; PT 26; S1.

Universitas MPU Tantular, Jl. Cipinang Besar 2, Jaktim, DKI Jakarta; YF 1984; EN 563; FT 38; PT 79; S1.

Universitas Muhammadiyah Gresik, Jl. K.H. Kholil No. 73-A, Gresik, Jawa Timur; YF 1980; EN 138; FT 20; PT 76; S1.

Universitas Muhammadiyah Jakarta, Jl. K.H.A. Dahlan, Ciputat, Jaksel, DKI Jakarta; YF 1955; EN 3,539; FT 191; PT 243; S1: Business Management, Criminal Law, Civil Law, Constitutional Law, Social Welfare.

Universitas Muhammadiyah Jember, Jl. Karimata No. 43, Jember, Jawa Timur; YF 1981; EN 3726; FT 121; PT 228; Dip.; S1.

Universitas Muhammadiyah Lampung, Jl. Raya Teuku Umar No. 14, Tanjungkarang, Lampung; YF 1987; EN 216; FT 25; PT 23; S1.

Universitas Muhammadiyah Magelang, Jl. Tidar 21, Magelang, Jawa Tengah; YF 1964; EN 1,015; FT 41; PT 130; S1.

Universitas Muhammadiyah Makasar, Jl. Ranggong 21, Ujung Pandang, Sulawesi Selatan; YF 1963; EN 2,412; FT 99; PT 102; Dip.; S1.

Universitas Muhammadiyah Malang, Jl. Bandung No. 1, Malang, Jawa Timur; YF 1966; EN 3495; FT 433; PT 234; S1.

Universitas Muhammadiyah Mataram, Jl. K.H.A. Dachlan, Pagesangan, Mataram, Nusa Tenggara Barat; YF 1980; EN 2,853; FT 41; PT 236; Dip.; S1.

Universitas Muhammadiyah Palembang, Jl. A. Yani No. 13 Ulu, Palembang, Sumatera Selatan; YF 1979; EN 7,413; FT 139; PT 270; S1.

Universitas Muhammadiyah Palu, Jl. Letjen Suprapto, Kampus Bumi Nyiur, Palu, Sulteng; YF 1983; EN 391; FT 14; PT 110; S1.

Universitas Muhammadiyah Ponorogo, Jl. Batorokatong No. 221, Ponorogo, Jawa Timur; YF 1983; EN 870; FT 14; PT 115; S1.

Universitas Muhammadiyah Pontianak, Jl. A. Yani Komp. Perg. Muhammadiyah, Pontianak, Kalimantan Barat; YF 1989; EN-; FT 24; PT 34; S1.

Universitas Muhammadiyah Sumatera Barat, Jl. A. Karim No. 4, Bukittinggi, Sumatera Barat; YF 1975; EN 2,598; FT 58; PT 188; Dip.; S1: Criminal Law, Civil Law; Administrative Law.

Universitas Muhammadiyah Sumatera Utara, Jl. Gedung Arca No. 53, Medan, Sumatera Utara; YF 1957; EN 3,506; FT 64; PT 159; Dip.; S1.

Universitas Muhammadiyah Surabaya, Jl. Pucang Adi No. 124, Surabaya, Jawa Timur; YF 1980; EN 3,185; FT 11; PT 330; Dip.; S1.

Universitas Muhammadiyah Surakarta, Jl. Achmad Yani P.O. Box I, Surakarta, Jawa Tengah; YF 1958; EN 10,608; FT 189; PT 326; Dip.; S1.

Universitas Muhammadiyah Tap. Sel., Jl. Sultan M. Arief No. 62, Padang Sidempuan, Sumatera Utara; YF 1983; EN 1,023; FT 16; PT 120; Dip.; S1.

Universitas Muhammadiyah Yogyakarta, Jl. HOS Cokroaminoto 17, DI Yogyakarta; YF 1981; EN 2,664; FT 50; PT 144; S1.

Universitas Muria Kudus, Jl. Gondangmanis, Bae P.O. Box 53, Kudus, Jawa Tengah; YF 1980; EN 1,724; FT 55; PT 79; S1.

Universitas Muslim Indonesia, Jl. Kakatua 27, Ujung Pandang, Sulawesi Selatan; YF 1954; EN 10,540; FT 206; PT 475; S1.

Universitas Narotama, Jl. Arief Rahman Hakim 51, Surabaya, Jawa Timur; YF 1981; EN 834; FT 14; PT 127; S1.

Universitas Nasional, Jl. Sawo Manila, Pejaten Ps. Minggu, Jaksel, DKI Jakarta; YF 1949; EN 4,718; FT 144; PT 442; Dip.; S1: Management, English Literature, Indonesian Literature, Political Science, Ecology, Zoology, Botany, Mathematics, Physics.

Universitas Ngurah Rai, Jl. Padma Penatih, Denpasar, Bali; YF 1979; EN 1,761; FT 61; PT 138; S1.

Universitas Nusa Bangsa, Jl. Baru Km. 4, Cimanggu, Bogor, Jawa Barat; YF 1987; EN 92; FT 48; PT 27; S1.

Universitas Pakuan, Jl. Pakuan, P.O. Box 353, Bogor, Jawa Barat; YF 1980; EN 3,839; FT 120; PT 313; S1.

Universitas Palembang, Jl. Dharmapala No. 1-A, Palembang, Sumatera Selatan; YF 1981; EN 1,508; FT 95; PT 249; S1.

Universitas Panca Bhakti, Jl. Yos Sudarso, Pontianak, Kalimantan Barat; YF 1983; EN 1,481; FT 27; PT 134; Dip.; S1.

Universitas Panca Marga, Jl. Yos Sudarso, Pabean Dringu, Probolinggo, Jawa Timur; YF 1984; EN 651; FT 16; PT 64; S1.

Universitas Pancasakti Tegal, Jl. Pancasila No. 2, Tegal, Jawa Tengah; YF 1980; EN 2,487; FT 62; PT 92; S1.

Universitas Pancasila, Srengseng Sawah, Ps. Minggu, Jaksel, DKI Jakarta; YF 1966; EN 10,695; FT 161; PT 547; Dip.: Mechanical Engineering; S1: Management, Pharmacy, Civil Law, Criminal Law, Constitutional Law, Architecture, Civil Engineering, Mechanical Engineering, Electrical Engineering.

Universitas Panji Sakti, Jl. Pramuka 5, Singaraja, Bali; YF 1959; EN 963; FT 29; PT 81; S1.

Universitas Pasundan, Jl. Tamansari No. 6-8., Bandung, Jawa Barat; YF 1961; EN 9,329; FT 140; PT 366; Dip.; S1: Public Administration, Management.

Universitas Pawyatan Daha, Jl. Soekarno Hatta, Kediri, Jawa Timur.

Universitas Pekalongan, Jl. Tentara Pelajar 49, Pekalongan, Jawa Tengah; YF 1982; EN 609; FT 25; PT 70; S1.

Universitas Pembangunan Panca Budi, Jl. Gatot Subroto Km. 4.5, Medan, Sumatera Utara; YF 1961; EN 1,739; FT 57; PT 69; S1: Criminal Law, Civil Law.

Universitas Pendidikan Nasional, Jl. Tukat Yeh Aye, Denpasar, Bali; YF 1969; EN 2,346; FT 71; PT 38; S1: Management, Public Administration.

Universitas Pepabri Ujung Pandang, Jl. Syarief Alkadri 32, Ujung Pandang, Sulawesi Selatan; YF 1978; EN 1,100; FT 32; PT 87; S1.

Universitas Persada Indonesia "YAI," Jl. Biru Laut, Kelapa Gading, Jakarta Utara, DKI Jakarta; YF 1985; EN 853; FT 55; PT 40; S1: Management, Accounting.

Universitas PGRI Batang Garing, Kampus Universitas PGRI Batang Garing, Palangkaraya, Kalimantan Tengah; YF-; EN-; FT-; PT-; S1.

Universitas Prof. Dr. Hazarudin, SH, Jl. Jend. A. Yani No. 1, Bengkulu, Bengkulu; YF 1984; EN 1,832; FT 43; PT 96; S1.

Universitas Prof. Dr. Moestopo (Beragama), Jl. Hang Lekir I/8, Keb. Baru, Jaksel, DKI Jakarta; YF 1962; EN 2,246; FT 289; PT 77; Dip.; S1: Administration, Dentistry.

Universitas Proklamasi 45, Jl. Dagen 219, DI Yogyakarta; YF 1964; EN 1,921; FT 37; PT 82; S1.

Universitas Putra Bangsa, Jl. A. Rahman Hakim 107-109, Surabaya, Jawa Timur; YF 1985; EN 2225; FT 78; PT 194; Dip.; S1.

Universitas Respati Indonesia, Jl. Karbela Timur No. 2, Setiabudi, Jaksel, DKI Jakarta; YF 1986; EN 1,342; FT 59; PT 46; Dip.; S1.

Universitas Saburai, Jl. Pagar Alam No. 259, Bandar Lampung, Lampung; YF 1989; EN 581; FT 39; PT 69; S1.

Universitas Sahid, Jl. Dr. Soepomo 84, Jakarta Selatan, DKI Jakarta; YF 1977; EN 926; FT 20; PT 140; Dip.; S1.

Universitas Sakhyakitri Palembang, Jl. S.M. Masyur, Kebon Gede 32 Ilir, Palembang, Sumatera Selatan; YF 1980; EN 514; FT 28; PT 95; S1.

Universitas Samudra Langsa, Jl. Iskandar Muda 3-4, Langsa, DI Aceh; YF 1976; EN 3,912; FT 30; PT 169; S1.

Universitas Sarjanawiyata Tamansiswa, Jl. Kusumanegara 121, DI Yogyakarta; YF 1955; EN 5,469; FT 93; PT 152; S1.

Universitas Satya Negara Indonesia, Jl. Makmur Baru, Keb. Lama, Jakarta Selatan, DKI Jakarta; YF 1987; EN 365; FT 32; PT 72; Dip.; S1.

Universitas Sawerigading, Jl. Sembilan 24, Ujung Pandang, Sulawesi Selatan; YF 1943; EN 193; FT 25; PT 54; S1.

Universitas Siliwangi, Jl. Siliwangi 24, P.O. Box 65, Tasikmalaya, Jawa Barat; YF 1978; EN 5,555; FT 155; PT 203; Dip.; S1.

Universitas Simalungun, Jl. Sisingamangaraja, Pematang Siantar, Sumatera Utara; YF 1966; EN 3,255; FT 97; PT 115; Dip.; S1.

Universitas Singaperbangsa, Jl. Wirasaba Johar I/1A, Karawang, Jawa Barat; YF 1982; EN 971; FT 69; PT 82; S1.

Universitas Sintumu Maroso, Jl. Pulau Timor 1, Poso, Sulteng; YF 1986; EN 488; FT 47; PT 52; Dip.; S1.

Universitas Sisingamangaraja, Jl. Urip Sumoharjo No. 9, Medan, Sumatera Utara; YF 1984; EN 2,758; FT 89; PT 112; Dip.; S1.

Universitas Sisingamangaraja XII, Jl. Siborong- borong, Padang Sidempuan, Sumatera Utara; YF 1986; EN 629; FT 7; PT 17; Dip.; S1.

Universitas Slamet Riyadi, Jl. Sumpah Pemuda No. 18, Surakarta, Jawa Tengah; YF 1980; EN 4,404; FT 100; PT 187; S1.

Universitas Sunan Bonang, Jl. Dr. Wahidin Sudirohusodo, Tuban, Jawa Timur; YF 1982; EN 155; FT 6; PT 59; S1.

Universitas Sunan Giri, Jl. Citarum No. 1, Surabaya, Jawa Timur; YF 1976; EN 980; FT 27; PT 64; S1.

Universitas Surabaya, Jl. Ngagel Jaya Sel. 169, Surabaya, Jawa Timur; YF 1968; EN 6,219; FT 115; PT 321; S1: Civil Law, Criminal Law, Constitutional Law, Administrative Law, International Law, Criminal Law, Economics and Development Studies, Management; S2.

Universitas Suropati, Jl. Budi, Dewi Sartika 184A, Jaktim, DKI Jakarta; YF 1983; EN 70; FT 12; PT 25; S1.

Universitas Suryo, Jl. Jurusan Kecepu Km. 3, Ngawi, Jawa Timur; YF 1981; EN 379; FT 25; PT 45; S1.

Universitas Swadaya Gunung Jati, Jl. Cipto Mangunkusumo, Cirebon, Jawa Barat; YF 1960; EN 1,834; FT 74; PT 238; Dip.; S1.

Universitas Tabanan, Jl. Ganesya 8, Tabanan, Bali; YF 1981; EN 364; FT 40; PT 87; S1.

Universitas Taman Siswa, Jl. Taman Siswa No. 9, Padang, Sumatera Barat; YF 1987; EN 419; FT 58; PT 120; Dip.; S1.

Universitas Taman Siswa Palembang, Jl. Taman Siswa No. 261, Palembang, Sumatera Selatan; YF 1987; EN 362; FT 41; PT 64; S1.

Universitas Tarumanagara, Jl. Letjen S. Parman 1, Jakbar, DKI Jakarta; YF 1959; EN 11,604; FT 221; PT 735; Dip.: Accounting; S1: Business Management Accounting, Civil Engineering, Architecture, Criminal Law, Civil Law, International Law, Constitutional Law; S2.

Universitas Tidar Magelang, Jl. Kapten Suparman, Magelang, Jawa Tengah; YF 1979; EN 2,247; FT 48; PT 88; S1.

Universitas Timor Timur, Jl. Kaikoli, Dili, Timor Timur; YF 1986; EN 853; FT 47; PT 41; S1.

Universitas Tirtayasa, Jl. Raya Jakarta Km 4, Serang, Jawa Barat; YF 1981; EN 1,691; FT 53; PT 259; Dip.; S1.

Universitas Tridharma, Jl. Mayjen Sutoyo No. 22, Balikpapan, Kalimantan Timur; YF 1978; EN 839; FT 23; PT 94; Dip.; S1.

Universitas Tridinanti, Jl. Kapt. Marzuki 2446, Palembang, Sumatera Selatan; YF 1984; EN 3,990; FT 197; PT 194; S1.

Universitas Trisakti, Jl. Kyai Tapa, Grogol, Jakbar, DKI Jakarta; YF 1965; EN 14,319; FT 672; PT 798; Dip.; S1: Criminal Law, International Law, Civil Law, Business Management, Accounting, Civil Engineering, Architecture, Mechanical Engineering, Electrical Engineering, Dentistry; S2.

Universitas Tritunggal, Jl. Jojoran IV/2-D, Surabaya, Jawa Timur; YF 1983; EN 228; FT 9; PT 25; S1.

Universitas Trunajaya Bontang, Kampus Universitas Trunajaya, Bontang, Kalimantan Timur; YF 1990; S1.

Universitas Tulungagung, Jl. Ki Mangun Sarkoro, Beji, Tulungagung, Jawa Timur; YF 1986; EN 611; FT 24; PT 51; S1.

Universitas Tunas Pembangunan, Jl. Walanda Maramis 31, Surakarta, Jawa Tengah; YF 1980; EN 2,587; FT 63; PT 161; S1.

Universitas Veteran Republik Indonesia, Jl. Gunung Bawakaraeng 72, Ujung Pandang, Sulawesi Selatan; YF 1960; EN 5,856; FT 61; PT 149; S1: Public Administration, Pancasila/Civics, Curriculum and Educational Technology.

Universitas Wangsa Manggala, Jl. Wates Km. 10, Pos Kemusuk, Bantul, DI Yogyakarta; YF 1986; EN 1,423; FT 38; PT 62; S1.

Universitas Warmadewa, Jl. Teropong, Tg. Bungkak, Denpasar, Bali; YF 1984; EN 8,847; FT 167; PT 506; S1.

Universitas Widya Gama, Jl. Borobudur No. 12, Malang, Jawa Timur; YF 1971; EN 2,295; FT 68; PT 110; S1: Economics.

Universitas Widya Gama Mahakam, Jl. Ruhni Rahayu No. 1, Samarinda, Kalimantan Timur; YF 1985; EN 1,506; FT 41; PT 218; S1.

Universitas Widya Kartika, Jl. Dharma Husada Indah VI/1, Surabaya, Jawa Timur; YF 1986; EN 336; FT 42; PT 37; S1.

Universitas Widya Mataram, Ndalem Mangkubumen KP. I/342, DI Yogyakarta; YF 1982; EN 1,110; FT 30; PT 85; S1.

Universitas Wijaya Kusuma, Jl. Darmokali No. 58, Surabaya, Jawa Timur; YF 1981; EN 6,300; FT 55; PT 173; S1.

Universitas Wijaya Putra, Jl. Raya Benowo, Surabaya, Jawa Timur; YF 1981; EN 782; FT 31; PT 79; S1.

Universitas Wijayakusuma, Kampus Karangsalan, Purwokerto, Jawa Tengah; YF 1980; EN 2,726; FT 69; PT 179; S1.

Universitas Wiralodra, Jl. Singaraja Km. 3, P.O. Box 17, Indramayu, Jawa Barat; YF 1982; EN 2,000; FT 63; PT 92; Dip.; S1.

Universitas Wiraraja, Jl. Dr. Cipto 35, Sumenep, Jawa Timur; YF 1986; EN 406; FT 25; PT 30; S1.

Universitas Wirawasta Indonesia, Jl. Achmad Yani 23, Pulo Mas, Jaktim, DKI Jakarta; YF 1983; EN 650; FT 67; PT 67; S1.

Universitas Wisnuwardhana, Jl. Dr. Cipto No. 17, Malang, Jawa Timur; YF 1981; EN 1,388; FT 12; PT 133; Dip.; S1.

Universitas WR. Supratman, Jl. A. Rahman Hakim, Surabaya, Jawa Timur; YF 1985; EN 862; FT 4; PT 65; S1.

Universitas Yarsi, Jl. Letjen Soeprapto, Jakarta Pusat, DKI Jakarta; YF 1967; EN 965; FT 83; PT 96; Dip.; S1.

Universitas Yos Sudarso, Jl. Sonokeling No. 1, Surabaya, Jawa Timur; YF 1981; EN 474; FT 18; PT 78; S1.

Appendix C. Grading Systems and Practices in Ten Tertiary Institutions

NOTE: The information in Appendix C comes from a study presented in two papers entitled "Grading Systems and Grading Practices in Some Indonesian Public and Private Universities, Parts I and II" by Dr. Sumadi Suryabrata of the Overseas Training Office of the National Planning Agency and also Professor of Psychology, Gadjah Mada University. Information was selected and condensed with Dr. Suryabrata's permission.

Background to Study

In order to investigate grading systems and practices in Indonesian tertiary institutions, 38 institutions were surveyed between 1987 and 1990 (when the 0-4 point scale replaced the 0-10 point scale). Because of space limitations, data from only eight universities and two institutes of the 38 institutions in the original study appear here. Institutional descriptions are presented with reference to GPAs (grade point averages) earned by graduates.

The first five institutions—University of Indonesia, Bogor Institute of Agriculture, Bandung Institute of Technology, Gadjah Mada University, and Airlangga University—are the oldest tertiary institutions in Indonesia; University of North Sumatra and Hasanuddin University are the largest universities outside Java; Diponegoro University and Brawijaya University are relatively young, fast-growing universities on Java. Bandung Institute of Teacher Training and Education is the last institution described. Candidates applying for graduate degree programs abroad will probably be graduates of these institutions.

Methodology

Data Collection. The majority of the data used in this study were obtained from secondary sources, including records on academic performance of graduates, institutional regulations and catalogs, and literature and documents on the tertiary education system. In addition, interviews were conducted to verify the data obtained and to facilitate interpretation.

Unit of Analysis. The faculty is the unit of analysis. Data on departments were pooled at the faculty level.

Discussion and Conclusions

This is a preliminary study. Further research using more complete data should be carried out to assure more objective consideration of Indonesian applicants to graduate programs abroad.

If GPAs are used as a basis for making decisions about Indonesian first-degree holders, caution must be used. No general rule can be applied to all graduates of Indonesian tertiary institutions. An application should be evaluated on the basis of data on the applicant's institution, faculty, department, and institutional policy. If a minimum GPA of 3.00 is used as a cutoff mark by graduate admissions committees abroad, almost all Indonesian first-degree holders would be rejected automatically. Means of GPAs and the appropriate standard deviations appear to yield the most informative data for graduate admission purposes.

Interpretation of data from selected tertiary institutions supports the following conclusions.

1. In theory, the grading system in Indonesian tertiary institutions is not significantly different from systems used by many American universities.
2. Actual grading practices in Indonesian tertiary institutions generally deviate from the formal system.
3. Significant differences in grading practices exist among Indonesian tertiary institutions.
4. There are also marked differences in grading practices among faculties within particular institutions and among departments within particular faculties.
5. In general, GPAs tend to underestimate actual performance.

How to Read and Interpret the Institutional GPA Tables

1. The interpretation of GPAs should be based on probability theory, using the normal curve model.
2. The reference of interpretation is the 5-point scale grading system ($A = 4$, $B = 3$, $C = 2$, $D = 1$, and $E = 0$).
3. Adjustment by linear transformation must be made where necessary. For example, if a particular institution uses an 11-point scale (ranging from 10 to 0) with a passing grade of 6, the GPAs should be linearly transformed 4 points downward. Thus, a GPA of 6.53 should be interpreted as 2.53.
4. For the Bandung Institute of Technology, which uses a 5-point scale ranging from 5 to 1, the GPAs should be linearly transformed 1 point downward: a GPA of 3.21 should be interpreted as 2.21.
5. Because GPAs from one institution are not compatible with GPAs from another institution, interpretation should be based on within-group comparison, using the faculty as the unit of analysis.
6. Using a mean, $\overline{X}$, and a standard deviation, s, an approximation of the proportion of the area in the normal curve can be made. Some of the points are presented in Table C1. Thus, for example, a student with a GPA of $\overline{X}$ or higher will be in the top 50% of the group and a student with a GPA of one standard deviation above the mean ($\overline{X} + 1.00s$) will be in the top 15% of the group.

Table C.1. Proportion of Area Under the Normal Distribution Curve Corresponding to Standard Deviation

Points in the Normal Distribution Curve	Area Included (% of students receiving grades in this range)
$\overline{X}$	top 50%
$\overline{X} + .25s$	top 40%
$\overline{X} + .50s$	top 30%
$\overline{X} + .65s$	top 25%
$\overline{X} + .75s$	top 23%
$\overline{X} + .90s$	top 18%
$\overline{X} + 1.00s$	top 15%
$\overline{X} + 1.25s$	top 10%
$\overline{X} + 1.50s$	top 7%
$\overline{X} + 2.00s$	top 2%

1. University of Indonesia (Universitas Indonesia/UI)

Complete data for 1975–88 from the faculties of dentistry, mathematics and natural sciences, and economics (see below) indicated marked differences a) in GPAs earned by graduates of different faculties, b) among faculties adopting the new grading system, and c) in the teaching staff's generosity in awarding grades. The mean GPAs of medical faculty graduates ranged from 6.040 to 6.161; the standard deviations ranged from .087 to .136. The ranges of grades awarded were very narrow. Figures for dentistry ranged from 6.051 to 6.356, and .76 to .767, respectively, and for mathematics and natural sciences from 6.173 to 6.566, and from .212 to .574, respectively. Although variations between GPAs from these last faculties were somewhat wider than those for medicine, they were still too narrow to allow a fine differentiation between graduates to be made. Dentistry began calculating GPAs according to the new system in 1988, mathematics and natural sciences in 1986, and economics in 1985; public health, and law in 1983. That law began using the new system early is surprising, since generally law in Indonesia is one of the more conservative faculties. With regard to generosity in awarding grades, the faculty of public health was the most generous, with a grand mean GPA of 2.783. The least generous was law, with a grand mean GPA of only 2.091.

No	Unit	St/Year	75	76	77	78	79	80	81	82	83	84	85	86	87	88
1	Fac. Medicine	N	153	103	128	58	132	90	94	71	128	50	123			
		$\bar{X}$	6.040	6.089	6.083	6.069	6.082	6.023	6.085	6.150	6.155	6.131	6.161	2.377		
		s	0.490	0.106	0.092	0.068	0.081	0.086	0.087	0.152	0.142	0.109	0.136	0.221		
2	Fac. Dentistry	N	43	40	39	49	44	57	52	33	50	27	77	73	45	46
		$\bar{X}$	6.056	6.077	6.051	6.098	6.123	6.105	6.130	6.127	6.266	6.356	6.248	6.323	6.278	2.578
		s	0.076	0.133	0.098	0.122	0.128	0.138	0.157	0.150	0.214	0.244	0.767	0.288	0.278	0.293
3	Fac. Public Health	N									54	58	68	58	52	
		$\bar{X}$									3.081	2.980	3.008	2.025	2.802	
		s									0.112	0.131	0.201	0.255	0.232	
4	Fac. Psychology	N								36	19	14	36	31	77	34
		$\bar{X}$								6.222	6.237	6.471	2.627	2.628	2.630	2.584
		s								0.533	0.522	0.390	0.259	0.226	0.263	0.222
5	Fac. Mathematics & Natural Sciences	N	57	40	56	49	35	31	29	52	46	60	139	120	214	74
		$\bar{X}$	6.285	6.550	6.566	6.449	6.173	6.237	6.314	6.238	6.384	6.261	6.447	6.455	6.463	2.534
		s	0.212	0.408	0.532	0.574	0.338	0.352	0.365	0.314	0.434	0.285	0.552	0.328	0.361	0.316
6	Fac. Economics	N	46	45	65	46	101	74	99	181	184	162	393	255	222	47
		$\bar{X}$	6.271	6.342	6.391	6.439	6.395	6.403	6.430	6.364	6.363	6.389	6.374	2.487	2.403	2.442
		s	0.166	0.233	0.255	0.248	0.250	0.271	0.261	0.219	0.216	0.251	0.196	0.263	0.267	0.395
7	Fac. Law	N	76	64	43	43	40	101	71	127	119	106	155	160	128	
		$\bar{X}$	6.500	6.505	6.530	6.453	6.638	6.506	6.394	6.291	2.264	2.204	2.058	1.960	1.971	
		s	0.322	0.334	0.304	0.268	0.369	0.287	0.369	0.326	0.497	0.324	0.361	0.338	0.304	

2. Bogor Institute of Agriculture (Institut Pertanian Bogor/IPB)

Data were obtained from the faculties of animal husbandry and agriculture/socioeconomics for 1975–88. Data from the faculty of veterinary medicine were nearly complete. Incomplete data were available from the faculties of agricultural technology, fisheries, and forestry. The data indicate most faculties had liberal grading practices. As a result GPAs were not exceptionally low (approximately 18% of graduates in agricultural technology had GPAs of 3.0 or higher). Agriculture had similar practices. Veterinary medicine was rather generous; the overall mean GPA of its graduates was 2.621. It can be estimated that the top 10% of this group earned GPAs of 3.00 or above. Forestry was far more stringent; only 1% of its graduates obtained GPAs of 3.0 or above. Animal husbandry seems to have grading practices similar to those of forestry. In general, grading practices at IPB appear similar to those of U.S. tertiary institutions.

No	Unit	St/Year	75	76	77	78	79	80	81	82	83	84	85	86	87	88
1	Fac. Agricultural Technology	N										29	38	46	88	19
		X̄										2.970	2.843	2.865	2.820	2.738
		s										0.301	0.350	0.300	0.356	0.337
2	Fac. Fishery	N				10									11	72
		X̄				6.000									2.525	2.657
		s				0.000									0.138	0.267
3	Fac. Forestry	N	50	25	32					14	70	92	148	154	133	
		X̄	6.691	6.853	6.726					2.403	2.469	2.464	2.436	2.462	2.495	
		s	0.344	0.302	0.245					0.258	0.255	0.217	0.212	0.224	0.211	
4	Fac. Animal Husbandry	N	28	29	6	14	14	25	86	106	129	148	60	126	135	52
		X̄	6.747	6.794	6.516	2.411	2.415	2.415	2.616	2.491	2.581	2.581	2.563	2.627	2.613	2.592
		s	0.274	0.328	0.210	0.198	0.220	0.220	0.250	0.238	0.238	0.253	0.276	0.297	0.287	0.243
5	Fac. Agriculture/Soil Sciences	N	5	10	10	10	15	19	53	72	65	41	83	73	77	42
		X̄	6.882	7.016	2.446	2.544	2.528	2.594	2.540	2.428	2.567	2.608	2.590	2.595	2.576	2.560
		s	0.228	0.629	0.186	0.359	0.187	0.378	0.283	0.233	0.271	0.249	0.281	0.295	0.309	0.220
6	Fac. Agriculture/Socio Economics	N	5	15	8	23	14	36	53	101	91	97	126	113	49	76
		X̄	6.680	5.473	4.853	3.068	2.570	2.475	2.424	2.455	2.533	2.555	2.612	2.635	0.723	2.700
		s	0.453	1.901	1.947	1.448	0.219	0.221	0.195	0.224	0.231	0.224	0.262	0.266	0.300	0.256
7	Fac. Veterinary Medicine Sciences	N	10	10	10	4	9	8	10	10	10	10	10	10	10	
		X̄	6.260	6.260	6.492	3.087	2.733	2.408	2.557	2.643	2.417	2.618	2.531	2.588	2.631	
		s	0.142	0.228	0.459	0.180	0.387	0.287	0.220	0.273	0.248	0.292	0.269	0.304	0.283	

3. Bandung Institute of Technology (Institut Teknologi Bandung/ITB)

The limited data available from ITB (1985–88) presents problems because the institute uses a 0–5 scale, while other tertiary institutions use a 0–4 scale. A linear transformation, where transformed mean GPAs will have a value of 1.00 less than the original value, must be made in order to interpret this data. The table below shows ITB teaching staff were very stringent in awarding grades. If mean GPAs are linearly transformed one value down, the possibility of an ITB graduate earning a GPA of 3.00 or higher is very small. An exception is the faculty of information technology, which was the most generous, with at least 10% of its graduates earning GPAs of 3.00 or higher.

No	Unit	St/Year	85	86	87	88
1	Dept. Mathematics	N	45	17	43	26
		$\bar{X}$	3.290	3.210	3.260	3.390
		s	0.390	0.210	0.380	0.450
2	Dept. Physics	N	33	35	21	14
		$\bar{X}$	3.270	3.210	2.460	3.470
		s	0.480	0.370	0.520	0.350
3	Dept. Astronomy	N	3	1	0	0
		$\bar{X}$	3.510	3.180		
		s	0.620			
4	Dept. Geo-Physics & Meteorology	N	19	23	26	9
		$\bar{X}$	3.050	3.130	3.210	3.230
		s	0.100	0.400	0.200	0.210
5	Dept. Chemistry	N	30	31	62	42
		$\bar{X}$	3.180	3.230	3.300	3.390
		s	0.370	0.280	0.380	0.380
6	Dept. Biology	N	34	28	30	5
		$\bar{X}$	3.280		3.360	3.660
		s	0.410		0.310	0.390
7	Dept. Pharmacy	N	58	65	44	31
		$\bar{X}$	3.250		3.390	3.420
		s	0.340		0.340	0.470
8	Dept. Geology	N	48	21	70	69
		$\bar{X}$	3.170	3.130	3.280	3.120
		s	0.220	0.180	0.270	0.250
9	Dept. Mining Engineering	N	29	13	43	22
		$\bar{X}$	3.070	0.308	3.120	3.190
		s	0.130	0.220	0.200	0.320
10	Dept. Petroleum Engineering	N	25	23	31	23
		$\bar{X}$	3.270	3.210	2.460	3.470
		s	0.480	0.370	0.520	0.350
11	Dept. Chemical Engineering	N	103	77	74	26
		$\bar{X}$	3.220		3.310	3.390
		s	0.230		0.340	0.430

(continued)

No	Unit	St/Year	85	86	87	88
12	Dept. Mechanical Engineering	N	123	58	98	47
		$\bar{X}$	3.050	3.130	3.210	3.230
		s	0.100	0.400	0.200	0.210
13	Dept. Electrical Engineering	N	123	58	98	53
		$\bar{X}$	3.340	3.430	3.270	3.380
		s	0.240	0.250	0.250	0.330
14	Dept. Physics Engineering	N	70	11	64	24
		$\bar{X}$	3.110	3.160	3.270	3.330
		s	0.150	0.180	0.310	0.490
15	Dept. Industrial Engineering	N	86	61	79	25
		$\bar{X}$	3.330		3.340	3.440
		s	0.230		0.220	0.260
16	Dept. Computer Engineering	N		5	14	8
		$\bar{X}$		3.480	3.680	3.680
		s		0.480	0.260	0.390
17	Dept. Civil Engineering	N	106	67	199	72
		$\bar{X}$	3.300	3.220	0.160	0.260
		s	0.200	0.190	0.160	0.260
18	Dept. Geodesy Engineering	N	37	16	31	21
		$\bar{X}$	3.270	3.210	2.460	3.470
		s	0.480	0.370	0.520	0.350
19	Dept. Architecture Engineering	N	46	56	39	39
		$\bar{X}$	3.030		3.190	3.510
		s	0.430		0.250	0.320
20	Dept. Enviromental Engineering	N	18	15	33	17
		$\bar{X}$	3.150	3.150	3.200	3.210
		s	0.310	0.110	0.340	0.320
21	Dept. Planology Engineering	N	20	35	47	34
		$\bar{X}$	3.180		3.270	3.270
		s	0.160		0.220	0.260

4. Gadjah Mada University (Universitas Gadjah Mada/UGM)

Despite its large number of faculties, UGM supplied the most complete data. The new (letter) grading system in general shows slightly higher results when compared to the old (numerical) system. Under the old system, mean GPAs were 6 or less. The lowest mean GPA was 5.01 in law; the highest was 6.378 in letters. After the system was changed, the mean GPA was around 2.5; the lowest, 2.453, was found in social and political sciences, and the highest, 3.030, was in psychology. UGM data also showed the narrow variability of the GPAs reflected by the size of the standard deviations which were generally small; the highest was only .570.

The data indicated grading practices have been consistent over the years. Consistencies occur within each faculty. Differences between faculties, however, should be noted. Teaching staff of the faculty of geography were in general more generous graders than those in social and political sciences. Teaching staff in mathematics and natural sciences were more stringent. The most conservative group was in law, where

No	Unit	St/Year	75	76	77	78	79	80	81	82	83	84	85	86	87	88
1	Fac. Pharmacy	N							36	92	69	69	23	56		
		$\bar{X}$							2.620	2.950	2.920	2.990	2.850	2.960		
		s							0.250	0.260	0.380	0.270	0.220	0.210		
2	Fac. Geography	N	26	33	48	41	15	48	83	48	126	211	83	113	43	2
		$\bar{X}$	6.182	6.232	6.277	6.407	6.507	6.616	2.715	2.949	2.915	2.981	2.943	2.998	2.995	2.670
		s	0.153	0.169	0.246	0.224	0.200	0.305	0.179	0.235	0.309	0.185	0.189	0.211	0.245	0.110
3	Fac. Biology	N											63	93	109	
		$\bar{X}$											2.470	2.600	2.710	
		s											0.250	0.320	0.280	
4	Fac. Social and Political Sciences	N	47	51	75	60	58	102	170	180	146	105	170	249	273	37
		$\bar{X}$	5.908	6.153	6.126	6.094	6.222	2.456	2.492	2.543	2.541	2.600	2.689	2.742	2.768	2.729
		s	0.155	0.202	0.212	0.154	0.208	0.215	0.282	0.280	0.278	0.280	0.200	0.261	0.288	0.156
5	Fac. Letters	N	15	13	17	19	30	32	52	54	68	102	119	93	126	14
		$\bar{X}$	6.234	6.305	6.378	6.183	2.393	2.458	2.709	2.665	2.657	2.696	2.678	2.755	2.788	2.654
		s	0.325	0.367	0.265	0.168	0.485	0.312	0.359	0.265	0.314	0.316	0.321	0.323	0.269	0.218
6	Fac. Mathematics and Natural Sciences	N	3	1	1	3	4	5	10	27	47	52	62	100	117	19
		$\bar{X}$	5.920	5.900	5.800	2.660	2.835	2.560	2.564	2.564	2.492	2.544	2.542	2.560	2.458	2.554
		s	0.000	0.000	0.000	0.150	0.044	0.160	0.238	0.277	0.287	0.343	0.325	0.331	0.320	1.154

(continued)

under the old grading system the grand mean GPA was less than 6.0, and under the new system the grand mean was less than 2.50. Other faculties with practices similar to law are animal husbandry, mathematics and natural sciences, and veterinary medicine. Faculties of psychology, economics, letters, forestry, and dentistry were more liberal than the above-mentioned faculties. The mean GPAs of graduates of these faculties were somewhat higher, ranging from 2.50 to 3.00.

The data suggest the results of grading practices at UGM were not as expected, possibly because the grading system was not applied according to the directives of both the university and the Directorate General of Higher Education. The GPAs of graduates were generally low, since most teaching staff tended to assign low grades to their students. However, considering UGM regularly admits only the top 5% of applicants for undergraduate admission, the low GPAs probably do not reflect the real ability or actual performance of the students.

No	Unit	St/Year	75	76	77	78	79	80	81	82	83	84	85	86	87	88
7	Fac. Philosophy	N												60	27	
		$\bar{X}$												2.600	2.800	
		s												0.250	0.380	
8	Fac. Economics	N											169	141	226	72
		$\bar{X}$											2.670	2.670	2.730	2.610
		s											0.280	0.300	0.300	0.270
9	Fac. Psychology	N	27	27	37	38	62	62	40	54	73	68	48	56	50	17
		$\bar{X}$	6.180	3.030	2.440	2.420	2.350	2.510	2.780	2.980	2.880	2.900	2.900	2.930	3.000	3.030
		s	0.230	1.400	0.670	0.230	0.190	0.330	0.320	0.220	0.200	0.200	0.240	0.220	0.230	0.250
10	Fac. Law	N	97	100	96	60	74	73	119	113	27	17	3	3		
		$\bar{X}$	5.960	5.970	6.000	5.980	5.950	5.910	5.950	5.970	5.970	5.930	5.890	5.970		
		s	0.150	0.170	0.160	0.150	0.400	0.120	0.140	0.150	0.150	0.300	0.090	0.080		
		N								120	175	216	197	213	155	58
		$\bar{X}$								2.440	2.390	0.470	2.440	2.510	2.490	2.530
		s								0.310	0.340	0.440	0.400	0.460	0.360	0.300
11	Fac. Forestry	N	75	86	90					23	38	48	82	58	82	33
		$\bar{X}$	6.200	6.210	6.240					2.980	2.790	2.930	2.980	2.950	2.740	2.540
		s	0.260	0.290	0.270					0.510	0.260	0.000	0.330	0.350	0.370	0.270
12	Fac. Medicine	N	90	124	118	104	122	86	114	176	78	95	143	140	150	35
		$\bar{X}$	6.140	6.130	6.360	6.160	6.070	6.150	6.020	6.130	2.710	2.550	2.500	2.530	2.510	2.190
		s	0.150	0.150	0.170	0.200	0.210	0.360	0.240	0.420	0.300	0.310	0.290	0.340	0.360	0.080

(continued)

4. Gadjah Mada University (Universitas Gadjah Mada/UGM) (continued)

No	Unit	St/Year	75	76	77	78	79	80	81	82	83	84	85	86	87	88
13	Fac. Dentistry	N	16	77	61	21	60	42	62	92	67	61	72	93	105	36
		X̄	64.310	63.210	63.410	63.530	64.180	2.420	2.440	2.730	2.690	2.740	2.810	2.830	2.670	2.550
		s	2.700	1.830	2.300	1.580	1.850	0.160	0.170	0.260	0.160	0.170	0.250	0.290	0.320	0.330
14	Fac. Veterinary Medicine	N					61	70	57	49	65	80	90	100	105	36
		X̄					2.210	2.400	2.420	1.980	2.360	2.590	2.480	2.580	2.460	2.510
		s					0.150	0.240	0.230	0.260	0.370	0.400	0.350	0.340	0.400	0.320
15	Fac. Agriculture	N	80	77	44	86	61	69	192	120	135	161	143	164	101	13
		X̄	2.310	2.560	2.700	2.900	2.900	2.970	2.650	2.560	2.620	2.790	2.730	2.630	2.780	2.930
		s	0.220	0.370	0.310	0.330	0.300	0.230	0.240	0.290	0.310	0.290	0.310	0.290	0.270	0.210
16	Fac. Agricultural Technology	N	19	31	39	50	113	55								
		X̄	6.040	6.260	6.260	6.320	6.250	6.140								
		s	0.200	0.290	0.200	0.340	0.190	0.150								
		N					15	42	118	97	126	97	67	111	65	20
		X̄					3.260	3.200	3.140	3.050	2.950	2.950	2.980	3.060	2.750	2.560
		s					0.190	0.210	0.270	0.310	0.250	0.250	0.300	0.320	0.350	0.300
17	Fac. Animal Husbandry	N	26	74	66	59	44	30	120	62	111	127	74	93	89	17
		X̄	5.920	6.000	6.040	6.280	6.430	2.430	2.470	2.530	2.570	2.510	2.490	2.450	2.480	2.570
		s	0.310	0.500	0.390	0.370	0.420	0.160	0.210	0.200	0.270	0.290	0.250	0.240	0.250	0.300
18	Fac. Engineering	N	46	43	36	77	106	217	151	168	172	139	337	217	249	52
		X̄	6.070	5.998	6.104	6.127	6.170	6.170	2.554	2.532	2.514	2.571	2.536	2.522	2.593	2.628
		s	0.450	0.748	0.155	0.180	0.188	0.463	0.199	0.251	0.202	0.295	0.181	0.252	0.244	0.281

5. Airlangga University (Universitas Airlangga/UNAIR)

Data from Airlangga faculties show that, under the old system, pharmacy used a 100-point scale, although GPAs ranged only in the 60s. If the means and respective standard deviations of GPAs of these graduates are adjusted by moving the decimal one digit to the left, the GPAs are then comparable to those awarded by other faculties. The generally conservative faculty of law was the first to change to the new grading system; the most conservative faculty appears to be medicine, which used the old grading system until 1986.

A common feature reflected in the GPAs is the narrow range of grades awarded. Under the old system, the standard deviations of GPAs ranged from .062 to .567 in medicine, from .030 to .153 in dentistry, from .026 to .035 in pharmacy, from .150 to .386 in veterinary medicine, and from .093 to .170 in law. In economics, the range was not so narrow. In 1978 the GPAs awarded had a mean of 6.261 and a standard deviation of .725; the figures were 6.200 and .877, respectively, in 1980. Even with the new grading system, the tendency to assign grades within a narrow range persisted. In pharmacy, for example, the standard deviations of GPAs ranged from .206 to .310, in law from .053 to .338. Data also indicated a general tendency to assign low grades. Observing the mean GPAs and the r respective standard deviations, the possibility of a graduate earning a GPA of 3.0 or higher is very small.

No	Unit	St/Year	75	76	77	78	79	80	81	82	83	84	85	86	87	88
1	Fac. Medicine	N	120	100	73	104	101	129	135	140	104	100	57	180		
		$\bar{X}$	6.064	6.060	6.037	6.037	6.037	6.025	6.048	6.038	6.032	6.077	8.082	6.061		
		s	0.078	0.085	0.062	0.066	0.067	0.058	0.071	0.056	0.567	0.114	0.107	0.077		
2	Fac. Dentistry	N	37	72	93	90	76	52	67	67	124	107	101	90	96	69
		$\bar{X}$	6.042	6.019	6.014	6.012	6.008	6.006	6.019	6.016	6.038	6.127	6.163	6.253	6.177	2.880
		s	1.586	0.047	0.047	0.042	0.031	0.030	0.058	0.053	0.063	0.130	0.271	0.234	0.153	1.318
3	Fac. Economics	N	42	68	72	69	62	49	145	241	109	120	164	161	98	40
		$\bar{X}$	6.040	6.448	6.410	6.261	6.323	6.200	6.314	6.220	2.758	2.426	2.468	2.421	2.475	2.402
		s	1.586	0.194	0.157	0.725	0.202	0.877	0.518	0.116	0.243	0.211	0.271	0.280	0.339	0.368
4	Fac. Pharmacy	N	24	24	29	13	35	42	28	26	20	15	16	66	79	55
		$\bar{X}$	62.167	62.500	63.793	63.077	64.686	64.738	63.571	63.571	2.388	2.379	2.269	2.441	2.295	2.299
		s	3.091	2.582	2.696	2.556	3.258	3.230	3.300	3.463	0.310	0.348	0.245	0.329	0.253	0.206
5	Fac. Mathematics and Natural Science	N												20	44	4
		$\bar{X}$												2.684	2.482	2.517
		s												0.282	0.271	0.379
6	Fac. Social and Political Science	N								15	13	29	23	30	17	42
		$\bar{X}$								3.045	2.991	2.902	2.817	2.823	2.921	2.771
		s								0.376	0.342	0.367	0.353	0.385	0.379	0.360
7	Fac. Veterinary Medicine	N		3	13	21	20	16	22	42	34	60	48	76	114	44
		$\bar{X}$		6.567	6.346	6.309	6.280	6.375	6.304	6.352	6.300	6.225	6.189	6.584	2.395	2.434
		s		0.386	0.213	0.148	0.150	0.222	0.136	0.211	0.251	0.197	0.240	0.358	0.322	0.321
8	Fac. Law	N	48	40	89	73	33	171	217	141	125	137	183	190	219	81
		$\bar{X}$	5.892	5.907	5.977	6.055	2.057	2.041	2.076	2.107	2.235	2.277	2.387	2.332	2.320	2.358
		s	0.170	0.134	0.141	0.093	0.068	0.053	0.086	0.118	0.249	0.300	0.338	0.303	0.308	0.274

6. University of North Sumatra (Universitas Sumatera Utara/USU)

Five faculties started using the new grading system in 1975. From 1975–84 the faculty of dentistry awarded the same grades to all graduates of the same year. Under the old system three faculties used a 100-point scale. The table below also shows students' tendencies to earn low GPAs. For example, for 14 years the highest mean GPA in the faculty of engineering was 2.299 with a standard deviation of .180 (1986). This indicates that no engineering graduates achieved a GPA of 3.0 or above. The faculties of medicine, dentistry, agriculture, and economics also tended to show low GPAs when they changed to the new grading system.

No	Unit	St/Year	75	76	77	78	79	80	81	82	83	84	85	86	87	88
1	Fac. Medicine	N	152	132	130	255	119	92	127	90	64	72	48	147		
		$\bar{X}$	55.855	56.212	56.269	56.370	60.000	60.000	59.991	60.000	56.230	57.640	2.037	2.020		
		s	1.883	2.143	2.176	2.231	0.000	0.000	1.176	0.000	2.154	2.496	0.043	0.036		
2	Fac. Dentistry	N	33	27	50	40	43	37	48	23	25	38	7	30	52	9
		$\bar{X}$	57.000	60.000	62.000	61.000	59.000	58.000	61.000	62.000	61.000	62.000	2.379	2.266	2.341	2.333
		s	0.000	0.000	0.000	0.000	0.000	0.000	0.000	0.000	0.000	0.000	0.095	0.123	0.297	0.147
3	Fac. Engineering	N	55	104	95	127	110	149	217	181	234	306	329	206	354	21
		$\bar{X}$	2.081	2.148	2.191	2.180	2.187	2.190	2.171	2.198	2.193	2.147	2.146	2.299	2.224	2.293
		s	0.210	0.101	0.140	0.095	0.104	0.108	0.118	0.119	0.117	0.115	0.146	0.180	0.181	0.143
4	Fac. Agriculture	N	53	57	103	76	131	34	41	80	83					
		$\bar{X}$	60.750	62.980	64.180	65.290	65.950	62.440	2.398	2.336	2.334					
		s	1.460	2.153	2.328	2.328	0.000	1.285	0.180	0.204	0.181					
5	Fac. Mathematics & Natural Science	N	9	19	24	31	51	47	38	74	94	198	76	85		
		$\bar{X}$	2.542	2.468	2.569	2.623	2.569	2.615	2.780	2.720	2.679	2.613	2.576	2.447		
		s	0.539	0.181	0.158	0.201	0.232	0.232	0.203	0.251	0.225	0.225	0.261	0.192		
6	Fac. Economics	N	30	24	36	63	30	21	38	30	30	59	58	34	77	43
		$\bar{X}$	63.600	59.910	62.269	62.610	61.790	62.800	62.340	62.020	63.530	63.340	2.574	2.475	2.558	2.602
		s	1.586	1.080	1.485	1.577	1.238	1.233	1.260	1.260	1.008	1.296	0.048	0.220	0.167	0.169
7	Fac. Letters	N											54	75	82	108
		$\bar{X}$											2.631	2.754	2.650	2.655
		s											0.333	0.340	0.315	0.300

7. Hasanuddin University (Universitas Hasanuddin/UNHAS)

Complete data were obtained from the faculties of agriculture and letters. Somewhat less complete data were available from the faculties of animal husbandry, and mathematics and natural sciences.

All faculties at UNHAS began using the new grading system for 1981 graduates (except for an mal husbandry, which began in 1980). Grading practices varied greatly under the old system. Two faculties, medicine and law, awarded the same grades to all graduates. When these faculties changed to the new system, the variation became smaller, and similarities between faculties became more apparent.

Data shows the faculty of public health was the most generous grader. The overall mean GPA was 2.961 with standard deviations ranging from .186 to .275. The next most generous was dentistry, where the overall mean GPA during a six-year period was 2.784 with standard deviations ranging from .153 to .502. The third most generous was animal husbandry. During an eight-year period the overall mean GPA was 2.682 with standard deviations ranging from .129 to .328. The most stringent grading was found in medicine, where the grand mean GPA for graduates during a seven-year period was 2.243 with standard deviations ranging from .132 to .502. It is clear that differences between faculties were significant. Despite differences between faculties, consistency across years within each faculty is also significant. It can be expected that this consistency will prevail in the coming years.

No	Unit	St/Year	75	76	77	78	79	80	81	82	83	84	85	86	87	88
1	Fac. Medicine	N		30	30	30	30	30	60	90	59	18	98	94		
		$\bar{X}$		6.000	6.000	6.000	6.000	6.000	2.104	2.147	2.246	2.379	2.352	2.377		
		s		0.000	0.000	0.000	0.000	0.000	0.237	0.132	0.209	0.212	0.168	0.221		
2	Fac. Dentistry	N				10				17	9	25	21	24	15	
		$\bar{X}$				6.000				2.827	2.817	2.867	2.621	2.858	2.716	
		s				0.000				0.153	0.205	0.226	0.502	0.263	0.248	
3	Fac. Public Health	N										120	164	161	98	
		$\bar{X}$										2.426	2.468	2.421	2.475	
		s										0.211	0.271	0.280	0.339	
4	Fac. Agriculture	N	21	18	23	48	58	38	70	125	117	186	398	265	191	
		$\bar{X}$	62.167	62.500	63.793	63.077	64.686	64.738	63.571	63.571	2.388	2.379	2.269	2.441	2.295	
		s	3.091	2.582	2.696	2.556	3.258	3.230	3.300	3.463	0.310	0.348	0.245	0.329	0.253	
5	Fac. Mathematics and Natural Sciences	N	12	18	29	26	21	31	5			5	59	97	58	5
		$\bar{X}$	6.167	6.322	6.624	6.552	6.479	6.535	6.416			2.596	2.594	2.539	2.576	2.614
		s	0.373	0.448	0.430	0.378	0.448	0.267	0.219			0.231	0.195	0.314	0.349	0.144
6	Fac. Economics	N					131	56	238	96	232	260	546	507	288	
		$\bar{X}$					6.335	6.506	2.299	2.258	2.229	2.206	2.200	2.210	2.304	
		s					0.330	0.409	0.200	0.089	0.071	0.030	0.031	0.232	0.206	

No	Unit	St/Year	75	76	77	78	79	80	81	82	83	84	85	86	87	88
7	Fac. Social and Political Sciences	N							65	63	59	59	215	330	340	
		X̄							2.444	2.406	2.258	2.792	2.551	2.540	2.689	
		s							0.209	0.292	0.089	2.418	0.292	0.296	0.379	
8	Fac. Law	N	36	32	80									146	274	
		X̄	5.892	5.907	5.977									2.592	2.138	
		s	0.170	0.134	0.141									0.415	0.297	
9	Fac. Letters	N	7	7	8	19	28	7	8	22	21	30	107	85	98	
		X̄	6.571	6.286	6.250	6.421	6.500	6.571	2.041	2.255	2.298	2.455	2.560	2.614	2.571	
		s	0.495	0.488	0.433	0.494	0.681	0.495	0.356	0.536	0.538	0.458	0.429	0.303	0.366	
10	Fac. Animal Husbandry	N	14		28	19	27	44	78	65	60	38	84	43	46	
		X̄	6.695		6.718	7.484	6.503	2.576	2.697	2.757	2.739	2.814	2.711	2.579	2.643	
		s	0.501		0.000	4.143	0.313	0.203	0.129	0.163	0.142	0.244	0.231	0.306	0.328	
11	Fac. Engineering	N	12	27	28						49		44	244	387	
		X̄	6.212	6.088	0.050						2.119		2.235	2.406	2.360	
		s	0.296	0.177	0.217						0.244		0.334	0.316	0.309	

8. Diponegoro University (Universitas Diponegoro/UNDIP)

The faculties of animal husbandry, law, and economics supplied complete data for 1975–84. Mathematics and natural sciences provided data only from 1982.

Data indicate some faculties started using the new system in 1980. During the transition period, 1980–84, some faculties used both systems. Mathematics and natural sciences is still using both systems. Medicine was the most lenient grader; the mean GPA in 1986 was very high, 3.034. In contrast, social and political science seemed to be the strictest. In 1980 the mean GPA was 2.066. The standard deviations were usually small. The standard deviation of GPAs in medicine was zero, because the same grades were awarded to all graduates.

	Unit	St/Year	75	76	77	78	79	80	81	82	83	84	85	86	87	88	89
1	Fac. Animal Husbandry	N	16	14	34	18	43	35	95	46	19	10	13	13		1	
		X̄	6.317	6.335	6.330	6.361	6.339	6.335	6.342	6.320	6.257	6.286	6.213	6.317		6.356	
		s	0.057	0.068	0.090	0.139	0.130	0.131	0.129	0.100	0.097	0.081	0.677	0.169		0.000	
		N							14	54	77	62	120	291	105	75	74
		X̄							2.323	2.285	2.308	2.271	2.331	2.308	2.375	2.440	2.584
		s							0.183	0.198	0.187	0.173	0.250	0.224	0.231	0.268	0.275
2	Fac. Medicine	N		82	97	165	101	92	64	111	83	64	64	90	91	115	151
		X̄		6.000	6.000	6.000	6.000	6.000	6.200	6.200	6.243	3.000	6.070	3.034	3.033	2.852	2.722
		s		0.000	0.000	0.000	0.000	0.000	0.000	0.000	0.239	0.000	0.317	0.180	0.180	0.355	0.448
3	Fac. Law	N	17	34	69	104	84	119	131	171	135	121	243	279	257	91	268
		X̄	6.222	6.238	6.292	6.319	6.331	6.281	6.487	6.407	2.333	2.217	2.287	2.304	2.449	2.612	2.674
		s	0.241	0.178	0.241	0.256	0.271	0.251	0.319	0.378	0.250	0.243	0.255	0.256	0.294	0.303	0.352
4	Fac. Mathematics and Natural Sciences	N								16	9	12	11	10	3	5	1
		X̄								6.482	6.318	6.326	6.196	6.196	6.197	6.126	6.000
		s								0.122	0.131	0.102	0.117	0.123	0.140	0.048	0.000
		N									3	8	14	13	15	33	18
		X̄									3.110	2.336	2.331	2.247	2.252	2.347	2.382
		s									0.236	0.122	0.134	0.229	0.322	0.279	0.284
5	Fac. Engineering	N		52	61	92	88	104	163	196	152	166	162	173	206	258	210
		X̄		6.518	6.077	6.505	6.629	6.222	2.478	2.486	2.257	2.321	2.307	2.344	2.338	2.512	2.479
		s		0.309	0.290	0.231	0.229	0.242	0.193	0.190	0.118	0.116	0.131	0.171	0.166	0.204	0.255

No	Unit	St/Year	75	76	77	78	79	80	81	82	83	84	85	86	87	88	89
6	Fac. Letters	N				2		5	4	4	11	1					
		X̄				6.250		6.540	6.360	6.500	6.277	6.000					
		s				0.000		0.206	0.207	0.212	0.284	0.000					
		N						2	8	15	31	31	45	42	56	80	97
		X̄						2.000	2.375	2.167	2.316	2.471	2.487	2.554	2.647	2.548	2.600
		s						0.000	0.331	0.236	0.322	0.387	0.375	0.292	0.310	0.272	0.358
7	Fac. Social and Political Sciences	N		39	38	74	95	80	19								
		X̄		6.269	6.147	6.146	6.136	6.214	6.137								
		s		0.365	0.217	0.339	0.271	0.346	0.200								
		N						22	69	100	128	87	93	106	133	89	123
		X̄						2.066	2.185	2.077	2.159	2.336	2.241	2.297	2.334	2.334	2.427
		s						0.272	0.292	0.321	0.327	0.317	0.310	0.277	0.281	0.289	0.295
8	Fac. Economics	N	9	5	4	17	48	39	64	111	95	8	26	2			
		X̄	6.050	6.048	6.203	6.088	6.098	6.093	6.108	6.099	6.077	6.029	6.014	6.020			
		s	0.065	0.201	0.081	0.106	0.132	0.174	0.125	0.089	0.089	0.095	0.076	0.080			
		N										2	56	164	255	291	133
		X̄										3.000	2.412	2.403	2.358	2.242	2.386
		s										0.140	0.301	0.294	0.289	0.294	0.335

9. Brawijaya University (Universitas Brawijaya/UNIBRAW)

UNIBRAW did not provide complete data about the old grading system, except in the faculties of economics and engineering. Some faculties documented not GPAs, but only the number of graduates each year. After UNIBRAW changed to the new grading system, each faculty began to record more data on graduates.

The highest mean GPA, 2.998 with a standard deviation of .247, was found in economics in 1985. Looking only at this figure, it can be easily estimated that the proportion of graduates obtaining a GPA of at least 3.0 would be about 49%. However, the overall data would tell a different story. There would probably be far fewer graduates obtaining a GPA of 3.0 or higher.

No	Unit	St/Year	75	76	77	78	79	80	81	82	83	84	85	86	87	88	89
1	Fac. Agriculture	N	17	28	56	65	79	51	96	251	136	94	86	130	40	161	77
		$\bar{X}$										2.933	2.783	2.676	2.69	2.774	2.771
		s															
2	Fac. Animal Husbandry	N						5	30	37	44	140	49	101	81	97	91
		$\bar{X}$											2.544	2.488	2.608	2.670	2.653
		s											0.279	0.277	0.294	0.255	0.252
3	Fac. Medicine	N	2	28	53	103	136	45	71	40	52	73	83	94	68	21	10
		$\bar{X}$															
		s															
		N													56	83	66
		$\bar{X}$													2.442	2.372	2.359
		s													0.207	0.228	0.144
4	Fac. Social and Political Sciences	N										18	202	339	267	200	298
		$\bar{X}$										2.822	2.565	2.463	1.500	2.552	2.615
		s										0.216	0.297	0.295	0.319	0.276	0.276

No	Unit	St/Year	75	76	77	78	79	80	81	82	83	84	85	86	87	88	89
5	Fac. Law	N						10	30	58	113	240	267	270	202	142	227
		$\bar{X}$										2,670	2,437	2,425	2,402	2,476	2,661
		s										0,000	0,187	0,196	0,225	0,214	0,245
6	Fac. Fishery	N	6	4	13	12	10	16	22	17	28	64	43	68	40	89	85
		$\bar{X}$											2,624	2,628	2,719	2,717	2,713
		s											0,312	0,294	0,289	0,212	0,226
7	Fac. Economics	N	42	42	58	77	65	123	197	258	180	188	15				
		$\bar{X}$	6,042	6,066	6,056	6,050	6,030	6,044	6,093	6,015	6,051	6,010	6,283				
		s	0,123	0,090	0,082	0,092	0,097	0,138	0,148	0,094	0,169	0,186	0,232				
		N									1	122	133	193	204	217	201
		$\bar{X}$									2,000	2,363	2,998	2,450	2,255	2,534	2,475
		s									0,000	0,272	0,247	1,217	0,280	1,562	0,319
8	Fac. Engineering	N	11	15	24	28	30	22	42	119	113	149	170	322	279	211	161
		$\bar{X}$	6,385	6,327	6,249	6,344	6,249	6,317	6,352	2,387	2,247	2,281	2,332	2,267	2,318	2,420	2,525
		s	0,201	0,179	0,170	0,140	0,175	0,176	0,139	0,137	0,150	0,175	0,255	0,204	0,238	0,241	0,283

10. Bandung Institute of Teacher Training and Education (Institut Keguruaan dan Ilmu Pengetahuan/IKIP Bandung)

IKIP Bandung, established in 1954, has produced over 11,000 *sarjana* degree graduates. When IKIP Bandung used the old grading system, mean GPAs of graduates ranged from 4.95 to 7.14, and standard deviations from .17 to 2.09. After IKIP Bandung changed to the new grading system, the figures ranged from 2.25 to 2.77 and from .13 to .34, respectively. Data in the table below shows that all faculties (except for sports and health education) began using the new system in 1982. This kind of uniformity is rarely found in Indonesian tertiary institutions. Under the new grading system, the faculties of social science education, general education, letters and fine arts education, and technological and vocational education show approximately the same GPA level. The overall mean GPA awarded by these four faculties was 2.485, 2.562, 2.474, and 2.529, respectively. Mathematics and science education was somewhat more stringent; the overall mean GPA of graduates of this faculty was 2.430. Even more stringent was sports and health education, with an overall mean GPA of 2.313. The grading practices do not seem significantly different from those of many U.S. universities. However, the reluctance to award high grades persisted, particularly in mathematics and science education, and sports and health education.

No	Unit	St/Year	75	76	77	78	79	80	81	82	83	84	85	86	87	88
1	Fac. Social Science Education	N	27	47	53	47	77	82	102	7	592	442	294	383	396	
		$\bar{X}$	6.740	6.450	6.550	6.490	6.510	6.610	4.950	2.460	2.420	2.410	2.500	2.530	2.590	
		s	0.590	0.240	0.310	0.240	0.300	0.330	2.090	0.290	0.240	0.280	0.280	0.290	0.280	
2	Fac. Education	N	27	23	24	44	69	130	115	120	341	388	370	442	282	
		$\bar{X}$	6.770	6.590	6.530	6.480	6.470	6.660	6.460	2.410	2.560	2.560	2.610	2.630	2.600	
		s	0.610	0.410	0.170	0.420	0.350	0.520	0.360	0.340	0.250	0.260	0.220	0.250	0.270	
3	Fac. Letters and Fine Arts Education	N	12	28	34	15	66	42	61		187	358	148	336	233	
		$\bar{X}$	7.140	6.720	6.970	6.570	6.520	6.650	6.790		2.440	2.380	2.450	2.530	2.570	
		s	0.520	0.620	0.560	0.360	0.320	0.360	0.450		0.320	0.290	0.330	-0.330	0.340	
4	Fac. Technological and Vocational Education	N	18	6	26	39		108	99		45	23	194	204	120	
		$\bar{X}$	6.550	6.490	6.830	6.750		6.390	6.420		2.770	2.670	2.500	2.460	2.520	
		s	0.460	0.400	0.510	0.520		0.400	0.370		0.200	0.280	0.260	0.250	0.310	
5	Fac. Mathematics and Science Education	N	15	11	23	23	23	62	30	75	115	191	104	115	152	
		$\bar{X}$	6.530	6.720	6.580	6.770	6.560	6.530	6.460	2.510	2.450	2.380	2.370	2.470	2.400	
		s	0.540	0.420	0.470	0.500	0.410	0.410	0.410	0.310	0.240	0.250	0.240	0.340	0.300	
6	Fac. Sports and Health Education	N				5		8	6				9	152	127	
		$\bar{X}$				6.890		7.220	6.580				2.520	2.340	2.350	
		s				0.260		0.570	0.460				0.150	0.230	0.250	

Appendix D. Sample Documents

SMA — 88	**DEPARTEMEN** **PENDIDIKAN DAN KEBUDAYAAN**	**Panitia EBTANAS** **1987/1988**

MENGESAHKAN

No. ..../R.SMA/SR ..../88

Salinan / fotocopi sesuai dengan aslinya

PANITIA EBTANAS
Tanggal _____

RAYON SEKOLAH MENENGAH UMUM TINGKAT ATAS SMA 3 Muhammadiyah

SUB RAYON .... Kebayoran Baru,

DAFTAR NILAI
EVALUASI BELAJAR TAHAP AKHIR NASIONAL MURNI
SEKOLAH MENENGAH UMUM TINGKAT ATAS (SMA)

Yang bertanda tangan di bawah ini Ketua Panitia EBTANAS Rayon SMA Sub Rayon .... NIP.

menerangkan bahwa:

N a m a	:	Student's name
Tempat dan Tanggal Lahir	:	Student's place and date of birth
Nomor Peserta	:	Student's registration number
Sekolah Asal	:	Name of school
Program	:	Ilmu-ilmu Fisik

telah mengikuti Evaluasi Belajar Tahap Akhir Nasional yang diselenggarakan dari tanggal .... s.d. .... berdasarkan Keputusan Kepala Kantor Wilayah Departemen Pendidikan dan Kebudayaan Propinsi .... No. .... Tanggal ....
dengan nilai sebagai berikut:

No.	Mata Pelajaran	Nilai Grades received	
		dengan angka	dengan huruf
1.	Pendidikan Moral Pancasila	723	tujuh dua tiga
2.	Bahasa dan Sastra Indonesia	617	enam satu tujuh
3.	Matematika	490	empat sembilan nol
4.	Biologi	600	enam nol nol
5.	Fisika	305	tiga nol lima
6.	Kimia	267	dua enam tujuh
7.	Bahasa Inggris	658	enam lima dilapan
	Jumlah	3660	tiga enam enam nol

.... 1988
Ketua Panitia EBTANAS Rayon SMA
Sub Rayon ....

Signature and civil service registration
number of examination committee head

NIP ....

Document 2.1. Upper Secondary School Leaver's Examination Results Certificate.

147

No. .... OC oh 0000000

DEPARTEMEN PENDIDIKAN DAN KEBUDAYAAN
REPUBLIK INDONESIA

Document name **SURAT TANDA TAMAT BELAJAR**

SEKOLAH MENENGAH UMUM TINGKAT ATAS
(S M A)

Yang bertanda tangan di bawah ini, Kepala Sekolah Menengah Umum
Tingkat Atas .... school name ....
di .... school address ....,
menerangkan bahwa

student's name
....

lahir pada tanggal .... birthdate .... di
.... birthplace ...., anak father/mother's name
...., telah

b e r h a s i l

dalam evaluasi belajar tahap akhir guna memperoleh Surat Tanda Tamat Belajar
Sekolah Menengah Umum Tingkat Atas, yang diselenggarakan berdasarkan
Keputusan Kepala Kantor Wilayah Departemen Pendidikan dan Kebudayaan
Propinsi ... province name ....
tanggal ... exam date ...., No. ... student exam # ....,
(vide Keputusan Direktur Jenderal Pendidikan Dasar dan Menengah tanggal
16 September 1989, No. 227/C/Kep/I/1989), sehingga yang bersangkutan
dinyatakan tamat belajar sekolah menengah umum tingkat atas.

Pemegang Surat Tanda Tamat Belajar ini terakhir tercatat sebagai
siswa pada Sekolah Menengah Umum Tingkat Atas ... SMA ....
.................................., di ..../........
SMA Address ...., dengan Nomor Induk SMA registration #

pas foto 3 x 4 cm

Cap tiga jari tengah
tangan kiri dan
tanda tangan
pemegang

Graduate Photo

...................., ... 1990
Kepala Sekolah,
Name, signature, civil service # of
principal of SMA issuing certificate

NIP

Keputusan Direktur Jenderal Pendidikan Dasar dan Menengah
Tanggal 20 Oktober 1989 No. 280/C/Kep/I/1989

PERUM PERURI

Daftar nilai tertera di balik ini.

Document 2.2a. Upper Secondary School Certificate of Completion.

Final Results   **D A F T A R   N I L A I**

HASIL EVALUASI BELAJAR TAHAP AKHIR SEKOLAH MENENGAH UMUM TINGKAT ATAS

(S M A)

School Year   **Tahun Pelajaran 1989/1990**

Program   : **Pengetahuan Budaya**

Nama Siswa   : Graduate's name ....

Nomor Induk : Student archive number ....

A. Daftar Nilai Mata Pelajaran yang di-EBTA-kan dan di-EBTANAS-kan   EBTANAS & SMA Final Results

Nomor Urut	Mata Pelajaran	Nilai	
		dengan angka	dengan huruf grades received
1.	Pendidikan Agama	....	....
2.	Pendidikan Moral Pancasila	....	....
3.	Pendidikan Sejarah Perjuangan Bangsa	....	....
4.	Bahasa dan Sastra Indonesia	....	....
5.	Sejarah Nasional Indonesia dan Sejarah Dunia	....	....
6.	Geografi	....	....
7.	Sejarah Budaya	....	....
8.	Sastra	....	....
9.	Sosiologi dan Antropologi	....	....
10.	Bahasa Inggris	....	....
11.	Bahasa	....	....
	Jumlah	....	....

B. Daftar Mata Pelajaran lain yang diperoleh di Kelas-kelas sebelumnya

Nomor Urut	Mata Pelajaran	Kelas	
1.	Ekonomi	I	—
2.	Pendidikan Jasmani	I	II
3.	Pendidikan Seni	I	II
4.	Pendidikan Keterampilan	I	II
5.	Matematika	I	II
6.	Biologi	I	—
7.	Fisika	I	—
8.	Kimia	I	—

Exam date

....................., ... 1990

Kepala Sekolah,

Principal's name

....

NIP

Document 2.2b. Reverse of 2.2a.

Nomor seri Ijazah : 1856

School name　　UNIVERSITAS KATOLIK PARAHYANGAN

graduate's name	Memberikan Ijazah kepada :
birthplace/date	Tempat dan tanggal lahir : Bandung, 23 Juli 1967
student number	NIRM : 86.4106078
program level	Program Pendidikan : Strata Satu (S-1)
faculty	Fakultas : Ilmu Sosial & Ilmu Politik
department	Jurusan : Ilmu Administrasi
study program	Program Studi : Ilmu Administrasi Niaga
accreditation	Status : Disamakan berdasarkan Surat Keputusan Menteri Pendidikan dan Kebudayaan Nomor 0527/0/1989, Tanggal 1 September 1989.
S1 statement	Ijazah ini diserahkan setelah yang bersangkutan memenuhi semua persyaratan yang ditentukan, dan kepadanya dilimpahkan segala wewenang dan hak yang berhubungan dengan Ijazah yang dimilikinya.

Graduate Photo.　　Institution 20 Agustus 1990
　　　　　　　　　　stamp
　　　　　　　　　　　　　　　　date of signature
　　　　　　　　　　　　　　Rektor, signature/name of rector

(Prof. Dr. Bunde Bunga Silalahi.)

NIP : 90410655211063519
　　　　　civil servant registration#
Disahkan oleh :
Koordinator Kopertis Wilayah IV date of signature
Tanggal 21 September 1990
　　　　regional Kopertis Coordinator's name

(Prof. Dr. H. Maman R. Rachmana),

Document 3.1. Sarjana (S1) from an Equalized Study Program in Business Administration, Parahyangan Catholic University. The S1 statement on the document indicates the graduate has fulfilled all conditions and receives all the authority and rights devolving to holders of such (S1) degrees.

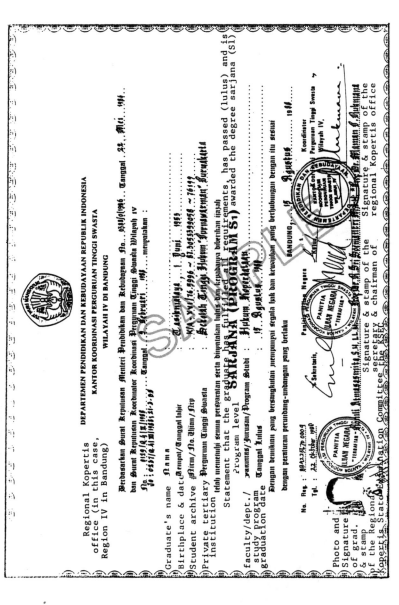

Document 3.2. *Sarjana* (S1) for a Study Program in Civil Law, with Registered Accreditation Status, Purnawarman Advanced School of Law. The certificate states the graduate has passed the state exams appropriate to registered/*terdaftar* study programs. The S1 statement on the document indicates the graduate has fulfilled all requirements, has passed (*lulus*) and is awarded the degree *Sarjana* (S1).

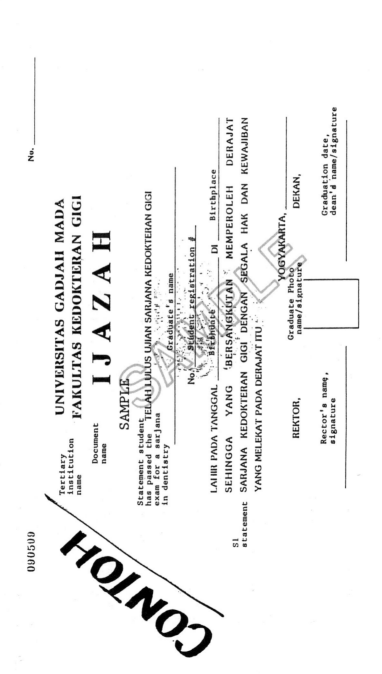

Document 3.3. *Sarjana* (S1) in Dentistry, Gadjah Mada University. The S1 statement on the document indicates the student receives all the rights and obligations that devolve to holders of the S1 degree.

Institution name **INSTITUT TEKNOLOGI BANDUNG**

Menyatakan bahwa

Graduate's name

Statement of pass *(berhasil)* *telah berhasil menyelesaikan program pendidikan*

Field of study Mathematics/ Natural sciences *pasca sarjana matematika dan ilmu pengetahuan alam strata kedua* Program level (S2)

Specialization area and honors *bidang Matematika dengan predikat Cum Laude*

Dan kepadanya diberikan ijazah ini yang dikeluarkan di Bandung

pada tanggal

Graduation date *20 Oktober 1984*

Rektor

Rector's name/signature *Harìadì P. Soepangkat, Ph.D.*

Document 4.1a. *Magister* (S2), Mathematics and Natural Science, Bandung Institute of Technology.

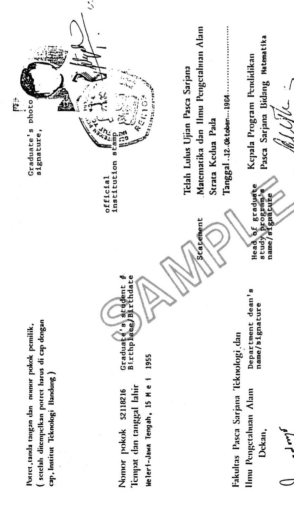

No: S2.11001/I/BAP-ITB/1984.

Potret, tanda tangan dan nomor pokok pemilik,
(setelah ditempelkan potret harus di cap dengan
cap, Institut Teknologi Bandung)

Graduate's photo
signature,

official
institution stamp

Nomor pokok S2118216   Graduate's student #
Tempat dan tanggal lahir   Birthplace/Birthdate
Weleri-Jawa Tengah, 15 M e i 1955

Fakultas Pasca Sarjana Teknologi, dan
Ilmu Pengetahuan Alam   Department dean's
Dekan,   name/signature

PROF. DR. MOEDONO.

Statement

Telah Lulus Ujian Pasca Sarjana
Matematika dan Ilmu Pengetahuan Alam
Strata Kedua Pada
Tanggal .12.Oktober...1984......

Head of graduate
study program's
name/signature

Kepala Program Pendidikan
Pasca Sarjana Bidang Matematika

DR. ACHMAD ARIFIN.

Ijazah ini diberikan berdasarkan surat keputusan Rektor Nomor : 338/PFK/ITB/1984.

Document 4.1b. Reverse of 4.1a. The statement on the document indicates the student has passed the appropriate graduate exams (*lulus ujian pasca sarjana*).

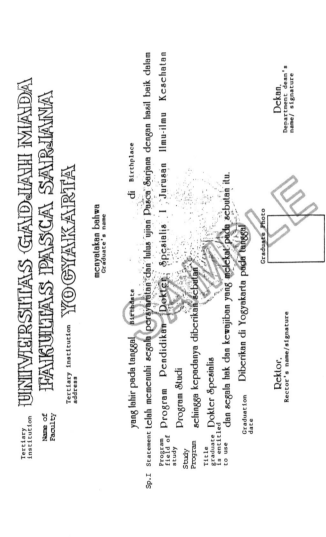

Document 4.2a. Specialist I (Sp.I) Diploma in Public Health, Gadjah Mada University. When this certificate was issued, graduate education was organized by faculty. Gadjah Mada University had not yet printed new diploma certificates. The document indicates the graduate has fulfilled all conditions and passed the graduate examinations.

Tahun Pendidikan
Academic year
  Diberikan oleh
  Institution awarding
  the diploma

Satuan Kredit Semester
Credit value of courses

Kurikulum dan Kegiatan
Specialist curriculum

SAMPLE

Kelua Program Studi
. Pendidikan Dokter Spesialis I.
Signature of the chairman
of the study program for Sp.I

Dekan Fakultas Kedokteran
Signature of dean of
medical faculty

Document 4.2b. Reverse of 4.2a.

Smalp II form

№ 005034   /........../........../19..........

Contoh

DEPARTEMEN PENDIDIKAN DAN KEBUDAYAAN

Institution name

INSTITUT KEGURUAN DAN ILMU PENDIDIKAN
SEMARANG

Memberikan kepada :

                                                                Graduate's name

Nomor Registrasi   :   Student registration #

Lahir di   :   Birthplace   , pada tanggal .... Birthdate

Fakultas   :   Faculty

Bidang Ilmu   : Kependidikan.   Field

I J A Z A H   :   **DIPLOMA II**   Name/level of diploma .

Program studi   :   Study program

Setelah memenuhi semua persyaratan yang ditentukan untuk memperoleh ijazah tersebut,

kepadanya diberi hak untuk memakai sebutan ahli muda pendidikan,

serta segala wewenang dan hak yang berhubungan dengan ijazah yang dimilikinya.   Statement

SAMPLE

Graduate Photo

Foto dan
tanda tangan
pemegang
Ijazah

Semarang, Date of rector's signature

Dekan Fakultas,

Faculty dean's name,
signature, civil servant
registration #

(..........................)
NIP. : ....

Rektor,

Rector's name/signature
civil servant registration #

(..........................)
NIP. : ....

Document 5.1. Diploma II in Education, IKIP Semarang. The statement on the document indicates the graduate has fulfilled all conditions set forth and has the right to use the title Junior Educator.

DEPARTEMEN PENDIDIKAN DAN KEBUDAYAAN REPUBLIK INDONESIA

INSTITUT KEGURUAN DAN ILMU PENDIDIKAN JAKARTA

Institution name

Dengan Rakhmat Allah Yang Maha Kuasa

Institut Keguruan dan Ilmu Pendidikan Jakarta
dengan persetujuan Senat Institut atas rekomendasi

Dekan Fakultas

Name of faculty

menganugerahkan gelar

SARJANA PENDIDIKAN

kepada

Graduate's name

Lahir di: ....   Birthplace   pada tanggal   Birthdate

Degree level
name

Statement that student
has fulfilled all academic
conditions/date of graduation

setelah menyelesaikan semua persyaratan akademik pada tanggal

S1 Statement   yang dengan demikian untuk selanjutnya dikukuhkan sebagai kesarjanaan,
hak dan kewajiban sesuai dengan gelar yang dianugerahkan.

Jakarta, ...   Date of rector's signature

Graduate Photo/signature

3 x 4

Dekan,
Dean's name/signature

Rektor,
Rector's name/signature

Document 5.2. *Sarjana* in Education, IKIP Jakarta. The S1 statement on the document indicates the student has earned the rights and obligations devolving to *sarjana* degree holders.

№ 005034 / .... / .... / .... / 19 ....

DEPARTEMEN PENDIDIKAN DAN KEBUDAYAAN

INSTITUT KEGURUAN DAN ILMU PENDIDIKAN SEMARANG

Institution name

Memberikan kepada :

Graduate's name

Nomor Registrasi : .... student registration #

Lahir di : .... Birthplace .... pada tanggal .... Birthdate

Fakultas : .... Faculty

Bidang Ilmu : .... Field of study

A K T A II Certificate name

IJAZAH :

Program studi : .... Study program

Setelah memenuhi semua persyaratan yang ditentukan untuk memperoleh Akta tersebut,

kepadanya diberi hak untuk mengajar dalam bidangnya pada .... Statement

serta segala wewenang dan hak yang berhubungan dengan Akta yang dimilikinya.

Semarang, ... Date of rector's signature

Rektor,
Rector's name/signature
civil servant registration **Number**

(................)
NIP. :

Dekan Fakultas Ilmu Pendidikan,
Faculty dean's name, signature
civil servant registration #

(................)
NIP. :

Foto dan
tanda tangan
pemegang
Ijazah

Graduate's Photo,
signature

SAMPLE

Document 5.3. Akta II Teaching Certificate, IKIP Semarang. The statement on the document indicates the graduate has fulfilled all conditions and gives the level at which the graduate can teach.

CONTOH   **- 65 -**
                                                          Lampiran 5.h
                        DEPARTEMEN AGAMA RI
          PANITIA PENYELENGGARAAN EBTAN MADRASAH ALIYAH
          ....
          DAFTAR NILAI EVALUASI BELAJAR TAHAP AKHIR NEGARA MURNI
                      MADRASAH ALIYAH (MA)
                        TAHUN 19   / 19

Yang bertanda tangan di bawah ini Ketua Panitia Penyelenggara EBTAN
Madrasah Aliyah ....
menerangkan bahwa :   Name of Examination Committee Chairperson

          N a m a Name of Candidate :
          Tempat dan Tanggal Lahir : Birthplace and Date
          Nomor Peserta Candidate # : Student number
          Sekolah Asal Name of Madrasah Attended by Candidate
          P i l i h a n Study Program : Ilmu-ilmu Agama (Program Khusus)
   Statement that the Candidate participated in the EBTAN Aliyah on the Dates Specified
telah mengikuti Evaluasi Belajar Tahap Akhir Negara yang diselenggarakan
dari tanggal .... s.d. .... berdasarkan Keputusan
Direktur Jenderal Pembinaan Kelembagaan Agama Islam Departemen Agama No.
52/E/1989 tanggal 4 Oktober 1989 dengan nilai sebagai berikut :

NO.	BIDANG STUDI Subjects Examined	N I L A I Grades received	
		Dengan Angka	Dengan Huruf
1.	F i q i h		
2.	Bahasa Arab		
3.	Pendidikan Pancasila		
4.	Bahasa dan Sastra Indonesia		
5.	Bahasa Inggris		
6.	Matematika		
7.	Tafsir-Ilmu Tafsir		
8.	Hadits-Ilmu Hadits		
9.	Ushul Fiqih		
	J U M L A H Total		

```
.--------------.
|              |                                    .................... 19 ...
|              |  Candidate's    KETUA PANITIA PENYELENGGARA EBTAN
| Pas Foto     |  Photograph     MADRASAH ALIYAH ................
|   3 x 4      |                 ................................
|              |
|              |                 ...........................
'--------------'                 NIP.
```
          Signature of Examination Committee Chairperson
          and civil service registration number

Document 6.1. EBTAN Madrasah Aliyah Certificate.

Nomor : ....

DEPARTEMEN AGAMA
REPUBLIK INDONESIA

IJAZAH

(SURAT TANDA TAMAT BELAJAR)

M A D R A S A H   A L I Y A H
(MADRASAH MENENGAH TINGKAT ATAS)

Yang bertanda tangan di bawah ini Kepala ..Name .of .MA................

.... menerangkan bahwa :

Student's name
....

lahir pada tanggal ..Birthdate................. di ....Birthplace......
anak ...Father/mother's name...telah

L U L U S

dalam mengikuti Evaluasi Belajar Tahap Akhir Madrasah Aliyah yang diselenggarakan berdasarkan Keputusan Menteri Agama RI Nomor 193 Tahun 1987, sehingga
yang bersangkutan dinyatakan tamat belajar dan berhak memperoleh ijazah ini
sesuai dengan Keputusan Menteri Agama RI Nomor 70 Tahun 1976 dan Keputusan
Bersama Menteri Agama, Menteri Pendidikan dan Kebudayaan dan Menteri Dalam
Negeri, Nomor 6 Tahun 1975, Nomor 037/U/1975 dan Nomor 36 Tahun 1975.

Pemegang ijazah ini, terakhir tercatat sebagai siswa pada Madrasah Aliyah
Name of last MA   di   . Location of MA   last
    attended   attended
dengan nomor induk : ...MA.registration.#........................

Graduate photo/fingerprints

..........................19....

KEPALA MADRASAH
MA head's signature/civil service
registration #

Pas Photo
4 x 6
Cap Tiga Jari
manis, tengah dan
telunjuk tangan kiri

(_____)
NIP.:

Statement that the graduate has passed the appropriate exams

Kep. Menag No. .... Tahun 1988   Daftar nilai tertera di balik ini.

Document 6.2a. Madrasah Aliyah/MA (Certificate of Completion).

D A F T A R   N I L A I
EVALUASI BELAJAR TAHAP AKHIR MADRASAH ALIYAH Name of certificate
(MADRASAH MENENGAH TINGKAT ATAS)
TAHUN AJARAN : ..School year.........

Stream

NAMA SISWA   : .....Student's name........   NO. INDUK : .Student's #..

PROGRAM PILIHAN : A. (ILMU–ILMU BIOLOGI)   NO. EBTAN : .Student's EBTAN #

JENIS PROGRAM.	NO	Subjects M A T A P E L A J A R A N	NILAI Grades rec'd	
			ANGKA	HURUF
PROGRAM I N T I		A. PENDIDIKAN AGAMA :		
	1	Qur'an – Hadits	....	....
	2	Aqidah – Akhlaq	....	....
	3	Fiqih	....	....
	4	Sejarah dan Peradaban Islam	....	....
	5	Bahasa Arab	....	....
		B. PENDIDIKAN DASAR UMUM :		
	6	Pendidikan Moral Pancasila	....	....
	7	Pendidikan Sejarah Perjuangan Bangsa	....	....
	8.	Bahasa dan Sastra Indonesia	....	....
	9	Sejarah Nasional Indonesia dan Sejarah Dunia	....	....
	10	Ekonomi	....	....
	11	Geografi	....	....
	12	Biologi	....	....
	13	Fisika	....	....
	14	Kimia	....	....
	15	Matematika	....	....
	16	Bahasa Inggris	....	....
	17	Pendidikan Olahraga dan Kesehatan	....	....
	18	Pendidikan Seni	....	....
	19	Pendidikan Ketrampilan	....	....
PROGRAM PILIHAN	1	C. PENDIDIKAN PENGEMBANGAN KEILMUAN : Matematika	....	....
	2	Biologi	....	....
	3	Fisika	....	....
	4	Kimia	....	....
	5	Bahasa Inggris	....	....
		J U M L A H	....	....

......................,........................19.....

....

KEPALA MADRASAH
Signature of Madrasan head and date

(_____)
NIP..........................
Madrasan head's civil service
registration number

Document 6.2b. Reverse of 6.2a.

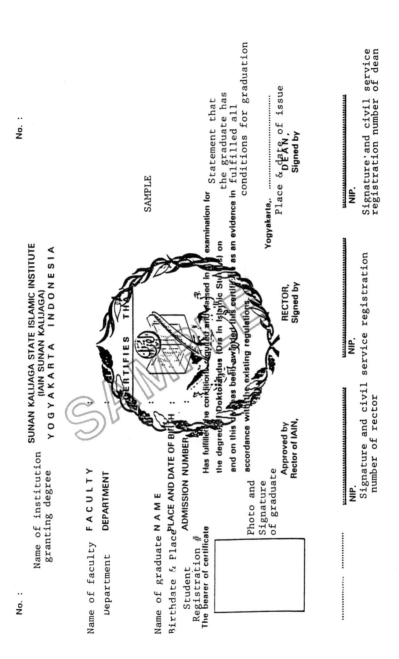

Document 6.3a. *Sarjana* **(S1) Diploma, IAIN Wali Songo, Semarang. The S1 statement on the document indicates the graduate has fulfilled all conditions for graduation.**

SUNAN KALIJAGA STATE ISLAMIC INSTITUTE
(IAIN SUNAN KALIJAGA)
Y O G Y A K A R T A   I N D O N E S I A

CERTIFICATE – SUPPLEMENT

F A C U L T Y :
DEPARTEMENT :
N A M E :
PLACE AND DATE OF BIRTH :
ADMISSION NUMBER :

S U B J E C T S   T A K E N

1. ....
2. ....
3. ....
4. ....
5. ....
6. ....
7. ....
8. ....

9. ....
10. ....
11. ....
12. ....
13. ....
14. ....
15. ....
16. ....

Thesis : ....

Yogyakarta, ...

Approved by
Rector of IAIN,

RECTOR,
Signed by

DEAN,
Signed by

NIP.

NIP.

NIP.

SAMPLE

Document 6.3b. Reverse of 6.3b.

Glossary

adab	Arabic language and Islamic civilization faculty in Islamic tertiary institutions
akademi	Academy offering tertiary professional nondegree programs
Akta	Teaching certification awarded to teacher training institution graduates in addition to the diploma or degree
akuntanasi	Accounting
asuransi	Insurance
bahasa	Language
bahasa asing	Foreign language
da'wah	Islamic propagation faculty in Islamic tertiary institutions
DI, DII, DIII, DIV	Diplomas I-IV; professional nondegree tertiary qualifications
diakui	Recognized; second of three accreditation levels for private educational institutions
Direktorat Jenderal Pendidikan Dasar dan Menengah/Dikdasmen	Directorate General of Primary and Secondary Education
Direktorat Jenderal Pendidikan Luar Sekolah, Pemuda, dan Olahraga/Ditjen PLSPO	Directorate General of Nonformal Education, Youth, and Sports
Direktorat Jenderal Pendidikan Tinggi/Dikti	Directorate General of Higher Education/DGHE
Direktorat Pendidikan Kejuruan	Directorate of Secondary Vocational Education
Direktorat Sekolah Swasta	Directorate of Private Schools
disamakan	Equalized; highest accreditation level for private educational institutions
disertasi	Dissertation for S3 tertiary degree
dokter/dr.	Title awarded to S1 graduates of a medical faculty before 1993
dokter Jawa	Name/term given to Indonesian graduates of NIAS and STOVIA medical schools during Dutch era
Doktor/DR.	Title awarded to an S3 degree holder
Doktoranda/dra.	Title awarded to female holder of a five-year tertiary degree (pre-1989)
Doktorandus/drs.	Title awarded to male holder of a five-year tertiary degree (pre-1989)

EBTA	Evaluasi Belajar Tahap Akhir; primary, lower secondary, and upper secondary year-end examination given by the particular school in preparation for the EBTANAS
EBTAN	Evaluasi Belajar Tahap Akhir Nasional; National School Leavers Examination for MOR schools
EBTANAS	Evaluasi Belajar Tahap Akhir Nasional; MOEC National School Leavers Examination
filsafat	Philosophy
FKIP	Fakultas Keguruan dan Ilmu Pendidikan; Faculty of Teacher Training (within a university)
grafika	Graphics
hubungan internasional	International relations
hukum	Law
IAIN	Institut Agama Islam Negeri; State Islamic Institute
ijazah	Term used to designate all diplomas and certificates in the Indonesian educational system
IKIP	Institut Keguruan dan Ilmu Pendidikan; Teacher Training Institute
ilmu	Knowledge, science
ilmu gizi	Nutrition
ilmu pengetahuan	Knowledge, science
Inpres SD	Presidential Instruction for primary schools; special government budget allocation for primary school construction
insinyur	Academic title adapted from the Dutch, the equivalent of a *sarjana* degree for engineering, architecture, and agriculture graduates
institut	Institute; offering tertiary academic degree and professional nondegree programs
IPK/IP	Index Prestasi Kumulatif; grade point average
kedokteran	Medicine
kedokteran gigi	Dentistry
keguruan	Teaching
kehutanan	Forestry
kejuruan	Vocational
kelautan	Seamanship
kepariwisataan	Tourism
kesehatan	Health
kesejahteraan	Welfare
kesenian	Related to the arts

ketatalaksanaan	Management
keuangan	Finance
kimia	Chemistry
Kopertis	Koordinasi Perguruan Tinggi Swasta; 12 Regional Coordinating Agencies for Private Education
madrasah	Nonresidential Islamic primary or secondary school
Madrasah Aliyah/MA	Islamic lower secondary school operated or accredited by the Ministry of Religion
Madrasah Ibtidaiyah/MI	Islamic upper secondary school operated or accredited by the Ministry of Religion
Madrasah Tsanawiyah/MT	Islamic primary school operated or accredited by the Ministry of Religion
magister	Title awarded to S2 degree holders
MOEC	Ministry of Education and Culture
MOHA	Ministry of Home Affairs
MOR	Ministry of Religion
NB/CHS	National Board of Evaluation, Consortium of Health Sciences
NEM	nilai EBTANAS *murni*; EBTANAS score (*see* EBTANAS)
non-gelar	nondegree
non-skripsi	nonthesis
olahraga	Sport, physical exercise (also *olah raga*)
Pancasila	Indonesia's 5-point state ideology; *see* footnote 1, chapter II
pasca sarjana	postgraduate education
pendidikan	Education
perbankan	Banking
perdagangan	Trade, commerce
perikanan	Fisheries
perkapalan	Shipping, shipping matters
perkebunan	Estate crops
perniagaan	Trade, commerce
pertamanan	Horticulture
pertanian	Agriculture
pesantren	Residential Islamic school, often rural
peternakan	Animal science, animal husbandry
PGRI	Persatuan Guru Republik Indonesia; Indonesian Teachers' Organization
PGSD	Pendidikan Guru Sekolah Dasar; special DII teacher training program for primary school teachers

PMDK	Penelusuran Minat dan Kemampuan; merit-based admissions system used by some tertiary institutions
politeknik	Polytechnic offering professional nondegree programs, usually in technical fields
S0	*Strata nol*; diploma-level (nondegree) tertiary programs
S1, S2, S3	*Strata satu, strata dua, strata tiga*; first, second, and third tertiary degrees
santri	A student attending a *pesantren*
sarjana	First academic degree; also holder of such a degree. *See also* S1, *doctoranda, doctorandus*
sarjana lengkap	Five-year tertiary degree awarded until 1989
sarjana muda	Three-year tertiary degree awarded until 1989
SD	Sekolah Dasar; primary school
Sekolah Tinggi	Advanced school, offering tertiary professional nondegree and academic degree programs in a single academic area
seni	Art
SGO	Sekolah Guru Olahraga; upper secondary teacher training school for primary school physical education and health teachers; discontinued in 1992
SGPLB	Sekolah Guru Pendidikan Luar Biasa; upper secondary special education teachers training school; phased out in 1992
SIPENMARU	Sistem Penerimaan Mahasiswa Baru; state tertiary institution admission examination used between 1984 and 88
skripsi	undergraduate thesis for S1 degree
SKS	Satuan Kredit Semester; a credit hour.
SLTA	Sekolah Lanjutan Tingkat Atas; upper secondary school. *See also* SMA
SLTP	Sekolah Lanjutan Tingkat Pertama; lower secondary school. *See also* SMP
SMA	Sekolah Menengah Atas; upper secondary school. *See also* SLTA
SMEA	Sekolah Menengah Ekonomi Atas; commercial upper secondary school
SMKK	Sekolah Menengah Kesejahteraan Keluarga; home economics upper secondary school
SMP	Sekolah Menengah Pertama; lower secondary school; *see also* SLTP

Sp.I	Spesialis I (Specialist I); two-year graduate-level professional diploma
Sp.II	Spesialis II (Specialist II); three-year graduate level professional diploma; no program yet exists
SPG	Sekolah Pendidikan Guru; upper secondary teacher training school for primary teachers; discontinued in 1992
STKIP	Sekolah Tinggi Keguruan dan Ilmu Pendidikan; private advanced school for teacher training
STM	Sekolah Teknik Menengah; vocational upper secondary school
strata 1, 2, 3	Academic degree levels *satu, dua,* and *tiga*
STTB	Surat Tanda Tamat Belajar; certificate of completion at primary, lower, and upper secondary school levels
syari'ah	Islamic law faculty in Islamic tertiary institutions
tarbiyah	Education faculty in Islamic tertiary institutions
tata niaga	Commerce
terdaftar	registered; lowest of three accreditation levels for private educational institutions
tesis	thesis for S2 degree
TK	Taman kanak-kanak; kindergarten
UM Politeknik	Ujian Masuk Politeknik; Entrance Examination for State Polytechnics
UMPGSD	Ujian Masuk Pendidikan Guru Sekolah Dasar; National Entrance Examination for Primary Teacher Training Program at tertiary level
UMPTN	Ujian Masuk Perguruan Tinggi Negeri; Entrance Examination for State Tertiary Institutions
universitas	University; offering tertiary academic degree and professional nondegree programs
ushuluddin	Theology faculty in Islamic tertiary institutions

Select Bibliography

Aanenson, Charles. 1979. *Indonesia*, World Education Series. American Association of Collegiate Registrars and Admissions Officers. Washington, DC.

_____. "Indonesian Educational Systems." June 1988. Presentation at the National Association for Foreign Student Affairs Conference, Washington, DC. Overseas Training Office/BAPPENAS. Jakarta.

Beeby, C.E. 1979. *Assessment of Indonesian Education: A Guide in Planning*. Education Research Series No. 59. New Zealand Council for Educational Research with Oxford University Press. Wellington.

Departemen Agama. 1990. *Buku Statistik Direktorat Pembinaan Perguruan Agama Islam Tahun 1989-1990* (Statistics, Directorate of Islamic Education Development, 1989-1990). Direktorat Jenderal Pembinaan Kelembagaan Agama Islam. Direktorat Pembinaan Perguruan Agama Islam. Jakarta.

_____. *Data Pendidikan Agama Islam Pada Sekolah Umum Tahun 1989-1990* (Data on Religious [Islamic] Education in State Schools, 1989-90). Direktorat Jenderal Pembinaan Kelembagaan Agama Islam. Direktorat Pembinaan Pendidikan Agama Islam Pada Sekolah Umum Negeri. Jakarta.

_____. 1988-89. *Information on State Institutes for Islamic Studies (IAIN)*. Direktorat Jenderal Pembinaan Kelembagaan Agama Islam. Direktorat Pembinaan Perguruan Tinggi Agama Islam. Jakarta.

_____. December 1990. *Petunjuk Pelaksanaan dan Instrumen Akreditasi Madrasah Swasta* (Implementation Guide and Accreditation Instrument for Private Madrasah). Direktorat Jenderal Pembinaan Kelembagaan Agama Islam, Jakarta.

_____. 1990-91. *Statistik Keagamaan Tahun 1989* (Statistics Concerning Religion, 1989). Badan Penelitian dan Pengembangan Agama. Jakarta.

_____. 1990. *Statistik Pendidikan Keagamaan Tingkat Dasar dan Menengah Tahun 1990* (Religious Education Statistics for Primary and Secondary Schools, 1990). Direktorat Jenderal Pembinaan Kelembagaan Agama Islam. Jakarta.

_____. December 1990. *Statistik Pendidikan Tinggi Agama Islam (IAIN, PTAIS, dan Pendidikan Agama Islam pada PTU) Tahun 1989-1990* (Statistics, Islamic Higher Education [State Islamic Institutes, Private Islamic Tertiary Institutions, Islamic Education in State Tertiary Institutions]). Direktorat Jenderal Pembinaan Kelembagaan Agama Islam Jakarta.

Departemen Pendidikan dan Kebudayaan. September 1990. *Data Perguruan Tinggi Negeri Tahun 1989/90.* (State Higher Education Statistics, 1989/90). Balitbang. Pusat Informatika. Jakarta.

_____. 1990. *Data Perguruan Tinggi Swasta Tahun 1989/90.* (Private Higher Education Statistics, 1989/90). Balitbang. Pusat Informatika. Jakarta.

_____. 1991. *Direktori Perguruan Tinggi Swasta di Indonesia 1990* (Directory of Private Tertiary Institutions in Indonesia, 1990). Direktorat Jenderal Pendidikan Tinggi. Jakarta.

_____. 1990. *Himpunan Peraturan Pemerintah No. 27, Tahun 1990; Nomor 28, Tahun 1990, Nomor 29, Tahun 1990* (Government Regulations Nos. 27/1990, 28/1990, and 29/1990; re: kindergarten and primary schools, lower secondary school, and upper secondary school). Sekretariat Direktorat Jenderal Dikdasmen. Bagian Tata Laksana. Jakarta.

_____. 1991. *Keputusan Direktor Jenderal Pendidikan Dasar dan Menengah No. 310/C/Kep/I/1990; No. 311/C/Kep/I/1990; No. 313/C/Kep/1990; and No. 345/C/I/ 1991*

(Decrees of the Director General of Primary and Secondary Education re: EBTANAS). Directorate Jenderal Pendidikan Dasar dan Menengah. Jakarta.

_____. 1986. *Kurikulum Menengah Umum Tingkat Atas (SMA), Garis-Garis Besar Program Pengajaran, (GBPP)*. (General/Academic Upper Secondary School Curriculum, Outlines of Educational Programs). Badan Penelitian dan Pengembangan Pendidikan dan Kebudayaan. Pusat Pengembangan Kurikulum dan Sarana Pendidikan. Jakarta.

_____. 1986. *Kurikulum Menengah Umum Tingkat Pertama (SMP), Garis-Garis Besar Program Pengajaran, (GBPP)*. (Lower Secondary School Curriculum, Outlines of Educational Programs). Badan Penelitian dan Pengembangan Pendidikan dan Kebudayaan. Pusat Pengembangan Kurikulum dan Saran Pendidikan. Jakarta.

_____. 1987. *Kurikulum Sekolah Dasar, Kelas 1, Garis-Garis Besar Program Pengajaran (GBPP)* (Primary School Curriculum, Grade 1, Outlines of Educational Programs). Direktorat Jenderal Pendidikan Dasar dan Menengah. Direktorat Pendidikan Dasar. Jakarta.

_____. 1986. *Panduan Belajar ke Pendidikan Kedinasan* (Guide to Government Service Education). Jakarta.

_____. 1986. *Panduan Belajar ke Sekolah Menengah Tingkat Atas Keguruan* (Guide to Upper Secondary Teacher Training School). Jakarta.

_____. 1986. *Panduan Belajar ke Sekolah Menengah Umum Tingkat Atas* (Guide to General/Academic Upper Secondary School). Jakarta.

_____. 1990. *Peraturan Pemerintah Republik Indonesia Nomor 30 Tahun 1990 Tentang Pendidikan Tinggi* (Republic of Indonesia Government Regulation No. 30/1990 Regarding Higher Education). Departemen Pendidikan dan Kebudayaan. Jakarta.

_____. May 1991. "Perkembangan Taman Kanak-Kanak, Tahun 1969-1989" (Expansion of Kindergartens, 1969-1989). Direktorat Jenderal Pendidikan Dasar dan Menengah. Jakarta.

_____. 1990. *Rangkuman Statistik Persekolahan 1989/90* (School Statistics, 1989-90). Balitbang. Pusat Informatika. Jakarta.

_____. 1991. *Struktur dan Deskripsi Matakuliah Program Penyetaraan DII Pendidikan Guru Sekolah Dasar, Universitas Terbuka* (A Description and the Structure of Education for Primary Teacher DII Upgrading, Open University). Proyek Penataran Guru Setara D-II. Jakarta.

_____. 1989. *Undang-Undang Republik Indonesia Nomor 2, Tahun 1989, Tentang Sistem Pendidikan Nasional dan Penjelasannya* (Republic of Indonesia Law No. 2/1989 Regarding the National System of Education and Clarification). Jakarta.

Editor. 23 November 1991. "Harga Seorang MBA" (The Value of an MBA Holder). No. 10/Thn. V. 11-26. Jakarta.

Florida State University, et al. March 1988. *Indonesia: Education and Human Resources Sector Review*. 3 vols. United States Agency for International Development, Bureau for Science and Technology, Office of Education, Washington, DC, and the Improving the Efficiency of Educational Systems (IEES) Educational Efficiency Clearinghouse. Learning Systems Institute. Tallahassee, Florida.

Hall, D.G.E. 1981. *A History of South-East Asia*. Fourth Edition. Macmillan Asian Histories Series. Macmillan Education, Ltd. Hong Kong.

Hill, Hal, ed. 1991. *Indonesia Assessment 1991*. Political and Social Change Monograph 13. Research School of Pacific Studies. Australian National University. Canberra.

Jakub Isman. 1988. "Indonesia's Higher Education System in Brief." Presentation at the National Association for Foreign Student Affairs Conference, Washington, DC. June, 1988. Overseas Training Office/ BAPPENAS, Jakarta.

Lewin, Elizabeth. 1992. "Animal Health and Livestock Science Education." Report for CIDA. Jakarta.

Ministry of Education and Culture. August 22, 1991. *Secondary Education in Indonesia in Brief.* Directorate General of Primary and Secondary Education. Directorate of General Secondary Education. Jakarta.

Muchsin Lubis, Suwardi, et al. 22 June 1991. "Antara Favorit dan Akreditasi" (Choosing Among the Best). *Prospek.* No. 37. Tahun 1. Jakarta.

Prospek. 27 July 1991. "MBA=Masih Butuh Akreditasi" (MBA=Still No Accreditation). 88-97.

Shaeffer, Sheldon. October 1990. *Educational Change in Indonesia: A Case Study of Three Innovations.* The International Development Research Centre. Ottawa.

Sumadi Suryabrata. June 1988. "Grading Systems and Grading Practices in Some Indonesian Public Universities, Part I." Presentation at the National Association for Foreign Student Affairs Conference, Washington, DC. Jakarta.

_____. March 1990. "Grading Systems and Grading Practices in Some Indonesian Public and Private Universities, Part II." Overseas Training Office/BAPPENAS. Jakarta.

van der Veur, Paul W. 1969. *Education and Social Change in Colonial Indonesia*, Southeast Asia Program. Ohio University Center for International Studies. Athens.

World Bank. December 22, 1989. *Indonesia: Basic Education Study.* Population and Human Resources Operations Division. Country Department V. Asia Region.

Index